OVER LAND AND SEA

Chelsea FC
in the
Great War

OVER LAND AND SEA

Chelsea FC
in the
Great War

Alexandra Churchill
with Andrew Holmes

The History Press

For John, Sam, Karen, Ken, Matt, Jamie, Sebastian, Kjell Arne, Garry, Carol,
Gray, Ian, Andy, Roy, James, Matt & Family, May, Mark, Brian & Family, Lee,
Paul P, Paul O, Big Steve, Tim, Little Steve, Lewis, Jan, Russ, Mark P, the mad lot
behind us, Arnie, Charlie, Trevor, Pete, Liz, Dave, Mark W, Scott, Emma, Joseph,
Nick, Christelle, Feisal, Tes & Regine, Shaz, Big'ed, Colin, Vic P, Cos, Jonny,
Lesley, Andrew, Matt, Alan, Mal, Karn, Cranny, Pippa, Cliff, Tony, Celia, Cookie
and dozens of others, some of them, including Kyle, Vic, Denis Leroy Bryan and
Blind Gerry, sadly gone but not forgotten. Because football done right isn't just about
the players, it's an extended family too.
A.C.

To Diane and Adam, for accompanying me on all those trips to the Western Front.
A.H.

In memory of William Hanna, nephew of Cecil Dean, who sadly passed away before
he could see the results of our research.

First published 2015

The History Press
The Mill, Brimscombe Port
Stroud, Gloucestershire, GL5 2QG
www.thehistorypress.co.uk

© Alexandra Churchill, 2015

The right of Alexandra Churchill to be identified as the Author
of this work has been asserted in accordance with the
Copyright, Designs and Patents Act 1988.

British Library Cataloguing in Publication Data.
A catalogue record for this book is available from the British Library.

ISBN 978 0 7509 6021 2

Typesetting and origination by The History Press
Printed and bound in Great Britain by TJ International Ltd.

Contents

Acknowledgements

First, this book would not have been possible without the dedication and assistance of some fellow Chelsea fans who have assisted with our research: Jonathan Dyer, Lesley Blacklaws and Stuart Disbrey, your efforts are much appreciated. Also, the team at The History Press who have brought it to fruition: Declan Flynn, Nicola Guy, Mark Murray, Emily Locke and Chris West – despite the fact that none of them are Blues fans they could not have put more into it!

Without the time and generosity given by the families of so many of the men who feature in the chapters we would have been unable to tell their stories. Huge thanks are due to the descendants and relatives of Thomas Bason, James Broadbridge, George Collison, Cecil & William Dean, William Hayes-Fisher, Sid & Herbert Jerram, Bert Palmer, Pat Ronan, Edwin Siveyer, Harry Trusler, Clifford Whitley and Bob Whiting.

At Chelsea, Ron 'Chopper' Harris and Jonathan Thacker. Writing this book would also have been impossible without the help and encouragement of some of our fellow fans: Graham Bush, Karen Halls, Dave Johnstone (only a pound!), John Sawyer, Sam Sawyer, Peter Trenter and Mark Worrall. Also, Scott Cheshire and David Hockings, without whose meticulous work we would have had a mountain to climb.

Elsewhere we also have cause to thank the staff at both the Imperial War Museum and the British Library, Gavin at the Royal Logistics Corps Museum for his time and interest, David Barber at the FA, Tim Carder and the Brighton & Hove Albion Supporters & Historians Society, Roger Wash at Luton Town, the document supply staff at the National Archive for their patience with huge lists of demands and in particular fellow Chelsea (and in particular JT) fan Grace Delahunty who has been cleaning up after us for months. Peter Devitt at the RAF Museum, Hendon, Mike Dottridge for material relating to the Irish Guards at the beginning of the war, Peter Hart for letting us pillage his work and for being rather Yoda-like and tolerant when I annoy him with inane questions, Fawziah Husain, Diane Holmes, Nadine Landrebe,

Timothy McCracken, Kevin Mason, who still doesn't understand the offside rule, Andy Pay at the very least for his help with the Rifle Brigade at Aubers Ridge and more importantly for being a true friend, Louise Provan, Paul Reed for his images and his assistance with the South Downs battalions as well as being an ever-supportive chum, David Simkin, Roger Stillman of Full Stop Photography for his assistance with our images and Alex Wood at Brechin City for his assistance on Colin Hampton. Finally, Mark Bavin, Paul Xavier Fernandes I, Nathan, the self-professed imp lord of Casterley Rock, Naz, Man of Steel, and Mike, the latter certainly not for his jokes.

About the Authors

ALEXANDRA CHURCHILL is from south-west London and has spent most of the last six years contributing to documentaries about the Great War and writing on the subject – her first book *Blood and Thunder: The Boys of Eton College and the Great War* was published in 2014. She is currently working on a book for the centenary of the Somme and a biography of George V, as well as trying her hand at some crime fiction set during the Great War. She has supported Chelsea since 1990 and her club heroes are Roberto di Matteo, John Terry and Branislav Ivanovic.

ANDREW HOLMES lives in south-west London and has spent most of his free time over the last ten years researching, visiting and photographing the Great War battlefields and cemeteries on the Western Front. He has been a Chelsea supporter since 1978 and his club heroes are Kerry Dixon, Gianfranco Zola and Eden Hazard.

1

'Entry by Storm'

In normal circumstances it would have taken years of growth and meticulous campaigning for a new team to finally reach the Football League. Not so with Chelsea. The process by which the club arrived on the football scene was rapid, described as 'entry by storm' by one early club historian,[1] as they flew through the required steps on their way to the highest echelons of the game. As the New Year was rung in at the beginning of 1905 the club did not even exist; nine months later Chelsea were playing in the Second Division.

Football clubs were springing up all over London at the turn of the century. High estimates put a figure of 100,000 Londoners playing for some 2,000 teams in the decade or so prior to the Great War. Despite this, top-level football in the capital developed at a slower rate than further north. During the 1900/01 season the southern limit of the First Division was Small Heath, who later became Birmingham City. The only Football League club south of them, never mind specifically London, was (Woolwich) Arsenal, midway down the second flight. Even if they were not contending for top honours, though, there were a number of clubs in the metropolis by the time Chelsea came about. Fulham were among the oldest, formed in 1879; Millwall had followed in 1885. Arsenal, the first to turn professional, had been formed in 1886, then West Ham United in 1895. Both Charlton Athletic and Crystal Palace were formed in 1905 but their births that year were far less dramatic than that of Chelsea.

In 1896 Henry Augustus ('Gus') Mears, of a family prominent in the building industry, had come up with the idea of turning the existing Stamford Bridge Athletic Stadium into a football ground. He had no intention of forming a club of his own; in fact his plan was to attempt to get Fulham to rent the space. He and his brother 'JT' had no easy time of it when it came to bringing their idea to fruition. First, they had to wait for the death of the freeholder, who wasn't interested in their plan, and then the lease had to expire. In the meantime they purchased the property next door, a large market garden and finally, in 1904 took possession of Stamford Bridge itself.

Even then, Mears almost sold off the land for use as a goods yard to the Great Western Railway, but a friend of his, a financial whizz, convinced him otherwise. They went up to Glasgow to meet an architect and look at stadia in the area. By February 1905 a huge new facility was being put up next to Brompton Cemetery back in west London, terraces being built on top of piles of clay that had been excavated during the construction of the Piccadilly Line.

In order to maximise the potential of their investment, Gus Mears was intending to offer a multi-purpose arena; a home for everything from polo and lacrosse to agricultural shows and military tournaments. Having come this far, though, the Stamford Bridge investors now hit a considerable snag in their enterprise. Fulham declined the opportunity to move from Craven Cottage. The venture took a new twist. If Mears wanted to have a football club call Stamford Bridge home, then it looked as if he would have to form one of his own. Not one to be dissuaded by such things, he did exactly that. At a meeting on 14 March 1905 a name was settled upon. Stamford Bridge FC did not work – it had too many confusing connotations with the site of the Yorkshire battle of 1066, the precursor to that at Hastings. London FC didn't sound right; neither did Kensington. Debating what would sound inspiring being chanted on the terraces, Mears and his cohorts went back to a suggestion that had previously been rejected. 'Come on Chelsea' had the ring to it that they were looking for.

Unless Chelsea Football Club could gain admittance to a league there was little point to its formation. The Southern League seemed like the best bet. A step below the two divisions of the Football League, it was the home of the likes of Fulham, West Ham, Brighton and Hove Albion and Reading. Entry was by election and although Norwich City had oddly been granted admittance for the 1905/06 season, when Chelsea began canvassing, it became apparent that only Southampton could be relied upon to vote 'yes'. Rather than be dismayed, it was decided that Chelsea would aim higher, for the Football League itself. This was ambition indeed. In comparison, Crystal Palace, also formed in 1905, made their debut in the second flight of the Southern League. Charlton, a third London side formed that year, would not even join the Lewisham League as a senior side until 1913, when Arsenal moved away from Woolwich to Highbury and enabled them greater freedom to develop in the area.

Frenzied canvassing was carried out by Chelsea before the various club representatives converged on the Football League's 1905 annual general meeting in Covent Garden. Chelsea's man had to bribe the barman to keep him sober so that he could keep his wits about him. The scene was tense, with rumours afoot that members would not vote this upstart new club in. 'The audacity of them, trying to gatecrash the league like this!'[2] Chelsea were convinced that despite £3,000 in the bank, a ground fit for the First Division and a powerful looking team already being assembled, they would not make it. Happily for Mears and his investment, this was not the case. Thus, before they had ever kicked a ball in serious competition, Chelsea were in the Second Division. 'Well that's that,' Gus Mears was said to remark, 'Now for the struggle.'[3]

John Tait Robertson of Rangers had been named as a prospective player manager while canvassing for the AGM was still in progress. The first two players came in, costing a total of £150, and others were arriving from Sheffield United, Manchester City and Everton. The top clubs in London could expect to draw average crowds of 20,000, even up to 30,000 and Chelsea's gate receipts did not disappoint from the off. In the first season, 1905/06; Chelsea scored 90 goals in 38 games to the surprise of everybody, a Chelsea league total only surpassed twice since, once in the 1980s and again in the double-winning season of 2009/10.

The club attracted media coverage in the early years on account of its fashionable location and big names. The press reported on their pre-match meals (roast mutton and dry toast at one away game), and there was much uproar on one occasion when one player was spotted kissing another in celebration when a goal was scored. The early playing staff was full of characters like William 'Fatty' Foulke, the 23-stone goalkeeper, original captain and fabled first victim of the chant 'Who ate all the pies?' Following him came Robert 'Pom-Pom' Whiting. He arrived from Tunbridge Wells in 1906 bearing his nickname on account of the sheer distance over which he could kick a football. Only 10 goals went by Whiting at Stamford Bridge all season in the league in 1906/07. So confident was he that he allegedly sent the ball boys up the other end of the pitch when he arrived between the posts, for they would not be needed on his watch.

Results were more than satisfactory for a new club, especially at home where visitors declared that the wide open spaces of Stamford Bridge beat them. In just two years Chelsea reached the dizzy heights of the First Division. Despite initially staying up, though, a succinct summary of the 1909/10 season that followed 'is that almost everything which could go wrong did so'.[4] The battle against relegation went to the wire. 'To the very last game of the season Chelsea players, officials and supporters were kept on the rack.'[5] The team only won away from home once and even with the arrival of England's famous amateur centre forward, Vivian Woodward, Chelsea tumbled back down to the Second Division that year along with Bolton Wanderers.

Despite this setback, Chelsea's popularity as a top-level club was growing. With nicknames such as the 'Pensioners' and the 'Buns', in 1912 the gate for one game topped 80,000. Back up they came to the top flight after narrowly missing out the year before. 'What a struggle that was, with the issue open, so far as the people and players at Stamford Bridge knew, until the last kick of the final game.'[6] The club bid a sad farewell to its founder that year. Gus Mears died of kidney failure and was buried next door to the ground in Brompton Cemetery, his funeral cortege stopping momentarily at the gates to Stamford Bridge on its way.

Thankfully for the nerves of the fans, the drama subsided in the 1913/14 season. Chelsea survived by 'steering a middle and not very exciting course',[7] with 16 wins, 15 losses and an eighth place finish as reward. There was a notable win at Villa Park too, which meant that in nine years, Chelsea had beaten every team in the First and

Second Division. The club's existence so far had been a whirlwind, full of highs and lows. Football, however, was about to recede into the background. The ebb and flow of Saturday afternoon fortunes on the terraces was about to be interrupted. On the horizon was a seismic event that made the worries of every club in the country seem petty and irrelevant. After less than a decade, a new page in Chelsea's history was about to become dominated by the most savage conflict the world had ever seen.

2

'A New Stick for an Old Dog'

The Outbreak of War

The *Chelsea FC Chronicle* marked the outbreak of war with contemplative thought at a friendly game against Fulham at the end of August 1914. The 1914/15 season was about to open 'under the shadow of the greatest and most momentous war in the history of the world'.[1] There had been preliminary suggestions that it was improper for the Football League to continue. But the few 'who publicly voted the view that the proper thing, under such terrible circumstances was to carry on a funeral face and mope were quickly silenced',[2] an outcome that was welcomed by those who called Stamford Bridge home. It was, however, clear to all those present that it was the responsibility of anyone not in uniform to at least support those who would endure hardship as a result of the war. The match with Fulham had been arranged specifically to raise money for the cause. From among 7,000 present, fans contributed money at this hasty additional west London derby and both Chelsea and Fulham dispatched the proceeds to the new Prince of Wales's relief fund. Some 5,000 more fans donated money at a match organised by Newcastle United at the other end of the country and in between, similar pre-season games were being played throughout England as the football season approached.

Despite these early gestures and deferential editorials supporting the war effort, the reprieve as far as those disgruntled by the idea of continuing the game in wartime was concerned was short. An impassioned campaign began to suppress the playing of professional matches in particular. How, it was asked, when there was a war on, could men justify watching a game of football? How too could all of these able-bodied young men, these professional athletes, decline the opportunity to display their physical prowess on a battlefield when their country was calling for them? Some newspapers began to refuse to publish match reports and a number of high profile men, such as Arthur Conan Doyle and the Dean of Lincoln, spoke out against such frivolity continuing in the face of war.

Early on, one notable campaigner managed to draw attention to the cause. Frederick Charrington was heir to the brewery of the same name, but at some point in his youth had had an epiphany about the evils of drink. He turned his back on the business and devoted his life to missionary work in London's East End with a special emphasis on temperance. Charrington obsessively led the charge against football and even petitioned the King to intervene in the matter. He asked Fulham if he could address the crowd at a match shortly after their visit to Chelsea at Craven Cottage, a mile and a half from Stamford Bridge. The club did not object to his presence so long as if he spoke he encouraged men to enlist, rather than attempted to attack the sport. He refused and was told that he would be removed if he attempted to protest. According to a friend who went with him, he intended to cause a scene 'even if the crowd tore him to pieces'.[3]

In front of some 12,000 present, including the secretary of the Football Association, Charrington was removed from the ground for getting to his feet and attempting to condemn football despite the club's warning. The savvy campaigner milked the incident for all it was worth, accusing Fulham's employees of beating him up as they tossed him out. On 23 September his farcical case pressing the matter came up in court and on evidence from the directors of the club and the FA's representative, as well as the Fulham manager, it all came to nothing. It transpired that despite being 'assaulted' Charrington's silk cap had not even fallen off and the magistrate subsequently ordered costs against him.

The reason that football was singled out as an example of unnecessary vice and pilloried at the outbreak of the Great War actually went all the way back to the origins of the modern game. The idea of kicking a ball to and fro had been in existence for hundreds of years, but it was not until the nineteenth century that the version recognisable as today's association football began to take shape. It did so at the instigation of the public schools, where it was believed that games should foster a team mentality, selflessness and courage. In the years following the formation of the FA in 1863 the rules began to be standardised and refined and the game was dominated by Old Etonians, Old Carthusians and the like.

Then things began to change. Embraced by the working classes, new teams from industrial areas like Birmingham, Blackburn and Wolverhampton began to dominate the upper echelons of the sport. The working classes had embraced the modern game wholeheartedly. Then came the crunch issue. It 'rolled up on football like a huge black cloud in an otherwise blue sky'.[4] After years of bickering and skulduggery revolving around the complexities of what might be construed as payment, the FA finally legalised professionalism in 1885.

It contradicted the very nature of the public school ethos as far as games were concerned. Playing for money was undignified and ungentlemanly, as were some of the rules that began to develop under the FA's banner. Penalty kicks were first seen in 1911 amidst much bluster. 'It is a standing insult to sportsmen', it was claimed, 'to have to play under a rule which assumes that players intend to trip, hack, and push their opponents and behave like cads of the most unscrupulous kidney.'[5] Also mystifying to those against professionalism in the game was the idea of paying to watch a match. Observation surely did not provide the benefits one would gain from actual participation? The partisan nature of the crowd was distasteful. Where was the sportsmanship when supporters were so clearly behind one team? To those who objected to the arrival of the professional footballer this was all highly offensive, 'another travesty of the game that was to be endured by the purists'.[6]

Thus, with the outbreak of the Great War, the screeching (as the *Chronicle* put it) for the abandonment of professional matches was largely coming from one upper-class corner. It ignored the fact that amateur players, who vastly outnumbered those who earned their living playing the game, were apparently enlisting in droves. 'Football proved to be the medium through which vocal elements of the middle and upper classes launched an embittered literary attack upon … the working-class reaction to the national crisis.'[7] It was to prove to be a 'time for paying off old scores' so to speak, as much as the outcry incorporated a genuine debate on the contribution of football to the war effort.[8] This underlying element had not gone unnoticed at Chelsea. 'It must not be forgotten', claimed the *Chronicle*:

> that some of the noisiest screaming for the instant abandonment of football –
> it is more especially professional football, mark you, that is aimed at – are those
> who have always been bitter opponents of the paid player and all connected with
> him. With him any stick is good enough to beat a dog with, and they are simply
> using the war as a new stick with which to beat the same old dog.[9]

There were, of course, two sides to the debate. Those involved with the game were being criticised for their lack of endeavour, but it would have been ludicrous to claim that it was only professional footballers and the spectators who watched them play that were staying away from recruitment offices. In fact, the reality was far from it.

This was the war to end all wars. At the outbreak of the conflict there was nobody in place at the highest government level to orchestrate proceedings and into the role came a national hero, Earl Kitchener of Khartoum. He took the cabinet post of Secretary of State for War on 5 August 1914 and was immediately a dominating figure. David Lloyd George said that his colleagues were thoroughly intimidated by him. 'A word from him was decisive and no one dared to challenge it at a cabinet meeting.'[10] Within a day in his new role, Kitchener had made steps to get approval for up to half a million men and his famous call to arms was first published, initially asking for 100,000 men to expand the regular army. He was under no illusions about a short war. Envisaging years of fighting and millions of combatants, Kitchener was hell-bent on forging a new force to join the one already across the Channel: a New Army.

In the first week of war some 8,000 men enlisted, a huge jump on peace-time figures, when the army could expect 30,000 a year. The machinery by which men were accepted into the army had immediately begun to expand. As early as 7 August a new recruiting station was opened in Fulham. The local Mayor, who was also a director of both Fulham Football Club and Arsenal, organised an office in the town hall, 500 feet from Stamford Bridge where existing reservists could report for duty. Soon afterwards a recruitment office for new soldiers was also operating out of Munster Road Girls' School, a mile from the ground.

Throughout August recruitment figures jumped to in the region of 50,000 a week. Kitchener quickly had his desired 100,000 men, but it was not until reports reached home, three weeks after the commencement of hostilities, of the less than satisfactory outcome of the Battle of Mons on 23 August that the nation was propelled into hysterical levels of enlistment. Before the British Expeditionary Force turned to begin fleeing from the German onslaught, while a significant and steady stream of men approached the colours, Britain was far from a nation where every man felt compelled to go and enlist.

In the week following Mons, recruiting figures boomed, 10,000 men enlisting in a single day for the first time. In total contrast to Frederick Charrington's evangelical claims that football was a nuisance to be done away with, despite the beginning of the season and crowds arriving to support their team of choice, in the week following his being unceremoniously dumped outside Craven Cottage the army recorded its highest recruiting figures for the entire war. Almost 175,000 men volunteered to join the army in a seven-day period, trebling figures from the week before.

On 31 August a second recruiting office opened at Fulham Town Hall, signing up men at trestle tables put up outside, where modern stalls now do the same to sell programmes and memorabilia on matchdays. On 3 September more than 33,000 men were recruited in a single day, the highest daily return for the war, and that week *The Times* reported that men were waiting up to eight hours to enlist at some locations in London. In the time it took the BEF to get from Mons to the Marne, then back up to the Aisne in mid-September, nearly half a million men answered Kitchener's call to arms – despite the continuance of professional football.

The FA itself had not simply ignored the outbreak of war. Its Vice President acknowledged the calls for the professional game to stop and did not agree with the sentiment. 'Having regard to the great anxieties which all must feel during the continuance of war,' he remarked, 'I think total suspension would be mischievous rather than good.'[11] The FA appeared conscious of its public image, though, as well as of a necessity to do the right thing. Frederick Wall, the Secretary and the same FA official who had witnessed Charrington's antics at Craven Cottage, had an acrimonious exchange with the Dean of Lincoln. He had made accusations of impropriety in connection with football betting and ludicrously recommended 'that you at once cancel all players' contracts, that those who are willing [this numbered many apparently] may go immediately to the front'. Ignoring the fact that this was a call for the immediate unemployment of some 7,000 men, he also recommended 'that you only admit men over 40 to your matches if you do not discontinue them altogether'.[12] Wall just about managed to remain polite when he pointed out 'agreements between clubs and players are binding at common law' and that the FA had already expressed a desire that clubs should release men for military service if they so wished.[13] He also requested a list of the many players that the Dean knew were being prevented from joining up. His opponent declined to provide one and cut off their correspondence.

The FA's Secretary did not shy away from the issue of suspending play either. He opened a public dialogue with the War Office in the second week of September and told the military authorities 'that the Football Association is prepared to request all its members to stop the playing of matches if the War Office is of the opinion that such a course would assist them in their duties'.[14] To the letter, the War Office replied:

> I am commended by the Army Council to inform you that they are very grateful to your association for its assistance in obtaining recruits for the army ... The question whether the playing of matches should be entirely stopped is more a matter for the discretion of the Association, but the Council could quite realise the difficulties involved in taking such an extreme step.[15]

All that the Army Council asked of the FA was that football clubs did not interfere with the recruiting process so as to hinder it; that they 'take all steps in their power to press the need for the country for recruits upon spectators who are eligible for enlistment'.[16] They could too, if at all possible, set aside some money for the charitable relief of those affected by the war.

The FA had been politically smart. To all intents and purposes the decision was not in their hands. The War Office would have to state they wanted play to stop and it appears that neither organisation yet wanted responsibility for making that landmark decision. So equilibrium reigned. 'As the War Office are satisfied,' [Wall] noted, 'the Football Association are of the opinion that its members should continue to play matches where by doing so they can assist and not hinder the authorities in recruiting'.[17]

As requested, the FA did encourage enlistment, and intervened as much as possible in respect of players' contract issues; but at this stage the FA made no desperate appeals for men to enlist for a simple reason. For now there was no shortage of men; in fact there were too many coming forward for the army to deal with. In the first week of September the recruiting boom reached its zenith and the War Office no longer had control of the situation. No administrative framework existed to process recruitment in such volume, or at such speed. It had taken less than a week to raise a second 100,000; in fact of the 500,000 Kitchener had laid the groundwork for on his appointment, 439,000 had been attested, *not* including those who had joined territorial units locally. In fact, when Frederick Wall offered on the FA's behalf to facilitate recruiting stations at matches, he was told there was no manpower available and that clubs should direct men to their nearest recruiting office. For those not waiting in eight-hour queues but already enlisted and languishing in depots, there were massive shortages of food, accommodation, uniforms, rifles and bedding, to say the very least. While of course logic would propel the authorities to take anybody who offered their services at this point while enthusiasm was high, 'on the other hand, it must be said that most of the early problems faced by the New Armies were the direct result of the failure to impose some sort of ceiling on enlistments until the War Office was in a position to cope with the influx of volunteers'.[18]

On 12 September Chelsea played Newcastle at home and it was noted in the programmes that Kitchener already had his half-million men, 'provided the army medical examiners and recruiting officers have been able to keep up *their* end'.[19] For now what was the point in more men rushing to enlist? 'If still more men are required the country has only to ask for them and they will be forthcoming – and from no section of the community more readily than the much maligned footballer or "follower".'

It was forcefully pointed out too, that it was not the War Office or the Admiralty lambasting professional football for failing to do its duty. 'First let us be told – by those who KNOW – not merely that it is necessary, but that the authorities are ready, and able to do THEIR part of drilling, clothing, arming and instructing an unlimited number of men.'[20] Indeed if everyone joined the army at once there would be several million for the authorities to deal with. 'It remains for the War Office to sound the call, not the cranks,' proclaimed the *Chronicle*:

> Far be it from us to minimise the gravity of the situation, or to deter one single man from flocking to the colours … [But] so long as the best class of recruits are coming forward faster than they can be enlisted, there is no need for hysteria or the slinging of verbal mud at players or spectators. When the War Office tells us that it is time to stop, there will not be a moment's hesitation in complying.[21]

As well as the failure of the press to observe the bigger picture as regards to the logistics of the recruitment process and that of turning men into soldiers, the *Chronicle* was much irked by the hypocrisy evident. It referred to journalists as 'hedging their patriotism'. The same newspapers slamming the continuation of professional football were, in most cases, still providing their readers with coverage of the game. 'Highly souled motives do not preclude them from giving the results of matches, the names of the goal scorers; or the league tables!' In addition to noting that those calling for the cessation of football were unconnected with the sport, the FA had remarked at a meeting that the game, 'which is essentially the pastime of the masses, is the only sport which is being attacked … although football has publicly stated its willingness to place its whole organisation and influence at the service of the War Office'.[22]

A fierce argument that appeared in the *Hull Daily Mail* contained elements that suggested that the author himself was closely connected with the game. 'Throughout the country we hear of teams enlisting in bloc, yet because a matter of 7,000 ... professionals do not sacrifice everything, the sport is condemned.'[23] Until such time as every other profession saw all of their number enlist, the debate was unbalanced. The wily editor of the *Chelsea FC Chronicle* went so far as to point out that these journalists, 'vehemently insisting that *every* man between 19 and 35 should either drop his work and rush helter-skelter to the nearest recruiting office ... or else be branded as a coward and wear a petticoat', worked in large offices staffed by hundreds. Who was inside? 'Young boys, old men – or business like girls while the young men are carrying out their editors precepts and flocking to the colours?'

He was indignant. There was a legend that Sir Francis Drake had seen out a game of bowls while the Spanish Armada approached England and more than one Chelsea fan remarked upon it. 'Luckily for Drake there were no half-penny papers in his time ... Just imagine what some of them would have said about him for coolly insisting on finishing his game ... when the "invaders" of his native land were actually in sight!'[24] Perhaps, it was speculated, he would have been just as defiant as they now were. 'Drake was about the last man to care a tinker's cuss for hysterical nonsense of any sort.'

It is important to remember that it was unequivocally a *choice* as to whether one wanted to go to war at this point and it was a choice that in no way did British men universally make in 1914. For all of the men that rushed to enlist, there were several more that would not volunteer to fight in the Great War. Who were *The Times* or the 'white feather brigade' to attempt to compel a man to put his life at risk if he did not want to? There were a number of reasons why not every footballer enlisted in the late summer of 1914. 'It must be remembered that they are bound by agreement to their clubs,' remarked one newspaper trying to argue the case for the professional footballer at the beginning of September. Certainly at least one player remarked on his club's reluctance to let him go. Charles Buchan, a Sunderland legend, who would spend a good deal of time playing for Chelsea during the war, claimed that when he expressed his desire to go and join the army he was categorically reminded that he was under contract.

For those men with families, the debate as to whether married men should enlist would not take hold until 1915 and they would not be compelled to serve until the middle of 1916. At the beginning of the war there was arguably no stigma attached to a man who chose not to leave his wife and children to fight. It has, too, been put forward that the direct correlation between the number of war widows relative to deaths in the war indicates that married men were on the whole 'much more reluctant' to go to war. This argument was true of a number of Chelsea fans, never mind players who, even if they did not object to being shot at for starters, were unwilling at this stage to leave their families.

Chelsea opened the floor for some of these men to defend themselves. The reasons cited were largely economic. One said that he was not enlisting because he was solely responsible for his widowed mother and his own wife and children. He had, however, no intention of staying out if the necessity arose. Another Chelsea fan made a similar claim, that his family was simply too large for him to entertain the thought of leaving them. Another had tried, but was unable to enlist 'because my patriotic employer has refused any facilities, [and] will not reserve my post or make my widowed mother any allowance'.[25] The fact that money was a mitigating factor when men were considering whether or not enlist was not lost on the press. *The Times* pointed out on 11 September that when the call for a public school's battalion yielded 2,000-odd men within days, 'they are all of the well-to-do class, and are paying their own expenses'.[26] It was a generalised assumption to make, but an interesting point nonetheless.

None of this was immediately visible to disapproving people on the street of course. A deaf supporter was not unused to people initially commenting on his non-military status. Other Chelsea supporters still in civilian clothing, fending off women with feathers, had indeed tried to join the army. One fan was turned away because his eyesight was deemed sub-standard, while another supporter stated that on his second application to enlist, his chest measurement was found to be slightly deficient and so they would not take him. He was still defiant. Many men who later served were initially turned away from recruiting offices. 'I am determined,' he wrote, 'to do my best by joining some corps, patronising home industries and supporting Chelsea.'[27] Added to that there were men in civilian clothing who had enlisted. Deferred enlistment was introduced in the first week of September as a means to ease the burden on the War Office. Men were signed up and then sent home on a tiny allowance of sixpence per day until the army could call them back and process them properly.

The future of the clubs themselves was threatened with potentially dire economic circumstances if they were immediately ordered to halt their business. The chairman of Millwall Football Club had meticulously compiled details of the potential cost of abandoning the football season. He calculated a loss of some £500,000, more than half of which was wages for players and trainers. That was to say nothing of others employed by the clubs. Chelsea were particularly mindful of the old gatemen, most of them 'too old' for their trade, who kept their heads above water by taking tickets on matchdays. These employees, others at the various grounds and the cash paid for a police presence at matches, amounted to another £12,500 of lost revenue. Some £17,000, the chairman claimed, would be lost in printing and advertising. Rents, rates and taxes came to £35,000 and he pointed out that a large chunk, some £115,000, was already accounted for in outgoings before a fan had come through a gate – money owed to banks in the form of loans and overdrafts.

'The increase of distress which would result from a complete cessation of professional football is ignored by these "dog-beaters",' proclaimed the *Chronicle*. 'It is not only the so called "pampered" professionals and their dependants who would suffer.'[28] And where would these men and women turn to in the face of their distress? Why a relief fund of course, to which Chelsea and other league clubs were religiously dispatching regular cheques; which would of course stop if there was no more money coming in.

As for men who were already at the front, the Chelsea contingent at least appeared to have no problem with the season continuing. Several regular soldiers who had already seen action wrote to the club to say that they eagerly awaited the football news when scarce newspapers arrived. As the war of movement on the Western Front came to an end and the combatants in France and Flanders began to dig trench lines that would largely hold each other at bay for years to come, so too the frantic recruitment boom came to an end. Unsurprisingly, while the War Office battled to process hundreds of thousands of existing recruits, the clamour for the cessation of football began to subside.

'The "Stop Your Games!" screech appears to have died down considerably of late,' remarked the *Chronicle*. Perhaps, it speculated, they had realised that not everyone could enlist at once. 'This side of the question must surely have been patent to anyone of even moderate intelligence.'[29] To those willing to listen to both sides of the argument, the image of the entire country flooding to the colours while footballers ignored the world falling down about them was patently unfair. The day might well still come when every man would be expected to put on a uniform. In 1914 though, Britain had not yet reached the point at which the principle of resisting conscripting her men into uniform would have to be abandoned. For now at least her men would not be forced unwillingly to shoulder a rifle and go to war.

3

'Cook's Tourists'

The Great Retreat

Like a string of dominoes falling down, Europe's great powers plunged into war in the summer of 1914. A feeling of inevitability had plagued the Continent for a number of years, 'for nations do not build up gigantic armies and navies beyond their defensive needs,' remarked the *Chelsea FC Chronicle*, 'for the mere pleasure of reviewing them occasionally – any more than football clubs would spend thousands of pounds in players' wages if they designed to play friendly matches only.'[1]

The order to mobilise was given on 4 August 1914 but before troops could begin the bloody business of war there was much organisation to be done; including the creation of large bases across the Channel to keep the army going when the fighting began. Little thought of, the work of the Army Ordnance Corps was in fact pivotal to the war effort. Before the end of 1918 it would move some 25.5 million tons of supplies, including, at random, 16 million mess tins, 5.5 million pick axes, nearly a million saddles, 13.5 million waterproof sheets, 35.5 million blankets, 108 million pairs of socks and 2.6 million pairs of rubber boots.

Among their number was a young Chelsea fan named Frederick William Brooks. Originally from Devon, the 21-year-old storeman had been stationed in his home county and at Tynemouth already in his short career, being introduced to London and Chelsea while seeing out another spell at Woolwich. The AOC's recent experience, gleaned while Fred was still a boy, was of providing for the army during the Second Boer War and so would prove largely irrelevant for what they now faced in 1914. Operations had been fluid and their supply solutions based on the fact that troops would be out of contact from the lines of communication in deepest Africa for long periods of time. They had also operated on the basis that they did not know where they would ultimately turn up. This would not be the case on the Western Front. The issue of supply had also been coloured by the fact that stores needed during the Second Boer War had had to travel thousands of miles to reach

The Great Retreat in the opening weeks of the war spanned from Belgium all the way to Paris as the German army attempted to carry out their 'Schlieffen Plan' and finish the war in the West. *(THP)*

the army from Britain, whereas now ships could be dashed across the Channel. Additionally, at the turn of the century there were no big battles requiring the expenditure of obscene amounts of ammunition and material which would need instant replacement. The Great War was going to be a steep learning curve for Fred Brooks and the AOC from the very beginning.

Havre, at the mouth of the River Seine, had been identified before the war as the main forward supply depot because it had good rail links via Rouen, which sat further upriver, and beyond that with Amiens, which was a convenient stop-off on the way to the BEF's intended concentration point at Maubeuge near the Belgian border. Before long the port would be taking in tens of thousands of tons of equipment destined for the front. With the responsibility for organising supplies once they arrived, unsurprisingly contingents of ordnance men were among the first to arrive in Havre on the outbreak of war, establishing their headquarters on the quays.

Fred Brooks arrived with No. 2 Company of the AOC on 15 August, charged with helping to bring the depot at Havre to order just as the bulk of the BEF began arriving. Almost immediately the British established a multitude of facilities including hospitals, aid posts, veterinary facilities, reserve baggage stores, a telephone exchange, two telegraph offices and latrines for more than 20,000 soldiers. Thousands of men staggered onto the quays in the sunshine after being stuffed into transports, falling on specially erected coffee shops to revive themselves. Fields full of white tents were springing up all around the hilly countryside surrounding the town and arrivals were of such a high volume that there were special marching routes in and out of Havre to avoid congestion.

As others passed through on their way to where the BEF was concentrating further inland, Fred and his fellow storemen were to carry out their backbreaking work right by the water in an immense storage shed named the Hangar Aux Cotons. Situated on the Quai de la Garonne, the building was more than half a mile long and 600 feet wide. The water ran along one side and on the other were rails which fed into the main railway network around Havre and onwards to the front. It was so vast that several thousand men, hundreds of horses, 2,000 huge barrels of beer and endless stacks of supplies only half filled it when the BEF first arrived. In this sweaty enclosure, the Base Supply Depot for Fred and his men to store everything coming off of ships was established at the eastern end.

The men worked hard, carrying thousands upon thousands of boxes off arriving transports as they steamed into Havre. The hangar was stifling:

Twenty five acres of airless cobble-paved, glass roofed heat, packed with a seething mass of sweating humanity, struggling with boxes and bales of every description, amidst a dust that parched out throats, so that many lost their voices, so great was the din in this place that the great thunderstorm we had in the first half of August was not even heard of in the hangar.[2]

Outside in the heat of summer, floating cranes removed heavier items from ships such as wagons and pontoons. The endless rattle of steam cranes on the quayside continued around the clock as holds were emptied. Ordnance men brushed shoulders with French aristocrats who had volunteered for the work. A grandson of Marshal Ney, 'the Duke of something', worked twenty hours a day in the mayhem 'as cheerfully as if he merely sauntered in the pleasure grounds of his chateau'.[3] The British Army dismissed him at 2 a.m. and he was on duty again eagerly three hours later.

But how to organise everything? Arrangements were already less than ideal, as the AOC was ignorant as to what would be arriving for them. Documents about supplies were withheld, despite appeals, in the interests of secrecy. 'The position might be compared to that of a manager sent to open a new branch of a bank whose liabilities ... were bound to be heavy; yet whose head office refused to help him ascertain either his available capital of further liquid resources.'[4] Littered about the gigantic hangar already, as well as in other sheds, workshops or wharves were some 20,000 tons of clothing, ammunition and stores of unknown quantities and more kept arriving:

> The articles were in miscellaneous heaps often buried under piles of forage; wagons had been dismantled for shipment, the bodies had not yet been erected on their wheels, machine guns had not been assembled with their mounts or cartridge belts, guns with mechanisms, cases of horseshoes with those of nails.[5]

The scene was one of slightly organised chaos. All of the extra space they had for now caused problems too. People kept trying to utilise it. 'In spite of protest, horses were stabled amongst the stores and French and Belgian soldiers encamped there ... lorries lodged under the same roof, thundered to and fro. Altogether the scene was one of great confusion.'[6]

A planned six divisions forming the British Expeditionary Force were to disembark at the onset of the war, at Havre, Rouen and Boulogne, which was a better destination for cavalry as it was situated further north and was therefore a shorter journey for the horses. Each division of infantry consisted of nearly 20,000 men but some 40 per cent of them were not in front-line regiments. The rest, no less crucial, consisted of troops like Fred Brooks, those who kept the men in the front lines supplied with everything they needed to function.

Key in providing for these soldiers was the Army Service Corps. Until the Corps of Royal Waggoners in 1794 there was no organised form of supply and transport to move with the army. It was not until the ASC was formed in 1888 that the concept of supplies and how to move them were linked together properly. They were also to be a corps trained for combat, not a mere logistical department, and would be capable for the first time of defending their own convoys in attack. The first test came during the Boer War and it was accomplished admirably in trying conditions.

A decade or so later, in 1914, the ASC consisted of seventy-one companies. The fact that this number was to expand to over 1,100 throughout the course of the Great War was indicative of how vital they were to the army in a multitude of different roles and how significant their contribution would be. In the matter of supply, once dispatched by the Army Ordnance Corps from a depot, a substantial proportion of the responsibility for delivering items into the hands of the troops at the front would be theirs. After being selected for dispatch, items were put on trains at the likes of Havre and sent inland to a railhead, 'the farthest limit of the railway that was considered advisable in the context of war being waged nearby'.[7]

Once it arrived at a railhead a delivery would ordinarily be routed to a supply park until it could be picked up. An ammunition park was a specialised type of storage facility close to the lines operated by a company of the ASC using motorised (as opposed to horse) transport. They accumulated 'dumps' of everything from shells to mortars and bullets for rifles ready for dispatch to fighting units. They would align themselves both with the railhead and in a position convenient for collections. Another Chelsea fan found himself at 1st Division's ammunition park: in his early 30s, Lawrence Catchpole was not a regular soldier. A significant proportion of the original BEF was formed of various types of reservists and Lawrence was one such man. By trade, he was a driver for the London General Omnibus Co. and as part of the Special Reserve was committed in peacetime to giving just three to four weeks a year to the army. At the outbreak of war Motor Transport units were scheduled to depart from Avonmouth.

Employed as a driver, Lawrence, 'willing, honest, sober, reliable' as one reference described him,[8] arrived on 6 August, leaving behind in the capital a son less than a year old and a heavily pregnant wife. After a week of preparation, he sailed for Rouen with the rest of his company; three officers and 350 men equipped with ninety lorries, seven motorcycles and four cars, responsible for keeping 1st Division able to fight off the German army.

A fellow Blues fan was present in France early on with another type of store. Born in 1895, Albert Ponman was the third son of a large Southwark family and having worked as an errand boy to bring money home, he had joined the ASC as a teenager. Albert's Company operated using horses and wagons and was officially classed as a 'Reserve Park', housing emergency supplies and performing admin and support roles. Prior to the war they had been trundling about Portsmouth on local transport duties with just thirteen pairs of horses. On 6 August at Hilsea almost 200 more animals arrived along with reservists, increasing the size of their unit massively. Before they departed yet more Special Reserve men had joined along with over a hundred more horses. It took eight trains at Fratton to carry them along the south coast a short distance to Southampton where they embarked on three ships that sailed into Havre on 21 August. On arrival in France, the 5th Reserve Park numbered a comparatively huge 155 wagons, but were consistently reporting that despite their influx of men and horses, they were still short of what was needed for a wartime complement.

While troops continued to arrive in France and make their way inland to Maubeuge, the Royal Flying Corps had already spied a long grey column of German troops threading its way westward towards Britain's small force. The Battle of the Frontiers was already taking place to the south and despite the efforts of the French it appeared that the initiative was passing into the enemy's hands. France's attempts to beat a path to Berlin through Alsace and Lorraine were failing and in the meantime multiple German armies were pressing down on the northern end of the Allied line. The BEF moved north from France into Belgium and cavalrymen encountered their German counterparts on 21 August. Two days later the British Expeditionary Force attempted to help put a stop to the German advance for the first time in their clash at Mons. Despite being vastly outnumbered they held their own until the afternoon when enemy troops began to force a way across the canal that ran through the town and forced a retirement south. The battle was not a loss, but the position at the canal had been so unsatisfactory by the close of play that there was little choice but to withdraw. The casualties had amounted to some 1,600 men killed or put out of action, but their loss was felt disproportionately as almost half of them had come from just two battalions. The German advance, however, had been delayed.

To the rear with their ammunition and reserve parks, Lawrence Catchpole and Albert Ponman had heard the artillery pounding away in battle and seen aeroplanes buzzing overhead. The lines of communication had had just a few days to assess how to move food, equipment and ammunition from Britain, through the supply depots and out towards the front, and little time to consider how to effectively distribute it. Now they would need to urgently replenish all of the above in the most chaotic of circumstances as the army fell back from the German onslaught.

Once supplies or equipment had gone past Fred Brooks and arrived at a park looked after by the ASC with the likes of Lawrence Catchpole or Albert Ponman, they would need to be collected by a fast-moving unit called a Divisional Supply Column for dispersal to their division, wherever it might currently be situated. Yet another Chelsea fan and reservist, Thomas Bason, found himself engaged with one, shuttling supplies frantically back and forth for the Cavalry Division. It was a significant responsibility to keep such a large formation fed, moving and capable of fighting off the enemy.

As the BEF picked up and began streaming away from Mons and its environs, the Cavalry Division could be expected to cover as many as 11 miles when stretched out on the road, comprising up to 9,000 men and nearly 10,000 horses as well as its collection of artillery and machine guns. Forty-year-old Thomas arrived in Avonmouth on the same day as Lawrence Catchpole, one of the first to join his unit. Like his fellow Chelsea fan he was a London bus driver, born off North End Road a few years before Stamford Bridge had been originally built. He was now settled with his wife and five children in a terraced house among the crisscrossing railway lines just south of the river, a stone's throw from Battersea Park and the Dog's Home.

Getting the Divisional Supply Column ready for departure was not easy, as many of the reservists were unruly and out of military shape and there were few officers yet present to bring them into line. The entire unit, led by five of them, comprised some 340 men divided into two sections. One section drove 3-ton lorries and the other, which Thomas joined, smaller ones that weighed just shy of three-quarters of a ton. As night fell on the battlefield at Mons, the Supply Columns began shuttling out towards the retreating troops laden with food.

Each division of the army had a significant amount of transport under its own command known as the Divisional Train and it was here that supplies were ideally delivered by the column. In peacetime these small horse-drawn companies were scattered throughout the Empire, engaged in local military transport, and yet another Pensioners fan had spent a significant amount of time abroad. Arthur Timoney had been born at the Curragh where his Irish father was stationed in 1891. Patrick Timoney had been one of the first men to join the ASC in the 1880s. Later he served in the Boer War where the new corps received its initiation as a Wheeler before retiring to become a pub landlord at the Old George in Holborn. Just as his father had retired, Arthur had enlisted in the Corps and quickly earned the tag as the fabled 'Timoney the Fiddler of 18 Company'.[9] Soon he was sent south to Pretoria and joined his father's old company. They dedicated much of their leisure time to football and Arthur was something of a star forward, despite the fact that their little company was facing other teams from such large groups as brigades and regiments, as well as prized civilian outfits. They won the Pretoria Wednesday Cup in 1911, defeating the favourites United Banks. Arthur scored the winning goal in an end-to-end game, prompting sticks and hats to go flying in the crowd after 24 Company ASC promptly 'parked the bus' to see out a 4–3 victory in extra time.

When war was declared four ASC companies were pulled into a 'Train'. There was much ignorance about what the term actually signified. 'What is a Train?' the commander of one was asked by a lady who took it literally. 'I should have thought Officers were too precious to waste as guards; but, of course, you couldn't possibly get to the war without them.'[10] Timoney's company was joining a group of ASC units that would constitute the Train for the 5th Division. It was a vitally important and significant formation, that when in procession on the road, created a line some 2 miles long when travelling with divisional ambulance units. Roughly 400 men had at least as many heavy draught horses to care for as they dragged well over 100 wagons along. They were the 'workhorse' of a Division, carrying everything from military supplies to food and baggage.

In the early hours of 24 August it was decided that the sharp removal from Mons was not enough. The commander of the BEF, Sir John French, wanted to retire some 14 miles south-west through Maubeuge and Bavay into France to protect his army. His orders were executed, but despite the best intentions it was not as well organised as staff officers might have hoped. Arthur Timoney and his Divisional Train were about to be tested to the utmost. What began as a tactical withdrawal from one town was about to descend into an epic march south, pursued by enemy troops in often blistering conditions as the enemy bore down on Paris and threatened to knock France, Belgium and Britain out of the war so that they might turn their attentions to the great numbers of troops the Russians could muster in the East.

The 24 August began with an immense amount of confusion as far as Arthur and his fellow men were concerned. At dawn they were issued complicated orders to make their way to Vendregies with their unwieldy transport. These were countermanded an hour later by new instructions telling them to take a different route. Five minutes after that they received yet more orders that had been issued as early as 5.30 a.m. but were only just reaching them and telling them *not* to go to Vendregies but to an alternative location. By the afternoon they had been given a third destination verbally before ultimately being rerouted to a fourth in an entirely different direction, where it was now intended that the 5th Division would attempt to concentrate somewhere else.

In contrast, Lawrence Catchpole and his ammunition park had not gone anywhere. They spent the whole day sitting still awaiting orders and it wasn't until 25 August that a car laden with three staff officers clattered past and said they had forgotten all about them. They went back on themselves to Landrecies, where they had waited throughout the battle on the 23rd but found it full of troops so went on to Étreux, arriving there instead at midnight.

Throughout the BEF it was a similar story for the Supply Trains. 'I stopped every dispatch rider who came through the town,' remarked one officer:

> and at last I got an order to march to Presleau ... Just as I was about to comply ... a motor cyclist despatch rider, streaking with sweat and covered with dust, dashed up to me cancelling ... and substituting an order to march at once to Villers-Pol, via Wargnies.[11]

The lack of distinct orders was hard on the physically drained men who had now gone as many as forty-eight hours without sleep. One train was pulled up by a staff officer just as they were about to bed down for the night and told that they had to move immediately:

> He said he would be back ... in three minutes, but it was not until 7am that he returned with the order to move; so that the whole night we were standing motionless on the road, and the drivers were falling off their boxes in their sleep. Another officer was so tired that he stood in front of a hedge and used the most appalling language at it for not obeying orders.[12]

It turned out that in his tired state the hedge looked to the officer like a horse and wagon.

Considering the circumstances, the first day of the retreat had been carried out without major mishap, even for Arthur Timoney's division, which was forced to attempt to defend 6 miles of front as they moved with the help of the cavalry and a smaller formation of infantry. The men were now desperate for both food and sleep, but despite their exhaustion there would be no rest forthcoming. As 25 August dawned, Sir John French was aware that the enemy had already moved 10 miles past the right flank of his little force and he decided to continue the retirement a further 15 miles to the neighbourhood of Le Cateau.

Picking up and preparing to move early in the morning was another Chelsea fan, named James Broadbridge. Although born in Fulham, 22-year-old James's large family had relocated to between Wimbledon and Tooting before he joined the Royal Field Artillery as a teenager. Third Division's artillery was overseen by a small headquarters of twenty-two men and a similar number of horses. Amongst their number, James had been stationed at Bulford on Salisbury Plain along with the rest of the division when war was declared. On 16 August approximately sixty guns were put aboard the SS *Californian*, notorious for not coming to the aid of the *Titanic* two years earlier. A week later their precious weapons had only been extracted with great difficulty at Mons from a salient, covered by a Highland regiment.

As the BEF's weary trek resumed on 25 August, both James Broadbridge and Arthur Timoney passed into the vicinity of the Forest of Mormal, 'a compact and well cared-for block of woodland, mostly oak and beech'.[13] Arthur and his Divisional Train passed down the old Roman road that ran past its western side. Conditions were trying, 'for the sun had beat down fiercely upon the interminable length of the straight, white, dusty road and under the tall trees … there was not a breath of air to relieve the stifling heat'.[14] During the afternoon dark clouds replaced blue skies compounding the misery of the fleeing Expeditionary Force. At about 5 p.m., just as Arthur's division finished trudging into the area about Le Cateau, the clouds broke and rain came down in torrents, soaking half-sleeping men to the skin.

The BEF had embarked upon a manic period of being constantly on the move pursued by a largely unseen, but huge enemy. One of the hardest tasks on this forced march fell to Thomas Bason and the Supply Columns, their role being to try and co-ordinate between constantly re-designated railheads and, as illustrated by the plight of Arthur Timoney and his confused Divisional Train, erratically controlled recipients with no definitive orders retiring away from them. Even when a column caught up with their allotted division, this huge formation consisted at full strength of thousands of men, thousands of horses, dozens of pieces of artillery and dozens of machine guns. Strung out on the road altogether they could cover up to 15 miles, the train somewhere among it all. The roads were jammed solid and on the first night of the retreat, the 5th Divisional Supply Column pulled to a stop and could not distribute their wares to Arthur and their ASC counterparts because of the magnitude of late night traffic struggling along. Lorries were already breaking down under the strain of constant movement and there were limited quantities of parts and equipment available for repairs. Drivers were being sent up from ammunition parks with their vehicles to try and cover the shortfall, but it was not enough. Almost immediately the ASC attempted to simplify the chain of supply. On 25 August the 5th Division Supply Column was ordered to go right up to the troops and begin distribution. Instead of Arthur and his fellow men driving up their wagons for loading, the Train would send their officers to orchestrate proceedings direct from the lorries.

I Corps, comprising the 1st and 2nd Divisions under the command of Douglas Haig, had travelled down the opposite side of the Forest of Mormal and with them was another Blues fan with the artillery. Chelsea-born Henry Jarvis was another reservist in his 30s who, since leaving the army, had been working as a postman. Married with a newborn baby boy when war broke out, he was summarily recalled to duty to serve as a driver with 2nd Divisional Ammunition Column. This kind of formation did not exist until the army was mobilised, when nearly 600 artillerymen were pulled together. They were equipped with over 700 horses and tasked with keeping tens of thousands of weapons firing, dragging along shells, as well as small arms ammunition and more for the machine guns. Unsurprisingly, the Column was a 'huge and unwieldy thing on the road',[15] and on those as congested as the ones running south of Mons, Henry's had been unable thus far to function in the normal way. They simply passed along with the rest of the traffic, 'bundled on out of the way as fast as possible so as not to block the road for others'.[16] Like James Broadbridge's guns, the 2nd Division's had been engaged at Mons. Two had come under particularly heavy fire from two German batteries and they had already suffered a number of men killed and wounded. On their way south on 24 August, the column met up with reinforcements in an orchard where they had been ordered to stand in readiness for action. All of the conversation among Henry and the men was of Mons. One of their guns had been pulverised by enemy fire, but was still being dragged alongside on the retreat:

> The only two survivors of the detachment filled us with stories of the fight but always kept coming back to poor Bill … and showed again and again the hole in the seat made by the [shell] which had first passed through [him]. They seemed a bit dazed by it all and certainly that gun with the still fresh marks of blood brought it home to us all for the first time.[17]

It was to prove a quick introduction to war, for at Le Cateau the German Army would catch up with the British in force. The German First Army was hard on their heels and the little BEF turned to attempt to help take the impetus out of the enemy's advance. Battle commenced not long after dawn on 26 August when the enemy came within close rifle range of some of 3rd Division's troops. They held their own but by 10 a.m. the British were being bombarded heavily along the whole divisional front. Half an hour later the Germans attacked again. Thanks in part to the artillery under James Broadbridge's care, spread about Audencourt, they were pinned from taking too much ground but pressure continued and at noon part of the village itself had to be evacuated.

Telephone wires which had been laid immediately for instructing James' batteries were cut early on in the battle by enemy artillery and messages had to be taken in and out on horseback. The same issue was evident up and down the front. 'The terrific nature of the battle that was taking place not only affected those bearing the brunt of the day's action, but the whole line of communications.'[18] Everywhere dispatch riders attempted to fill the void left by the destruction of field telephones. Counter-attacks relieved the situation slightly, but shortly afterwards word arrived that the whole division was to fall back. Some troops did not get the order and found themselves lost, but the whole mess was covered by artillery and the Germans did not attempt to give chase as the men retired. James Broadbridge's guns had not fared well. Some, dug in on forward slopes and highly exposed, had covered the infantry retirement with a rapid fire that managed to halt the enemy advance completely; but German rifles meant that they could not safely be removed. Three more were left when no horses could be found to pull them out.

Units like Arthur Timoney's and Thomas Bason's were further to the rear, but they had seen the effect of the fighting. Civilians in the area had been helping to dig trenches, but had largely begun fleeing as battle commenced. General Headquarters had been based at St Quentin, 70 miles to the south-east of Le Cateau, and had begun hurriedly packing up to leave. This added to the panic among the locals. 'Outside, the town was in the greatest state of excitement; it was in the air that we had been completely annihilated at Le Cateau and the populace stood about bleating and baaing; some literally too terrified to move.'[19] As the army men walked about people grabbed at them in hope of receiving instruction.

Arthur Timoney had continued down the Roman road early in the day with his train and now, with paranoia that these vital supplies were about to be taken over by German cavalry, staff officers attached themselves to it to ensure that it kept moving in the darkness. Confusion was rife as the road was choked to capacity with transport wagons and lorries. Tiresome, constant security checks were carried out and blockages repeatedly occurred. Finally, by midnight, soaked through, the men had arrived at Estrees, 15 miles south-west of Le Cateau. Troops, transports and animals were a hopeless jumble. In the dark a complicated exercise was undertaken to try and sort the BEF back out into their respective units. In the rain, staff officers stood at the crossroads hollering orders to the arriving men. 'Transport and mounted troops straight on, 3rd Division infantry to the right, 5th Division infantry to the left.' More officers attempted to separate them into battalions, then came the laborious task of parking up the transports:

Parking was a complicated process. Wagons were formed up by the side of the road, or a field alongside if there was one to be had. More often than not they formed a hollow square, they were positioned so that they could move again quickly if necessary. Then the horses were unhooked and tied up. At this point the men were largely past caring what they were doing. As soon as the order to halt was given, they had begun falling asleep on the spot. There was no rest for those with the artillery and the cavalry who had horses to look after though; as officers shook them awake again to feed and water the animals.[20]

'All of this had to be done in inky darkness, under drizzling rain.'[21] There were injuries as a result of the confusion. One man of Henry Jarvis's ammunition column had already been stabbed in the leg with a bayonet because another thought that he looked like an Uhlan. The reservists lent a large, out of practice or inexperienced contingent to the column and this too could be dangerous in times of panic. A group of them were ordered to unload their weapons as they began pinging off shots in a panic and one flew too close to an officer's head. Then the ammunition column had been lulled to sleep, wet and huddling together for warmth by a heavy battery in the next field which kept banging away into the dark.

Sir John French's 'Contemptible Little Army'[22] was now midway through the most stressful part of the retreat. Empty wagons of the likes of the Divisional Train had begun to be utilised for carrying the infantry's packs, but it could not alleviate the strain of constant motion, skirmishing as they went. Despite efforts, the BEF was still in disarray. Rain hounded the men on the 27th August as they moved off. It had still proved impossible to get the whole of Timoney's division linked up together. They roamed the countryside looking for their missing counterparts. James Broadbridge's artillery kept having to stop to take up covering positions, often not being required to fire at all before the laborious process of limbering up and moving off came again. Injured men were bundled into Thomas Bason's lorries as they emptied out their supplies and then ferried them out towards the railheads. The following night an urgent message arrived at Albert Ponman's Reserve Park to say that 200 stragglers in the rear of the 5th Division were starving and that food must be kept for them at all costs. In the event it was impossible to distinguish bedraggled infantry, who had now marched nearly 70 miles in fifty hours, as they passed by. The paved roads were terribly hard on their tired feet and throwing supplies from their wagons, Albert and his fellow men ended up feeding more men of 3rd Division than their own. It was deemed to matter little at this stage, as long as they could keep the flow of traffic moving.

As 28 August continued the sun added to the men's woes again. 'The weather was terribly hot: and our boots felt as if they had been filled with hot marmalade. All our clothes stuck to us, and we had not got used to the weight [of equipment].'[23] With their wagons, Albert Ponman's unit had been ordered to travel back along the road and pick up stragglers who could not continue under their own steam. They passed out oats, preserved meat, biscuits and thousands of gallons of petrol to motor transport and filled their empty wagons with their footsore compatriots. As they left they dumped more supplies by the side of the road for those in the rear to come upon as they followed them down the never-ending path of retreat. Just how confused the BEF was was evident on this day when they picked up almost 500 passengers. Their collection of exhausted men was diverse, including seventy from 8th Field Ambulance, eleven artillerymen, fourteen from the Veterinary Corps, a number of cavalry from scattered regiments to a whole host of infantry soldiers, ranging from big groups of the Middlesex Regiment and Scottish Rifles to a lone man of the Norfolks.

The dust kicked up along the route had given the staggering men of the BEF a ghostly pallor, a 'paste of dust and sweat'.[24] Their boots were in an appalling state and yet there seemed no end in sight. 'Hours passed as a week will at home; and never till now had one learnt the meaning of the phrase about time standing still.'[25] French cavalry crossed their path at one point. 'They looked more as if they were fighting at Waterloo than in this war. They had shining breastplates on, and manes of horsehair streaming from their helmets, and were riding beautiful horses.'[26] It was the first time that some of the men had seen the nearby French forces at all since the beginning of the retreat and it was a relief. Every hour a halt would occur to give the men a short time to rest and refresh themselves. Unless a hapless cow was wandering nearby, the tea that they hastily brewed in tins was always black and overly sweet, 'as the sugar was chucked in out of a sack, more or less anyhow; and there was always little bits of bully beef floating about, as we used to put [it] in water, and some of it always got left'.[27]

Marching did not stop at night, the skies often lit up by burning stacks and villages in the distance:

How many people at home realise what marching at night means, without any lights, and on unknown roads with ditches on either side … the checks, the swearing of drivers … the everlasting rumble of wheels and rattle of pole chains; the noise of the horses' feet; eyes straining into the darkness … throats dry with the constant question; 'Who are you? Who are you?'[28]

The roads were not only packed with the BEF. 'From the moment we started the backward move the natives came with us.'[29] Even as the British fell away from Mons itself, houses appeared shuttered and civilians were seen loading every valuable they could aboard carts, prams and other available vehicles. They trudged along dejectedly, asking the army 'a thousand questions. "Shall we go? Shall we stay? What about the little ones? Our houses? Are you beaten? What shall we do?" How to answer them when we ourselves were in ignorance?'[30] One particular officer with a supply train was attempting to remain positive in front of them. 'We did our best to cheer them up, and to show no anxiety ourselves; but the strain of this can be imagined [when] every minute we expected the Germans to come pouring into [St Quentin] in overwhelming strength, bringing fire and rape and pillage with them.'[31] The natives were understandably terrified, but it was frustrating for the soldiers, for they knew very little about what was happening in the grand scheme of things and could provide no answers:

> We used to get awfully bored with the word 'peur'. The fugitives were always using it. Were we afraid? Need they be afraid? They were afraid for the little ones. Would the children have their fingers cut off as they had had in Belgium; they were afraid so ... It was peur, peur ...[32]

Fraying tempers were in part a result of the terror at the threat of the enemy overrunning the mass of Allied humanity streaming south. Who was to say that there were not already spies among them, infiltrating the procession and passing unnoticed with the retiring army, feeding back information to the enemy? Whenever the buzzing of aeroplanes was heard overhead it meant that soon information about their whereabouts would be relayed back and the German artillery would be trained on them. There was little way to tell between fact and rumour and it all contrived to incite panic. One Commander found his own train galloping towards him 'with the spare men sitting on the boxes beside the drivers, pointing their rifles all over the place ...'[33] He joined them and off they rode, until 'after a wild gallop of about a mile ... we pulled up, and I found that a bogus order had been passed up from the rear to gallop off at full speed'.[34] They thought it was down to spies.

Night skirmishes were far more frightening than those occurring by day. Shots would fly out of the dark and the artillery would be put on alert. Shadows played tricks on the men in the blackness as they took cover. Woe betide any man that lost track of his fellow soldiers in the night, for he could be left behind. 'I found to my horror,' said one man, 'that the section with my horse were going on at the trot so I and the men had to sprint for the last wagon on which we jumped exhausted'.[35] Security was paramount every time the precious supply wagons trundled to a halt. The usual escort afforded to Divisional Trains had been neglected in the confusion for some days and Arthur Timoney and his Company had already been required to defend the entrances to towns en route themselves. Roads in and out of towns would be blocked with wagons and sentries, patrols engaged. Locals would have to put out their lights. Mixed with whatever infantry elements were present, the ASC were to sleep by their rifles and remain on alert throughout the night. The lack of escort remained deeply disturbing given the potential consequences. Much of the defence was being undertaken by reservists worryingly out of practice with their weapons. 'Under other circumstances, it would have been amusing to watch them.' There was no question of letting the enemy get hold of supplies. 'Before ... ever surrendering, the horses [would] have to be shot, and the wagons burnt.' The men were pulling together. A feeling of camaraderie was beginning to develop among all the elements of the BEF, infantry, ASC, artillery, cavalry.

The British Army had been shedding equipment ever since Mons. Both James Broadbridge and Henry Jarvis's units had lost precious guns. Without adequate spare parts and under incredible strain, or even for want of petrol, a demoralising amount of lorries belonging to Thomas Bason's Supply Column had had to be abandoned in the heat. Items would arrive at a railhead designated the day before, only for it to turn out that this was now an area that was too far away for a supply column to get to, or worse still, an area that had now been overrun by the German army. Everything from boots, to baggage, to greatcoats, to field kitchens had been discarded along the way. Unsurprisingly space on the surviving lorries was coveted. Stores were turned away in favour of food and one of the Directors of Ordnance Services found that he couldn't even find a vehicle to get to the railhead on a daily basis. Whole rail trucks full of supplies were turned away for lack of transport. Divisional Supply Columns argued that they should not carry anything other than food and that military supplies and clothing were not crucial enough to take up space. The Ordnance men shouted them down in protest. What stores did get through arrived in a haphazard manner, composed of random bales addressed to all different types of units. Trying to find the recipients was next to impossible and slowed down distribution or ended up in items being delivered to the wrong place.

As August came to a close, the first, crippling phase of the retreat from Mons came to an end and the BEF found time to take a short breath. General Smith-Dorrien's II Corps, Timoney and Broadbridge amongst its number, were utterly spent and he issued a message to all of them as they collapsed into billets:

> The commander of the corps desires to let troops know that the object was to delay the advance of a far superior force of the enemy to enable our allies to conduct operations elsewhere ... General Sir Horace Smith-Dorrien, whilst regretting the terrible heavy casualties and the weary forced marches, in which it has been impossible to distribute enough food, begs to thank all ranks and to express his admiration of the grand fighting and determined spirit shown by all ranks, and his pride in being allowed to command such a splendid force.

There was little time left for any self-congratulation, though. The exhausting march towards Paris was far from at an end. So far some 15,000 men were estimated to be gone from the strength of the British Expeditionary Force, although many of them were simply misplaced along the path of the retirement. By 29 August the terrain became markedly more difficult for the shattered men. The bridges over the Oise blown up behind them, Sir John French's force reached the River Aisne, climbing into forested areas. Inside the air was close, suffocating. The countryside comprised steep hills, thick woodland and narrow valleys. The roads were parched and dusty. Many men were unable to climb up and down the harsh gradients and they were loaded onto empty supply wagons to be carried along. Arthur Timoney's company was detached to march along with some infantry. In command of the French, General Joffre had deemed it necessary to yield more ground before a satisfactory blow could be dealt at the Germans going back in the opposite direction. The British complied and began making their way towards Villers-Cotterêts. The ground was soft and men sank up to their ankles. Transports were stuck fast, 'and only by the drivers putting themselves round the wheel like flies were they able to move the wagons'.

Debris littered the road, broken wagons and dead horses. It was, and continued to be, a very difficult thing to replace them both. Officers were continually on the lookout for horses of any description that had been left in the fields. If the men were in a considerable amount of discomfort after more than a week of marching, then the thousands of animals being driven along on the Retreat were in a worse state. The flies pestered them constantly, 'but the poor jaded brutes after a day or two got too fatigued to trouble about them, so they glued on round their eyes'.[36] The terrain, as well as the state of the roads, caused them considerable discomfort but there was nothing else for it, the horses simply had to be walked along until they dropped dead or had to be put out of their misery. The line of the BEF's retreat was littered with their corpses, limbs sticking out at odd angles.

Still trudging alongside the army were the thousands of refugees abandoning their homes in the face of the oncoming German forces. At each village or town more joined the procession. 'One of the things that all of us noticed was the wonderful welcome we got everywhere and the simple faith these poor people had in the power of the British to protect them ... Bread, eggs, wine, cider, fruit of all sorts, cigarettes, matches, milk.' But water was the prized gift of all. 'The dust on the roads dried up the throat till one could hardly swallow.'[37] Even live chickens were thrust on them if the farmers could not ferry them along with the assurance that it was better the British have them than the Germans. Though their plight was tragic, certain sights were so bizarre that they had to elicit humour. 'To see a huge farm cart drawn by a huge Flemish stallion, a milk cow and a dog, no matter under what circumstances makes you smile.' British soldiers took pity on the smallest children, taking them from the arms of their exhausted families and carrying them along, or putting them on wagons, giving up their own seats and walking alongside. 'This was no slight thing as it meant a walk of thirty miles for the man himself.'

The situation further inland had not escaped those back on the coast at Havre such as Fred Brooks. As early as 24 August the military authorities were contemplating evacuating the bases. The Director of Transport was hurriedly ordered to halt all incoming stores and troops on their way to Havre and Boulogne, devise a list of all equipment currently on hand at the ports and sites nearby and assess what they had that was immediately required by the retreating army.

To clear out Amiens was a relatively simple matter. 'We held nothing beyond some half-dozen lorries fit for little more than the scrap heap, which were abandoned without qualm.'[38] On 27 August the contents of the small depot at Boulogne and its

AOC detachment piled on to the SS *Inventor* and sailed for Havre with 3,000 tons of supplies. At Rouen the stores were shipped down the River Seine towards the main base at Havre too. Any lorries were handed over to the ASC to evacuate and the Ordnance personnel immediately jumped on trains and left.

At Havre, by 29 August the situation was deemed 'so grave' that the decision was taken to entirely abandon the setup on the Seine, and install a fresh line of communication based on Nantes and St Nazaire at the mouth of the Loire. Le Mans would act as headquarters for the Inspector General of Communications and his directors. Some 450 miles south-west of Mons, where the retreat had begun, and 150 miles inland from St Nazaire, it had become worryingly clear that its creation this far south was an operational necessity with the speed of the retreat.

In the meantime, security was heightened at Havre. Cavalry began forming up squadrons for patrols of the area, the infantry furnished outposts, all available pilots ran observation. While troops guarded the countryside against the rumour of enemy attack, Fred Brooks's job, dishearteningly, was to help pick up everything that had been unloaded at Havre and put it back onto ships as fast as they could be got into harbour. It was to be frenzied work. In all, to the main base some 65,000 shipping tons of material, 22,200 people and 3,500 horses would have to be put to sea. All of the infantry reinforcements collected at Havre of the highest military value were to go first. They would be followed by the rest of the unmounted men: specialists such as artillerymen and sappers if there were enough ships for them all. Hospitals, that is, injured men not fit to fight, were to follow those and only then would the time-consuming cavalry be evacuated. All the remaining men staffing HQs and Base units, such as Fred Brooks, were to leave last.

The Ordnance Depot would remain the biggest concern until the end of this ordeal, with its burden of tens of thousands of tons of valuable supplies. Nothing like this evacuation had been attempted by the army before and it was happening at the worst possible moment. The move was occurring just as the army was in a semi-disorganised retreat and known to have sustained serious losses of equipment. 'No other source existed from which these could be made good.'[39] The Havre Depot was not yet organised after three weeks of backbreaking effort and now the men would have to begin all over again elsewhere.

'*Suave qui peut*' was the motto of the day: every man for himself. Panic had begun to strike the town owing to the frenetic military activity and French troops were sent to guard approaches and erect barricades. As Fred and the rest of the Ordnance men at Havre began hurriedly reloading stores, the authorities began trying to impose some structure as to how items were piled up on transports. Small arm ammunition was put on as deck cargo on each vessel but broadly speaking the most important stores were loaded first: ammunition, smallest calibre up to shells and then lastly the cumbersome guns. Any specialist engineering equipment followed and finally general stores: clothing, vehicles, etc. Obviously once reaching the Loire this meant that everything in principle that was most crucial was going to be buried at the bottom of holds. 'Nothing was taken into account beyond the saving at all hazards of equipment of primary military value.'[40] The stores were in a state of hopeless confusion. 'There were cases of service dress caps, parts of guns and machine guns, bales of horse rugs and blankets, ammunition, tentage, signalling gear etc. – much in broken packages, mingled with forage, medical, veterinary and other goods, just as they had been indiscriminately bundled in the hold.'[41] Trying to sort it all at the other end was to be a monumental task that would delay the items reaching the still moving BEF. There was no rest for Fred Brooks, but by 4 September the last of the stores had been cleared. The telegraph offices were closed and the base shut down. On the following day the last ship, the SS *Inventor*, backed away from the quays at Havre laden with depot staff and sailed south.

Back on the retreat, frenzied, localised clashes had occurred for both infantry and cavalry and rumours abounded that German horsemen had entered the ranks of the BEF at the onset of September. On the road the strain was becoming too much for the hollow men still trudging away from the oncoming enemy. Members of Arthur Timoney's train were punished for looting and twenty-four hours later three men of his own company were being readied for a court martial for being drunk on the line of march. Sir John French's force was a wretched sight:

> The men had given away their badges, etc. in exchange for [French girl's kisses] and this made identification very difficult … many men [were] so weakened by the forced marches as to be almost past giving any assistance of identification. They were complete wrecks, these batches of stragglers. Often we came across them huddled up by a signpost, in a little green island of grass, like a little flock of sheep, and about as wilted. 'We want our units, we've lost ourselves.' 'What do you belong to? What is your regiment?' No answer … They seemed to collapse when they saw khaki again. Some we put up in the wagons – those too weak to shuffle along; and others we marched along till we could find a regiment to tack them onto. 'Cook's Tourists' we called them, till the term with us became almost an official one.[42]

By 2 September, nine days into the retreat, railheads were situated only 15 miles north-east of Paris. Rifle shots could be heard in the near distance and aeroplanes buzzed overhead, disturbing the peaceful surroundings: 'an "old worldy" looking place … very like Herefordshire, with its laden orchards and pretty flower gardens'.[43] Arthur Timoney and his company marched off at 3.40 a.m. behind the division's medical personnel to take over guard duty from the infantry at a nearby village. That afternoon all surplus gear not actually used for fighting began departing. As night fell, Arthur's train moved off to cross the River Marne, nearly 200 miles from where the Battle of Mons had been fought ten days earlier. The rest of the British force followed cautiously, French patrols hovering on the periphery; the men trudging across bridges in yet more brilliant sunshine before explosions rocked the countryside behind them as the bridges were destroyed.

The BEF had now reached the suburbs of Paris itself, so critical a prize in the German plan to knock her Western enemies quickly out of the war. Unsurprisingly, efforts had already been made to protect it but they frustrated the weary men and horses traipsing in. The French had dug a myriad of trenches which threatened to not only hinder, but injure British soldiers and wagons as they endeavoured not to fall into them. 'It was pitch dark, and we were very nearly shot, time after time, for blundering [about] … and not hearing the challenges owing to our sleepy condition and the noise of the wheels.'[44] From the city itself long processions of lorries and omnibuses hurried past overflowing with blue-clad Frenchmen on their way to do battle with the approaching Germans. They were cheered loudly on by the BEF, who at last were coming to the end of their ordeal. On 5 September Arthur Timoney's retirement came to an end. At Courcouronnes to the south of the French capital, the Train distributed more than 5,000 grocery rations and almost 300 cases of biscuits to exhausted troops.

Despite the Germans' rapid advance they were just as tired as the Allies. Gaps had begun to open between their troops and for all their forward momentum the French Army was still a huge obstacle to overturn in order to divert their attentions to the Eastern Front. Joffre had decided that the time was right to turn and make a stand. Siphoning off men he created a new army on the left of the BEF. The British contribution was small, but on 6 September together with the French they began to do battle on the Marne. Three days later a German retirement was ordered. The Allies now turned to begin marching back in the direction from which they had come, but morale soared. It was far from the same thing as their tiring retreat:

> It sounds a little thing to march back along the road you came down the day before, but I can't say what it meant to us. We heard nothing, only on marching out of the field we turned to the right instead of the left we had expected and found ourselves going towards the Germans.[45]

Disaster at the very onset of the Great War had been averted. For the likes of Lawrence Catchpole, Fred Brooks, Arthur Timoney, Henry Jarvis, James Broadbridge, Thomas Bason and Albert Ponman it had been an unexpected, frantic induction. Soon, though, this elaborate game of cat-and-mouse across the French countryside that they had supported would be all but forgotten by these men. The nature of warfare that all expected was to prove hugely different from the ensuing years of conflict that they had yet to experience. The opening throes dispensed with, it was now up to not only those at the front, but those at home too to begin to adjust to a new life at war.

4

'England Expects Every Man to Do His Shooting'

The Home Front

At home, Chelsea FC were beginning to feel the strain of wartime operation. Advertisements disappeared from the boards at Stamford Bridge as people found more important things to do with their money and crowds were thinner. The club had calculated that a minimum turnover of £700 per game was required to keep it afloat and although the initial impact of the anti-football campaign eased and attendances went back up, it was not to last. As winter approached crowd figures were low. A direct comparison before Christmas noted that by the same point in 1913, 228,000 fans had passed through the gates. So far in 1914 the figure was just 75,000. The team contributed little to driving people in, failing to win a match until mid-October.

For those that did attend, there was a heavy emphasis on fundraising for the war effort. By the time the fans were able to celebrate just a second victory against Bolton on 7 November, the club reported that a sum of £500 had already been raised for the charity. That did not include another £700 banked at a specially organised event in conjunction with Spurs. That week alone £50 had gone to the aid of Belgian refugees and £57 to the Prince of Wales's Fund. A small legion of local young ladies wearing bright sashes had volunteered to help convince supporters to empty their pockets. At a 1–1 draw with Sheffield United at the end of September they collected £30 alone. Dominated by a trio of sisters, Nellie, Grace and Phyllis Jefferies, they had their own league table. They floated through the crowd at matches, backed by slogans such as 'Pay up and look pleasant!' and 'Do your bit for the boys who are doing their bit for you!'[1]

Charity did not end with cash either. Wounded soldiers were entertained at Stamford Bridge, as were numbers of Belgian refugees who were most enthusiastic about the team's fortunes. Thousands of soldiers were encamped about London with Kitchener's new battalions and a trip into town for the football was a welcome weekend outing.

A group of Gordon Highlanders made the journey for the Sheffield United match. When the final whistle went, a makeshift game on the pitch descended into a jovial brawl with hundreds on each side until a police officer picked up the ball. The soldiers then claimed it from him and 'went off in high glee' declaring that it was going to the front with them. 'It'll dae fine tae kick along the Unter der Linden when we get tae Berlin!'[2]

While the 'screeching' of the anti-football contingent had appeared to die down in conjunction with the overwhelming response to Kitchener's appeal for men, the campaign began in earnest again as recruitment figures tailed off. In the House of Commons debate raged about football. Should they impose a special taxation on all gate money at professional matches? As Chancellor of the Exchequer, David Lloyd George thought not. One Member of Parliament said at least 50 per cent should be claimed, likening people 'so satiated with luxury and laziness' to those that had paid others to entertain them in a Roman arena.[3] Should the government take away the concessions given to fans travelling on trains to matches now that they had taken them over? It was pointed out by the President of the Board of Trade that the railways had been commandeered to an extent to facilitate the easy movement of troops and supplies, but that interfering with this was beyond their control.

On 23 November, *The Times* reported in a bitter tone that recruitment drives at Football League matches were having dismal results, despite large crowds. On Saturday 21 November, only six volunteers allegedly came forward from the crowd at a game between Cardiff and Bristol Rovers. This figure was cited by a Member of Parliament, who asked whether it was time for the government to order the cessation of professional matches. The Prime Minister was adamant that discussions that had thus far taken place between the War Office and the Football Association had covered the issue, and that he did not think that the playing of professional football matches should be banned by government legislation.

In fact, much of the press coverage aimed at the haranguing of professional football was dubious to say the least. The MP for Hammersmith and Fulham, William Hayes Fisher, also heavily involved at Chelsea, was not without cause when he labelled the press attacks on the game as 'some of the worst nonsense I have ever read in my life'.[4] Frederick Charrington was still going strong in his vehement attack on the game. He had had produced a photograph of a shirking football crowd in the national press, only for it to be pointed out by the editor of the *Chelsea FC Chronicle* that said image of Hampden Park had been captured as far back as April 1914. Lord Northcliffe received scathing reproach from the club, too, for producing a 1913 photograph of the crowd at Stamford Bridge and highlighting the lack of uniforms. The editor was of a mind to send him a gift, 'A copy of the Ninth Commandment suitably illuminated and framed.'[5]

At the time of these false revelations Chelsea published a photograph of their own, showing the crowd at the match against Sheffield Wednesday. While it could of course have been a selective shot, almost to a man those of military age were watching the game in uniform. At about the same time, William Hayes Fisher visited Stamford

Bridge to make a half-time speech aimed at recruitment and decided there really wasn't any point. On careful assessment of the crowd it seemed to him that those of military age were already wearing khaki or navy blue. At the Oldham game a few weeks later, it was noted that the crowd was thoroughly dominated by a military presence. On the terraces, in the stand and along the enclosure the khaki-clad spectators appeared to be quite as numerous as the 'civvies'.[6] Of course it too was a mistake to judge those out of uniform too quickly. The editor of the *Chronicle* was sitting next to two young men in civilian attire. On chatting with them he found out that they had both enlisted and that they were still awaiting arrival of their uniforms.

Even with regards to recruitment claims, the press could not always be relied upon for a balanced view. At one match a newspaper claimed that an MP had asked men to come forward to see two recruiting sergeants present at half-time and that none had bothered. In fact, the two men were not even there as they had been called away that afternoon and several men making enquiries had had to be turned away. On another occasion, the press made much noise about a Chelsea–Arsenal fixture that only yielded a single recruit. What the paper did not admit was that this was a match between the club's reserve sides with a tiny crowd, not the impressive fixture that was implied.

Of course despite this, at the forefront of those being publicly bludgeoned for football's perceived lack of sacrifice were the players who had not yet enlisted. As at the end of November, in Scotland the entire Hearts team had joined the Royal Scots. Apparently only Southampton players had enlisted in significant numbers of the southern clubs, although it was later added that eleven Plymouth Argyle players had joined up. A high figure of twenty Hull City players was given, eight from Everton, and West Bromwich Albion had established a company attached to the 5th South Staffordshire Regiment which included eight of their players. But of several other clubs that responded to the paper's enquiries, only nineteen other players had enlisted. 'It has a moral effect,' claimed *The Times*:

> These professional footballers of England are the pick of the country for fitness. Nobody has a right to say that any body of men are not doing their duty, and there may be excellent reasons why every one of these thousands of players does not enlist. But when young men week after week see the finest physical manhood of the country expending its efforts kicking a ball about, they can't possibly realise there is a call for every fit man at the front.

While the press continued their endeavours to demonise football, the players themselves at Chelsea had joined those of clubs up and down the country in preparing for the eventuality that they may have to go to war. In the opinion of the *Chronicle*, it rendered the argument for cutting off professional competition absurd. 'Almost without exception, the league clubs are giving their players rifle practice and military drill under competent instructors regularly – just as much as they would get it if they enlisted.'[7]

Bob Whiting had since moved to Brighton and Hove Albion but he was just one player that, it was argued, would be better off for not enlisting as he was getting a better military education at his place of employment:

> When the season ends these men will be so far advanced that another month of the 'polishing' process would find them as ready for the field as any man who enlisted now – for we are told it takes a good six months to make a new recruit into the finished article.

The editor of the *Chronicle* had it on good authority that men who had enlisted nearly three months previously had not yet fired a rifle, let alone received their uniforms. 'Actually,' he claimed, 'these "soldiers" are not so far advanced as the football players, some of whom are showing remarkable ability as rifle shots as a result of daily practice at the targets.'[8]

After comedic beginnings rifle drill at Chelsea was beginning to yield results. Presided over by the apparently terrifying figure of a Colour Sergeant Meacher, a 'very candid critic', the awkward 'regiment' of players, club officials and friends who were too old to enlist lined up in front of him. Bravely they weathered his booming voice under the floodlights in front of the club's offices. 'And so we go for a full hour; no half time interval in *this* game.' The players found the physical aspect easy enough, but the same could not be said of the elder gentlemen who suffered much as a result of the bending and stretching exercises. 'Fuller comment when the poor editor's back has ceased from aching!'[9]

Initial attempts at shooting were mildly hilarious. 'One well-known player (never mind his name!) stolidly fired his ten rounds to discover, at the finish, that his card had come through quite [unscathed].' Steadily, though, the players improved. Goalkeeper Jim Molyneux had had mixed results. 'He had one dead centre "bull" two wide "outers" and seven "blowed-if-I-know-where-they-wents."' He was happy enough. 'He bore his card away in triumph. And next morning it appeared on the club notice-board in the dressing room – with the following exhortation to his fellow players. "England expects every man to do his shooting' (signed) J.M."'[10]

By comparison, Kitchener's recruits sat still largely unequipped, largely untrained in camps throughout the country. Enlisting was categorically still a choice, not an obligation. The married population of Britain was not expected to leave their families to go and fight but all such rules did not, apparently, apply to the professional footballer. Chelsea opened the pages of the *Chronicle* for fans to have their say and only one man advocated bringing a halt to the football calendar. In total contrast, another supporter went as far as to say that to end the league and leave a player unemployed, so as he had no choice but to take up a rifle, amounted to little more than forced conscription levelled unfairly against one occupation.

'Chelseaites' at the front remained unanimous in their support of football. One regular soldier in the Rifle Brigade painted a picture of fevered excitement on the rare occasion when a newspaper arrived in the trenches. 'They are passed down, one many to another, till everybody knows how their teams are getting on.' He could not abide the idea of halting the league season. 'YOU DON'T KNOW HOW FOOTBALL GIVES ENCOURAGEMENT TO OUR TROOPS IN THE TRENCHES! It cheers every man who takes an interest in football, and I can tell you, Sir, that I feel downhearted if I do not hear how ... Chelsea are getting on.'[11]

Alf Porter was a sailor aboard HMS *Sappho*, a veteran troop ship of the Boer War being hastily converted as a minelayer. He was in total agreement. Cigarettes and *Chronicles* were the contents of his aunt's care packages from home:

> Being a constant supporter of Chelsea I should like to say a word or two in praise of your support of football. Seeing I am unable to see the Pensioners playing, I do the next possible thing, and that is to have the Blues programme sent to me ... Even at the present time our lads look forward to the football results as eagerly as ever and all I come in contact with say the following. 'Let football continue.'[12]

Despite the support of the men who were fighting the war, however, anti-football proclamations rose to hysterical levels. A well-known Lord was reported to have said that 'he almost hoped a zeppelin would drop a bomb' on Sunderland's ground.[13] Chelsea responded in early November by producing a sarcastic zeppelin insurance coupon in the programme for the fans in attendance. But 'the absolute limit' appeared in the form of a letter from Sir Whitworth Wallis, on headed paper from the Garrick Club. He suggested that a 'Remember Antwerp' poster be put up at football grounds to rouse shirkers towards a sense of responsibility. The editor of the *Chronicle* was incensed. 'The "responsibilities" of the players are, apparently, to enlist and to leave heir wives and families.' He ended with a stereotype of his own:

> Gentlemen of [his] type loll at their ease in their comfortable chairs in their clubs and recover – by the aid of whiskey and soda and a cigar – from the exertion of writing (on club notepaper) letters to the press explaining in courtly terms to the 'common people' what is their duty in the national crisis.[14]

As Christmas approached, though, the colour of the landscape was changing. This war was not going to end any time soon. Any patriotic enthusiasm that had driven initial recruiting figures was ebbing away. Footballers and their supporters, it had been claimed, could not deny King and Country if indeed the need for their service arose. The likelihood of this was entirely plausible now, conflicting with the continuance of professional competitions. At the front a stalemate had been reached that would take four years for one side to overcome. And it had come about in October and November thanks to the bloody destruction of the original British Expeditionary Force, thanks to one clash that had almost brought the Germans victory: the first battle for Ypres.

5

'Thus Far Shalt Thou Go and No Farther'

The First Battle of Ypres

Prior to the Great War, pushing his way through the turnstiles at Stamford Bridge with his two sons was a retired army man and football supporter who had served Queen Victoria, Edward VIII and George V for almost twenty-eight years as man and boy.

William Alfred Dean's father had left Buckinghamshire as a young orphan to escape a pre-ordained life at a paper mill with the rest of his village, joining the Coldstream Guards in the 1850s. William, his fourth son, was born a stone's throw from Chelsea Barracks and fourteen years later he joined his father's battalion at the end of 1884, becoming a fully fledged private four years later. Promotions followed steadily: lance corporal, corporal, sergeant. Alongside his advancing career, William's own family grew. Married in 1891, a son, Ernest Stanley, died before he reached his first birthday but another boy, Cecil Patrick William, was born in 1894 while his father was stationed in Dublin. A third son, Reginald Noel, followed three years later in Chelsea, before a daughter known as Elsie was born in 1899.

The Foot Guards of the British Army were among the oldest regiments in existence and had a proud history with roots in the Civil War era. When the future Charles II fled the country in 1651 the king of Spain, whose territory he settled in, gave him permission to raise a regiment of them for his protection out of loyal men who had followed him into exile, the future Grenadier Guards. The Coldstream Guards began life on the other side of the Channel as part of Cromwell's New Model Army until his death, when their commander marched them south to London to help enable Parliament to be dissolved and Charles to be invited back to England as king. After his restoration, Charles very soon commissioned a regiment of Scots Guards too.

There were eleven regiments of Irish designation at the approach of the twentieth century but they did not include one of the Irish Guards, although there had been a

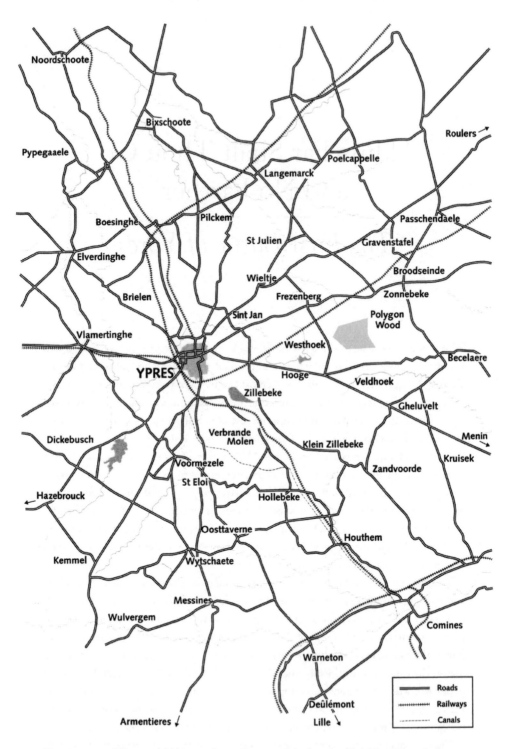

The area around Ypres would become home for tens of thousands of British soldiers during the Great War. *(THP)*

version of such a thing some 200 years before. At the turn of the twentieth century, though, as the Second Boer War raged in southern Africa, the contribution of these various Irish regiments had not gone unnoticed either by Queen Victoria herself or in public circles. In February 1900 it was proposed in *The Times* that there should be some sort of recognition for their service. 'There are Scotch Guards and English Guards – why not add to the toll of glory a regiment of Irish Guards?'[1] The notion had apparently already occurred to Her Majesty and by April it was made official. 'Having deemed it desirable to commemorate the bravery shown by the Irish regiments during the operations in South Africa in the years 1899–1900,' she proclaimed, '[She has] been graciously pleased that an Irish Regiment of foot guards be formed, to be designated the Irish Guards.'[2]

The practicalities of getting the new regiment together were quickly carried out. As soon as they were formed it was decided that they would join the Grenadiers, the Coldstream and the Scots Guards in the Brigade of Guards. Field Marshal Lord Roberts, a veteran of Indian, Afghan and South African campaigns spanning nearly half a century, was an obvious choice of colonel, 'as no greater Irishman lived'.[3] Officers were transferred in from elsewhere in the brigade. As for the men, almost 150 with Irish heritage transferred from other Guards units. More came from the existing Irish regiments and regimental #1 went to a soldier arriving from the Royal Munster Fusiliers. The doors to Irish and Scottish recruiting centres were also thrown open to men of the appropriate ethnicity. On 21 April 1900 James O'Brien of Limerick became the first man to enlist in the Irish Guards. By September enough men had been assembled to begin forming a battalion. A regimental orderly room at Horse Guards was opened and Queen Victoria approved the star of the Order of St Patrick as their cap badge. After sixteen years' service with the Coldstream, 30-year-old William Dean made the transfer into the Irish Guards, who were quartered at Chelsea Barracks, next to the Royal Hospital and 2 miles from Stamford Bridge, receiving a warrant as a superintending clerk on 26 November 1900.

The existing ancient battalions in the brigade were somewhat bemused by the newcomers and regarded them 'with a benevolent, if somewhat quizzical eye'.[4] In January 1901 the Irish Guards turned out for the first time as part of a guard of honour for Lord Roberts's return from South Africa, a motley crew with unfinished uniforms, missing some of their ceremonial equipment but proud nonetheless. Elements of the regiment were sent in the opposite direction to Africa as part of a mounted infantry collaboration among the Guards and became the first modern Irish Guardsmen to see active service, though William was not among the 150 or so chosen. In their absence the regiment continued to expand, not least with the important addition of regimental #1463, an Irish wolfhound mascot chosen from a parade of potential recruits at Crystal Palace and named 'Brian Boru'. The following year William was awarded a medal for long service and good conduct and in 1905 Sergeant-Major Dean became the first warrant officer to get his photo published in the *Household Brigade* magazine.

Ceremonial duties dominated regimental life before the war, the men standing guard at Buckingham Palace and the Bank of England, finding themselves stationed at the Tower, doing their musketry in the damp ditch that had formed the moat or doing drill in Hyde Park wearing short white monkey jackets. Home for the Dean family was just south of the river in Brixton. Every now and again, the quartermaster would organise family outings; the wives were kept occupied doing laundry and for the men their leisure time was spent in sports and the regiment quickly became famed for its boxers and its tug-of-war team as well as some of their officers featuring as prominent runners.

St Patrick's Day was the most important day of the year. William's eldest son Cecil had experienced a few before war came. In 1908 he followed his father into the army as one of the battalion's 14-year-old drummer boys. They would wake everybody up with an Irish military fanfare as they marched through the barracks. It quickly became a tradition for the Queen to issue shamrocks for the men to wear for the day and these would be passed out at morning parade. After mass there would be an enormous lunch followed by an afternoon full of sports. A grand tea followed before a concert which would go on well into the night. Football had been a lifelong passion of William's and one he keenly shared with his boys. An 'ardent devotee'[5] of the game, he had proudly supported the Brigade of Guards' football league but after 1905 he added weekly outings to Stamford Bridge to their family interests away from the army and he, Cecil and Reg became keen Chelsea fans.

On 4 August 1914, now numbering one large battalion of over a thousand officers and men, the Irish Guards were quartered at Wellington Barracks next to Buckingham Palace, where bank holiday crowds were excitedly assembling to await the news. Would Britain declare war on Germany? All of the company commanders disappeared into the orderly room during the hot summer afternoon. Outside the men, including Cecil Dean, who was now 19 and had replaced his retired father as a fully fledged member of the battalion, waited on tenterhooks. When the officers emerged in the early evening it became official: for the first time in their history the whole of the Irish Guards was mobilising for war.

In just eight days everything was prepared. Reservists arriving at the barracks watched enviously on 12 August as the battalion left for the front. And so did Cecil, as for now he was to be left behind. To the tune of the regimental band his fellow soldiers marched proudly off in the direction of Vauxhall Bridge. Nearly 1,100 men entrained at Nine Elms station in Battersea with thirty-two officers, 98 per cent of them Irish in origin, and set off for Southampton and beyond that, Havre and the war.

The Irish Guards formed a rearguard as the BEF began to fall away from Mons, coming under fire together for the first time at Landrecies. Exhausted, they trudged the entire length of the retreat until the army reached the environs of Paris. It was a trying experience for the battalion's young Kildare-born machine-gun officer, Eric Greer. 'During the first 6 days we marched about 95 miles and had 14 hours sleep. During the whole retreat of 150 miles in 10 days (with pretty incessant fighting) we hardly ever marched later than 3am, sometimes at 1am. I could easily sleep for a week.'[6]

At the Battle of the Marne, when the German advance was finally checked, the battalion played its small part by forcing the crossing of a river named the Petit Morin. In his absence, Cecil Dean's fellow Guardsmen crossed the Marne itself on the way north again at Charly on 9 September using a bridge that the Germans had failed to detonate properly. Then came the advance, pushing the Germans back towards the River Aisne.

It seemed to all that the enemy were on the run. Nobody had grasped the magnitude of the effect that defensive weapons in the main artillery would have on a modern war and how the fighting would grind to a stalemate across Europe. Even the Commander of the BEF, Sir John French, claimed later that he expected to be fighting a moving war. 'We fully believed we were driving the Germans back to the Meuse if not to the Rhine, and all my correspondence and communications at this time with Joffre and the French Generals most closely associated with me, breathed the same spirit.'[7]

The Aisne was a slow-moving, 'sluggish' waterway, nearly 200 feet across but deep enough to require proper bridges. On either bank the ground rose steeply hundreds of feet. The Germans had established themselves in a strong position that was duly noted by Sir John French:

> One of its chief military characteristics is that, from the high ground, on neither side can the top of the plateau on the other side be seen, except for small stretches. This is chiefly due to the woods on the edges of the slopes. Another important point is that all the bridges are under either direct or high-angle artillery fire … What astonished me was the volume of the fire. Between Soissons and Compiegne the river seemed ablaze, so intense was the artillery fire on both sides.[8]

The question was, though, would the enemy merely use the position as another stop on their retreat or would they make a stand? The Irish Guards crossed the Aisne on 14 September. There they followed a battalion of Grenadiers up a steep hill to help fight for a farm named Le Coeur de Soupir. 'The heavily wooded country was alive with musketry and machine gun fire, and the distances were obscured by mist and heavy rain.'[9] Elements of the Coldstream Guards had failed to take the farm. They found themselves outflanked from a ridge on their right, and so three companies of Irishmen attempted to force the issue. They reached to within a couple of hundred yards of a wood surrounded by the farm's cultivated fields and the battalion commenced pouring rifle fire into the trees. 'They did an awful clever thing,' wrote Eric Greer. 'For they left snipers behind, who shot officers actually behind the firing line and then shammed dead till they escaped or were captured … Of course, we did not know what was happening or where the bullets were coming from.' Three of the battalion's officers were killed by them. 'They nearly got me,' he recalled. 'For I thought the wood was cleared and pushed on to the edge of it to mount my guns for firing over the open turnip fields.' He stood talking to an old schoolmate in the Coldstream. 'Suddenly a hail of bullets arrived from somewhere. Poor Dick pitched over and died in a minute or two.'[10]

Eric and his two machine-gun crews were heavily fired upon by concealed enemy troops. One team was entirely wiped out and a gun put out of action. Speedily reorganising the men that he had left, he called for volunteers from the company nearby to retrieve their equipment. He lacked any sympathy for the hidden sniper menace that continued to pick off members of the battalion. He went out with a friend, the future Field Marshal Alexander of Tunis to find one. 'He was shamming dead under an oil sheet among all the other dead men. We shot him.'[11]

Four days after the clash at Soupir the first reinforcements arrived, Cecil Dean among them. He found the battalion holding some frantically scraped trenches at the summit of a flat-topped hill. It was a harsh introduction to the reality of war for the teenager. The men holding the trenches, those he knew so well, were in an awful, filthy state but that was nothing compared to the corpses that littered the hillside. A new adjutant had also arrived and he was repulsed by what he saw. 'There were many dead Germans lying out in front, and .... the whole place is littered with dead cows and smells most unpleasantly.' Eric Greer was already having 'the horrors' thanks to the constant onslaught.[12] Snipers still plagued the makeshift lines, but more terrifyingly, Cecil was introduced to the nightmare of high explosive shells. For three hours during his first evening the German Army pounded the hilltop with them.

Cecil and the other replacements were quickly incorporated into the battalion. The campaign was as yet only four weeks old and already the Irish Guards had suffered casualties, a worrying number among the officers in particular. They still lacked a commanding officer, having lost their pre-war incumbent and his subordinate during the retreat at the beginning of September. Officers were being borrowed from the other Guards battalions to make up for the shortfall but they were still under strength. For nearly three weeks the Guards remained in their positions in the neighbourhood of Soupir on its bluff above the Aisne. It was becoming increasingly apparent that a stalemate was ensuing. 'I began dimly to apprehend what the future might have in store for us,' claimed Sir John French in retrospect. Ditches that had been frantically scraped into the ground to gain some cover during the Battle of the Aisne grew into more elaborate trenches and more permanent as the British, Belgians, French and Germans began indiscriminately carving up the landscape of Western Europe.

This task in itself was enough to keep Cecil and his fellow Guardsmen busy. They foraged for wood and other useful things in the nearby country and built shelters, dug deeper trenches and communication lines and fixed roads needed to bring up supplies, pitching in with other units nearby as well as organising their own front. The Germans were so close in their own trenches that the Guardsmen could hear them chattering among themselves. Back behind their own lines they heard of fighting elsewhere, rumours of the French overrunning Arras and seizing prisoners, or of them moving on to Verdun to do the same, but in truth they knew nothing of what was happening on a wider front than the hillside they were perched upon. At first the German artillery wreaked havoc, a 'furious' fire day and night, but as shelters and trenches were improved and the front settled down, casualties and artillery fire decreased. Any spare time was spent with the new company commanders, for they were strangers to Cecil and the men and it was deemed important that they get to know each other as best they could.

With the advent of autumn came persistent heavy rain. Cecil remained in bright spirits, at least on paper, and his father forwarded one of his letters on to Stamford Bridge. 'Hope to be back before the football season ends,' he wrote cheerfully. 'I'd like to know how Chelsea are going on. Good luck to them!' William was proud that in the midst of war his eldest son breezed past his hardship and merely wanted to know of his team's fortunes. 'We feel it shows a fine spirit … He is not quite nineteen years of age and has always taken the greatest interest in the Chelsea club.'[13]

More troops, both cavalry and infantry, would land on Belgian shores at the beginning of October, but by this point Sir John French, 120 miles south on the Aisne, was already anxious about the safety of the Channel coast. He began to covet a move north for his force, closer to supply lines, closer to the area of vital national importance and closer to the Royal Navy so that they might fight the Germans with their support if it came to it and force them back on a better footing.

On the evening of 9 October cheering erupted in the trenches opposite Cecil Dean and the Irish Guards. Rumours shot up and down the line: Antwerp had fallen. 'If [it] is true,' wrote their adjutant, 'what difference it will make I am not quite clear.'[14] The French ultimately concurred with the idea of replacing the BEF so that they might travel north and so Cecil's time on the high chalky woodlands of Picardy was about to be severed rather abruptly. The Irish Guards were about to exchange the relative quiet of the Aisne for the relentless, violent carnage that was beginning to unfold on the Flanders plain, crammed on wet lowlands among Belgian farmlands.

The Germans had indeed struck north, heading for the immensely valuable Channel coast, and the Allies went with them, each attempting to outflank the other and get behind their enemy to deliver a decisive blow. It was becoming a race toward the sea with catastrophic consequences for the British Army not only in terms of supply routes, but also an invasion threat if the Germans got access to the coastline in its entirety. 'I think it is reasonable to deduce,' wrote Sir John French in the aftermath, 'that the stakes for which we were playing … were nothing less than the safety, indeed, the very existence, of the British Empire.'[15] Throughout October and November the battle would rage around one town whose name would become synonymous with the war for Britain. In order to stop the enemy from crashing through Belgium and northern France and winning the war before the year was out, it would become absolutely vital that the little town of Ypres, which happened to stand in between the German Army and ports such as Dunkirk and Calais, did not fall.

At this point, the BEF was still theorising about attacking the enemy towards Roulers, with its vital collection of railway lines. 'In my inmost heart,' wrote Sir John French, 'I did not expect I should have to fight a great defensive battle … Nothing had occurred, so far, to raise any great doubts in my mind as to the possibility of prosecuting the offensive which we had arranged to put in movement.'[16] The cavalry departed north from the Aisne by road on 3 October and the French began relieving the infantry so that they might entrain. While they waited to leave, the Irish Guards received supplies of new clothing before handing over their trenches after a short delay on the 13th. Cecil trudged back into billets on a particularly dark night, heavy gunfire becoming more distant and the whole of the front lit up by German star shells and lights. Most of the battalion slept on straw in the open before they boarded trains on a brilliant autumn morning.

The battalion chugged through Amiens, Boulogne and Calais on the way to Hazebrouck where they arrived on the evening of 15 October. They were among the last to reach this new front, and by this point it had become apparent that German opposition was fierce. Reports reached GHQ that the German Army was planning a powerful assault towards Ypres. All focus had remained on continuing to attempt an advance eastward but it was now that Sir John French later claimed that he became anxious at continuous news of German troops flowing into the area. If these reports were true, then the Allies could be in grave danger. French troops to the north of Ypres were not great in numbers and comprised, in the main, of territorial soldiers. The Belgians, having been driven out of Antwerp, were spent.

Even with the arrival of most of the BEF before that of the Irish Guards, the length of the line that the British Army was holding was daunting. Even more so were the consequences if the Germans managed to get through it. If the enemy broke through the left flank the whole force might be turned, the Belgians and the French troops would be cut off and the coast would be gone. French was not enthusiastic about the prospects of his troops making up the southern area of the battlefield towards Armentières either. In his opinion:

> the enemy was daily and almost hourly getting stronger in front of our line, which was held by the cavalry and by the 2nd and 3rd Corps. The endurance of these troops had been heavily taxed, and I had practically no reserves. Moreover, they were extended on a front much too wide for their numbers, especially north of the Lys.[17]

The centre of the line was being held by the newly arrived 7th Division who were receiving a baptism of fire, strung out on an impossibly long front running in front of Ypres from Langemarck, past Zonnebeke and on to Zandvoorde. This was a huge distance to be covered by their dwindling numbers. If, before a single casualty had been suffered, half of the fighting men were equally spread out to defend their front, the other half being left in reserve, each man would have stood 8 feet from the next in line. They were being repeatedly bludgeoned by the enemy, yet somehow holding their ground. The arrival of Haig with his corps then, the Irish Guards among its number, was more than timely. They began marching toward Ypres on 17 October and awaited further instruction at Boeschepe, where the locals spoke a guttural mixture of Flemish and French that made them difficult to understand.

While they were waiting for relief, 7th Division's ordeal continued. For four days they had been under a constant and fierce storm of German fire. Sir John French still wanted to attempt to push home an advance and, despite their wretched condition, they were ordered to attack towards Menin on the 18th. It became apparent that there were large numbers of undiscovered Germans on the left flank of the advance. Fighting broke out up and down the line and rendered the British attempt a failure. By the 19th, having suffered heavy losses, the division fell back to its original line.

At 6 a.m. on 20 October, Cecil Dean and his fellow Guardsmen began advancing to their aid through a damp cold mist. Along the narrow twisting road north-east to Vlamertinghe their adjutant spied cows with sacks tied to their backs, he assumed to keep them warm. At 11 a.m. they reached Ypres itself, the medieval cloth hall still looming in the town square. Here they came to a halt until late afternoon. Refugees from Roulers streamed past them and locals brought Cecil and the other soldiers hot coffee. Men amused the natives by dancing Irish jigs on the cobbled paving stones. It was clear, though, that they were moving closer to the fighting. French territorials passed through, then extravagant looking Cuirassiers. The guns boomed in the background; motor cars laden with staff officers clattered past and the men were warned: beware of the possibility that the enemy may attack you through a screen of women and children. If so, it might be necessary to fire through them.

In principle the Guards were going to help continue the attack, but given the uncertainty of all that was occurring in the area, Haig was given some leeway. With cavalry, the 7th Division were still battling the German onslaught in front of Ypres, but outnumbered some four to one and with heavy artillery raining shells down on them it seemed their situation was becoming more perilous by the hour. The two Coldstream Guards battalions of Cecil's brigade were sent up to try and help the flailing attack; while the battalion in which Cecil's father and grandfather had given some thirty-five years' service between them went forward, the Irish Guards moved to the north-east of Ypres with the remaining Guardsmen, the 2nd Grenadiers. The men of the Irish Guards waited nervously for events to transpire around them in the rain. 'We alone remain in reserve and expect to go out at any moment ... One hears of the Germans advancing and burning everything as they come ...'[18]

The following day, Cecil Dean would see battle for the first time. In hindsight Sir John French claimed that the magnitude of the situation was now beginning to sink in. 'All my worst forebodings as to the enemy's increasing strength were realised.'[19] Intercepted messages going over the wireless revealed that reinforcements were coming up behind the German force pressing on the northern part of the British front, including the shattered 7th Division. Although not the best calibre of troops, the German numbers were becoming overwhelming. 'The strength they actually reached astounded me,' French claimed. 'This, taken with the speed in which they appeared in the field, came like a veritable bolt from the blue.'[20] Plans for any kind of Allied offensive were evaporating. It was simply 'up to us to hold on like grim death to our positions by hard, resolute fighting, until relief in some shape could come'. The British commander was startled by his own later admission. With the fate of the Empire in his hands, he could cling to one positive. As far as events were playing out, he appeared in his opinion to have deployed Haig's corps, the last significant British force to arrive, in the best manner to try and stem the German tide.

The Irish Guards had moved towards Passchendaele and taken up a defensive position east of the main road running between Zonnebeke and Langemarck. A great number of enemy troops were apparently driving south through Houthulst Forest towards them and the Guards were ordered to stand in their way. While their cohorts dug their heels in, Cecil was in reserve with the rest of his battalion, listening to the sound of never-ending gunfire pounding the surrounding countryside, eclipsing anything he had heard on the Aisne. At 4.45 his turn came. Elements of the 7th Division in front were at breaking point. It was a concern that one particular brigade might come apart at the seams and the Irish Guards were ordered forward to support the tattered remnants of it by the railway station in Zonnebeke. They moved up in a jovial manner. The Guardsmen spied a hare crossing their path and went bounding after it, 'to the scandal of discipline and the delight of all'.[21] Then it was time for the business of war.

Cecil Dean stepped out into a hail of artillery fire and side by side with the rest of his battalion, perilously trudged through exploding shrapnel and twisted metal. The men threw themselves down in a ploughed field and helplessly lay there for fifteen minutes in the hope that it would subside. Then they got up and carried on; 500 yards later rifle bullets also began whistling past their ears. They came to a halt just past the village of Zonnebeke and prepared to scrape themselves some cover in the wet ground. The night lit up by the flames engulfing a nearby house, they helped bury some of 7th Division's dead and probed haystacks looking for snipers illuminated by a red glow.

At GHQ Sir John French was tentatively assessing his resources. What he had now was it. The French had promised to bring up reserves but in terms of British troops he had a corps of Indian soldiers being hurried up from the south of France and a handful of territorials from home, but there would be no more reinforcements in the immediate future. 'Doubtless,' he later wrote, 'if we could keep our positions for two or three weeks, much larger reinforcements would be forthcoming.'[22] Unfortunately for the commander of the BEF, he was becoming aware that in the coming days the ability of the Allies to hold the line in front of Ypres in the face of overwhelming German force was going to be calculated in terms of hours, not weeks.

The following day, Cecil and his fellow Guardsmen crouched in their primitive trenches and listened to an immense battle going on beyond Zonnebeke. The 7th Division retired out of the town and the Irish Guards were forced to go with them. After being hounded by shrapnel and maxims for another day, French troops arrived on the northern part of the battlefield to ease the burden on the battered BEF. On the 23rd October they seized Zonnebeke and took over the line, allowing the tired, hungry Irish Guards to trudge away. There was to be no respite for them, though. Every man Sir John French had available to him was valuable and they were immediately ordered to march 5 miles to the south-west, across the soon to be famed Menin Road on their way to Zillebeke to support a stretched Cavalry division. Arriving in the middle of night Cecil and the rest of his battalion collapsed into a brick yard to get some rest.

The following day was wracked with uncertainty, with continued fighting and the BEF trying to organise themselves on their new contracted front. After a few snatched hours, at dawn on the 25th the whole of Cecil's division was called out to advance again. This time the attack would actually be led by the Grenadiers and the Irish Guards themselves as they attempted to clear the enemy out of the upper half of Polygon Wood and advance on Reutel beyond, Cecil's first experience of assaulting the enemy in a leading wave of troops. The day began with a heavy bombardment by 1914 standards. Cecil and his cohorts climbed through the undergrowth to a spot at the western edge of the wood and lay down to wait for the rest of the brigade, sending the odd patrol out past the trenches in front to assess the whereabouts of the enemy. The attack finally got underway mid-afternoon. The Irish Guards put their heads down and went forwards into a storm of metal, passing over trenches occupied by the Worcestershire Regiment. Bitterly opposed they struggled on. Shells continued to explode overhead and among them. One devastated one of the companies advancing alongside Cecil's, killing four and leaving nearly twenty more writhing on the ground. Their officer fled back to the company behind, warning them to change course as best they could 'for the ground was a slaughter-house'.[23] On the right the Grenadiers were having even less success. The whole advance finally ground to a halt 200 yards short of Reutel. There the Irish Guardsmen were subjected to continuing rifle fire from enemy troops hidden behind a small ridge, 'which kept our heads down very low!'

Cecil was in for a long exhausting night. As darkness began to fall the realisation dawned on those commanding the battalion that the Grenadiers had disappeared somewhere in the undergrowth. Unbeknown to the Irishmen, their fellow Guardsmen had been held up and had lost track of them. The battalion adjutant began to get nervous at the lack of support. 'The Germans had come between us and the Grenadiers, or rather we had advanced beyond a German trench on our right without knowing.'[24] The situation was even worse on the left, where it transpired that the Irish Guards had lost touch with the brigade next door by a full quarter of a mile, leaving a huge gap for the Germans to exploit. 'Isolated in darkness and dripping autumn undergrowth,' the rain began to cascade down.[25] A patrol had been sent out in search of the Grenadiers but all they stumbled upon was the German trench. Reports arrived that the enemy was massing on the other side of the ridge ready to attack. Frantically the adjutant ran back to brigade headquarters for instruction. Through dense, boggy terrain he fought his way back where he was told that in spite of the confusion their orders were simple: hold the ground gained at all costs.

Blinded by darkness, wet, terrified and highly exposed, Cecil and the Irish Guards formed a 'P' shape, holding their ground but forming a tail 600 yards long back to link up with the Worcesters. The men stood back to back in the pouring rain all night, rifles poised in the pitch dark as they withstood probing German counter-attacks and snipers trying to get around their flank. They were utterly drenched and exhausted when the Coldstream Guards emerged, coming through the thick woods to their aid just before dawn; but their work was not yet done. From the tip of the little salient that their lone advance had formed, the Irish Guards moved forward again with their Coldstream counterparts. Severe machine-gun fire pelted them from all angles as they attacked and ensured that neither Cecil's battalion, nor any other troops could make much headway. One company managed to seize two farmhouses but were eventually shoved back out of them taking heavy casualties. More than fifty men were put out of action with no tangible result. All day conflicting orders arrived to confuse them. 'Once to resist a desperate counter attack, supposed to be commenced by the enemy; then to be prepared to assist another brigade who was going to advance and then to hold our ground.' Not until another part of the division arrived to help did the pressure ease and enable the Guardsmen to settle down and make contact with the rest of their brigade. The survivors were ready to drop. Finally they were allowed to eat their emergency rations. 'We had been digging all day, no sleep or food for at least 36 hours, so we were all rather fatigued.'[26]

Allied attempts to effect a movement around the German flank were in tatters. Having failed to push the enemy away from the Channel coast it was absolutely imperative that they did not now manage to charge forward and seize it. The Germans were about to commence repeated, desperate attempts to break the Allies and strike out for victory in the west. The defensive line had been formed, 'which, if it could be held, brought the Germans face to face with the challenge: Thus far shalt thou go and no farther.'[27]

Enemy reinforcements poured into the area, detraining at Lille and Courtrai ready for a tremendous attempt at overrunning Ypres and the surrounding area. The Irish Guards took advantage of the lull to expand their meagre trenches and firm up their defences as best they could. They were hardly left in peace, the days were 'expensive in blood and exhausting to nerves'.[28] The men could not show their heads above their trenches owing to enemy snipers but they retaliated by posting marksmen of their own. British artillery was also redirected onto an area proving to be a nuisance to the safety of the working Guardsmen and harrying attacks were driven off. Cecil and his fellow men might have expected some respite when they were finally relieved from the trenches by the Coldstream, but no sooner had they returned to the safer side of Polygon Wood and settled down to tend to their wet, swollen feet, than the enemy began spraying this rear area with shrapnel. Every fifteen minutes a round would be loosed off at them and although casualties were minimal, it put paid to the idea of any decent night's sleep and prolonged their ordeal. Numbers of officers continued to dwindle with sickness owing to the constant bad weather and wounds, including their third commanding officer already and Eric Greer, who was hurt while operating his machine guns alongside the Coldstream Guards.

On 29 October the Germans smashed violently through the join between two of Haig's divisions at the point where they met on the Menin Road. The day was spent fiercely fighting to gain back lost ground but by nightfall the British troops had succeeded in claiming Gheluvelt from the enemy. Although the attack did not take place on their front, Cecil's battalion was ordered to lightly assist the 1st Division near Polderhoek before tramping back again in the pouring rain. The adjutant of the Irish Guards was relieved that the enemy had been unable to press home their early advantage. 'They must have lost very heavily, but it was a bore they got through at all.'[29]

The most critical juncture of the battle for Ypres had now commenced; the most momentous period, claimed Sir John French, that he would ever direct in the field as commander-in-chief. The moment was not lost on the Irish Guards. The battalion had spent the 'beastly, dark, cold, wet morning' of 30 October digging in west of Polygon Wood, in case the exhausted troops to the south of them caved and let the enemy through. Their adjutant was wary of events to come. 'They are pressing hard and I hear this is supposed to be their final effort in this part of the field. I hope it is and that we are able to keep them off.' At lunchtime, along with the brigade's battalion of Grenadiers, the Irish Guards were ordered south-west again to Klein Zillebeke which was being pressed heavily. As evening came on half of the battalion advanced through heavy shrapnel fire to the aid of the cavalry, moving up 'in a perfect hail of shrapnel and big gun fire'.[30] The cavalry, apparently thinking that they were being relieved, simply left and the Grenadiers had to be summoned to fill the consequent gap in the line and reorganise the front. It was nearly midnight when the men began digging in, but by daybreak they had fashioned mildly adequate cover.

'October 31st and November 1st will remain forever memorable in the history of our country,' wrote Sir John French. 'For, during those two days, no more than one thin and straggling line of tired-out British soldiers stood between the Empire and its practical ruin as an independent first-class Power.'[31] The Irish Guards had dug all night and were prepared to support a French attack in the morning but the Germans beat them to it. At 7 a.m. shells began dropping into the Irish lines, 'the most terrific bombardment with guns of every calibre' and they would not cease for another sixteen hours. 'Not a house within a range of three or four miles was left untouched,' wrote the battalion adjutant. 'The incessant roar went on all day',[32] and was coupled with constant machine-gun fire and increasing numbers of troops building up opposite.

Again, officers were hard hit and the battalion was suffering mounting casualties among the men, but this was nothing to what was being experienced by the BEF further south. Crushing German blows were being dealt on Messines and at Gheluvelt on the Menin Road. At 12.30 p.m. the 1st Division faltered. The road to Ypres, the Channel coast and Britain lay exposed to the German army. In Ypres itself, shells were dropping in the centre of the town and the civilian population had caught wind of impending doom and began to panic. 'I saw loaded vehicles leaving the town,' wrote Sir John French, 'and people were gathered in groups about the streets chattering like monkeys or rushing hither and thither with frightened faces.' As the commander departed towards Gheluvelt himself, the BEF seemed to be unravelling around him:

> It looked as if the whole of the First Corps was about to fall back in confusion on Ypres. Heavy howitzers were moving west at a trot – always a most significant feature of a retreat – and ammunition and other wagons blocked the road almost as far as the eye could see.

His motorcar crawled along the congested road. In the midst of the press of traffic, and along both sides of the road, crowds of wounded came limping along as fast as they could, all heading for Ypres. Shells were screaming overhead and bursting with reverberating explosions in the adjacent fields. To compound the dire state of affairs, at lunchtime shells struck a nearby chateau being used as a headquarters, wiping out a number of immediately irreplaceable staff officers in the midst of battle. It was over, so far as Sir John French could see, the British had been broken. 'Personally I felt as if the last barrier between the Germans and the Channel seaboard was down, and I viewed the situation with the utmost gravity.'[33] But then something quite incredible happened. The BEF's commander was at Douglas Haig's headquarters at 3 p.m. when a staff officer came galloping up and declared that they had been saved. The Irish Guards' former lieutenant-colonel, Brigadier General Charles Fitzclarence VC had walked the remnants of a battalion of Worcesters to the edge of the woods and dispatched them in the direction of Gheluvelt chateau. Somehow, they managed to push forward and stabilise the situation.

On the Irish Guards' front, the shelling finally subsided at 11 p.m. The moon lit up the battlefield and bringing up supplies was awkward. Everyone was eventually fed but only the men in reserve got cups of tea. 'I think this was one of the worst days I ever spent,' wrote their adjutant. 'Both with anxiety as to what was going to happen, and the great strain on one's nerves to say nothing of want of food …'[34] In shelling and merely clinging to the line, in one day the Irish Guards had lost some 10 per cent of their strength. To compound their misery, French troops arrived to relieve the Guards from the lines, but only the Grenadiers escaped. The Irish remained in their wet ditches, shrapnel shells bursting overhead.

There was no let up in the German artillery bombardment as November dawned. So confident were they of victory, so it appeared, that rumours shot up and down the British front that the Kaiser himself was apparently at Courtrai, 'no doubt with the intention of heading a "triumphal entry" into Ypres'.[35] On the morning of the 1st, Cecil Dean was 'drenched' by shrapnel from a field gun that had been brought up to within five or six hundred yards of the Irish Guards and pointed right at them. Heavy artillery kept up a steady fire on the battalion's positions and if the guns stopped, machine-gun fire occupied the gap until the artillery resumed. Early on, almost an entire platoon of one company was wiped out by a single shell that blew up in the trench that they were occupying. The surviving officer and a handful of men scrabbled out of the dirt and made their way back to the rest of the battalion. The cascading metal was of such unheard-of intensity that there was no hope of their being joined by any reinforcements. The enemy had forced through south of Ypres and taken significant gains early in the day. The cavalry, minus their horses and doing battle in the Messines area, were utterly spent, clinging on for dear life and fighting as infantry. To the south of Cecil and the Irish Guards, the 7th Division now had just 2,000 men remaining. All along the Allied front it was proving impossible to make any headway against the German onslaught.

At 3 p.m. the enemy launched a fierce attack and seized a damaged Irish trench. All of the front companies were forced to retire, apart from a single platoon under the command of a teenage subaltern who missed the order and remained steadfastly until they could crawl back under cover of darkness. Meanwhile the Guardsmen making their retreat inched back, falling to the ground as they were picked off by enemy fire. As soon as they emerged from their trenches there was a machine gun trained and waiting to unleash fire on them. Their commander and the adjutant tried to rally the retiring men. Officers, troops, the wounded, cooks, orderlies, anyone who could grip a rifle joined in and tried to help hold the enemy at bay. 'Twas like a football scrum,' one man recalled. 'Everyone was somebody … if he dropped there was no one to take his place.'[36]

Covered by their reserve company, which had been sent up when battalion headquarters realised what was happening, the retiring Guardsmen occupied a new line and the adjutant was sent off to find the brigadier to find out what to do next. When he was finally apprised of the situation he sent up the Grenadiers and some spare cavalry to help. The adjutant returned, rounding up stragglers and putting them back into the line. Eventually he had managed to get 300 men together. The survivors, including Cecil Dean, had been stretched to breaking point. The dismounted horsemen held the trenches long enough for the Irish Guards to be fed, as they had now been some thirty-six hours without anything to eat and that night French troops arrived to help hold the line.

Lord Cavan, commanding the brigade, later issued a special note to their commanding officer:

I want you to convey to every man in your battalion that I consider that the safety of the right flank of the British section depended entirely upon their staunchness after the disastrous day, 1st November. Those of them that were left made history, and I can never thank them enough for the way in which they recovered themselves, and showed the enemy that Irish Guards must be reckoned with, however hard hit.[37]

The ranks of the Irish Guards had been decimated. Nearly half of the battalion had been put out of action in a single day. Eleven officers had been killed, seven more wounded, nearly all of them that were available. A nineteenth, listed as missing, had last been seen shooting at a German who was bayonetting one of his men and was feared dead too. The battalion was unrecognisable from that which, over 1,000 strong, had marched to Nine Elms station just two months before. At nightfall on 1 November it numbered just 300 men and a handful of officers, though the adjutant hoped that others would drift in over time. The following day the Irish Guards was reduced to three companies, the fourth being a shadow of itself with only twenty-six men answering roll call and all of the officers being gone. The reorganisation took place under unrelenting shellfire which continued for days following their landmark scrap of 1 November. Cecil and the other bedraggled survivors rotated in and out of the front line for their share of the punishment. They could still hear their wounded friends calling out in front and at night they went out to try and bring them in. On the first night, one wailed continuously until the Germans turned a machine gun on him. Under cover of darkness the men went out and buried their unfortunate friends and strung wire up in front of the meagre, wet trenches to help to try and stave off the enemy when they inevitably came at them again.

The shells pounded on. Help arrived in the shape of some Life Guards who, resigned to their fate as infantry for now, trudged up in pouring rain to boost their numbers. A new field gun was dragged up to try and put German machine guns out of action, and a new one of their own arrived to hold off the enemy at close range. A few dozen replacements came too. They were jumpy, terrified and imagined crowds of German soldiers coming at them, constantly raising the alarm. 'This was a popular obsession, but it led to waste of ammunition and waking up utterly tired men elsewhere in the line.'[38] The odd straggler found his way home. After three days without food or water one wounded Guardsman, who had been refused food and water by the enemy apparently because they were convinced that he was done for, finally managed to drop into the Irish lines. The shelling went on, and on, obliterating a farm behind them but missing the British artillery piece it was aiming for. More casualties slowly mounted up, but French troops were detraining in the area to continue picking up the slack caused by the BEF's comparatively massive casualty figures.

In hindsight, Sir John French claimed that at headquarters he was hopeful that news of Russian successes in the east meant that the pressure on the Allies around

Ypres would be relieved, and was buoyed by reports of large numbers of German troops being thrown on trains at the likes of Roulers and Tourcoing and spirited away. 'Whatever may have been really going on,' he later wrote, 'our hopes were, as usual, doomed to disappointment, for the pressure on our front became greater and greater. But our eyes were always turned towards the East … the Russian "Will-o'-the-Wisp" continued to uphold us and keep our eyes centred upon it.'[39]

On 6 November it became abundantly clear to the Irish Guards that the Germans had not given up on the French and Belgian coastline beyond Ypres just yet. After a quiet morning, shells began to drop again. Cecil and his fellow Guardsmen sat as they flew over their heads and exploded in the support trenches. Then fire opened on the front lines and machine guns began peppering them. An hour later a German infantry attack blew through the French troops on one side of the battalion and the right hand company of the Irish Guards was completely overwhelmed. One company was forced to fall back to the support line to protect itself but it left the remaining men in the front line completely isolated. Few of those would be seen or heard from again. As the enemy jumped down into the captured French position they set up a machine gun and began raking the Irish ranks with dire consequences for the retreating Guardsmen.

The cavalry came swiftly up to help. The Irish Guards' adjutant had returned from seeing the brigadier to find men streaming past him on their way back and he grabbed a sergeant and began trying to form them up into some sort of line. With the cavalry, who jumped from their horses, these 100 or so Irishmen advanced, thrusting at the enemy with their bayonets. The Germans continued to come on, driving towards the trenches and by early evening the smattering of Irish Guards survivors had been driven back 200 yards behind. Had there been any reserves available they might have been able to have taken back their front lines, but there was nobody left. The Irishmen were in such disarray that for now the adjutant counted just 200 men, 'most of them suffering from nerves'.[40] By sheer luck, more than anything else, Cecil Dean was still among them.

Four more officers were gone, including two who had brought up the battalion reinforcements just five days before. The battalion was spent. To compound the utter misery of the fortnight they had endured, another commanding officer fell the following day. He had been depressed for several days, his adjutant recalled. 'And told me, that without relief, he could not stand it much longer.'[41] Having never expected to find himself in charge he had seen the entire pre-war battalion annihilated in just a few weeks, in fact largely in the previous seven days. Since 31 October the battalion had lost over 600 men. Their leader, Major Stepney, had admitted that, however silly it seemed, he blamed himself for many of the losses. The adjutant sent men out to find him in the dark. He was lying to the left of his battalion, his head and chest riddled with bullets. The Irish Guards now boasted enough men to form just two meagre, under-strength companies. They were led by just four officers, one of whom, commanding their tattered remains, was borrowed from the Scots Guards.

On 9 November the Irish Guards were given rum and pulled back into reserve in deep trenches back towards Ypres itself. The following day Cecil was given blankets and his first hot meal for days. On the 11th the exhausted German Army launched its final large-scale attempt to break the deadlock in front of Ypres. The harshest blow fell on troops under Brigadier General Charles Fitzclarence, the Irish Guards' former commander: a fierce bayonet attack that came bursting through the morning mist. It was thought that the Kaiser had sent up his prized Guards to see to it that the Allies were firmly and finally overrun on the Western Front, but the impetus of the enemy attack waned and the offensive fell away. The Irish Guards had been summoned to Nonne Bosschen Wood to help force the Germans out of it. They supported the Ox and Bucks Light Infantry as they managed to repel Prussian Footguards from among the remains of the trees, but despite being shelled they managed to come away without a single casualty and were not heavily engaged.

Taking up a spot near the headquarters of 1st Division, to whom they had been temporarily attached, Cecil and his fellow guardsmen awaited further orders. The battalion might have thought that it had got off lightly, but they happened to be sitting in the wrong place at the wrong time. Having lingered in the rain for hours they were told that they could go back and take on hot tea and supplies. They waited till past midnight for anything to arrive and having bedded down in the mud, the clock had barely reached 2 a.m. when they were to drag themselves up again and report for an attack. Fitzclarence had decided to organise a counter-attack to recover the part of his line lost throughout the day's fighting. He planned to take a bundle of survivors from different battalions, including Cecil's Irish Guardsmen and seize it back.

The men waded up through thick mud bunched together in fours, led by the Irish Guards. Soon they reached open ground. Just as the leading company passed a farm house by the side of the road, fire erupted both in front and on their right flank, some of it later thought to be friendly fire. The whole column veered off to the left. They scattered, flinging themselves into nearby shell holes. In the darkness and confusion Fitzclarence's body was lost and never recovered and he would become the highest ranked man to have his name inscribed on the Menin Gate in the aftermath of the war. The idea of an attack petered out without him and the Irishmen trekked back to the woods by Hooge Chateau, crammed with a miscellaneous collection of hollow survivors from various decimated battalions, from fellow Guards to French North African troops in their brightly coloured uniforms. As they collapsed back down the Irish Guards now numbered just five officers and 162 men. Against all odds, Cecil Dean was still physically unscathed among them.

The First Battle of Ypres had all but run its course. A small draft of men arrived on 13 November, taking the battalion's strength back over 200 and for now the adjutant, Captain Trefusis, was in charge. He was feeling the pressure of having so little support in command of the battalion and thought that all of the decent NCOs had gone along with the officers. Those coming up to replace them were lasting a matter of days before being carried off by sickness in the damp conditions or by German fire. 'It is frightfully lonely and depressing here,' he wrote, 'with practically no one to talk to. I cannot describe my feelings … when only a few days ago there were 25 of us [officers], and all such a happy family. It is too sad.'[42] It was the same for Cecil and the men. The drafts that arrived comprised men whom none of them had ever met before.

They felt as if they could sleep for a week. Time in a rest camp had been promised but for now they suffered in torrential rain and mud. Cold northerly winds blew across the front and snow made its first appearance on the battlefield. Then a hard frost set in. The conditions had generated a mud so thick and all-consuming that the men's rifles were too clogged to fire and their bayonets were rusting. After intermittent shelling and probing attacks, the final German attempt on Ypres came on 17 November. The Irish Guards were shelled from dawn until dusk but managed to help hold up the enemy advance with their rifles. 'Altogether this has been a rather unpleasant day,' reported Trefusis. He didn't much rate the experience of the NCOs and officers left in the lines and just hoped they would be able to hold the men together. Finally, during the night of 18 November, Cecil Dean's Ypres ordeal was over. The ragged remains of the Irish Guards were removed from harm's way and trekked into billets where they scoffed down hot food. The following day there was a heavy snowfall, but soon Cecil and the other Guardsmen marched into Méteren, back across the French border and almost 13 miles south-west of Ypres. Exhausted, so cold that their water froze in their bottles, not a man fell out.

Drafts would bring the Irish Guards back up to three-quarters of their original strength, sixteen officers and 750 men. For now, though, Cecil and nearly 400 others began the laborious task of getting themselves clean and free of vermin again after weeks of squalor and nerve-wracking torment. The army replaced everything from their clothes to the ground sheets that they slept on. Grand Duke Michael of Russia, the Tsar's brother, sent them mittens and mufflers to keep the winter weather at bay.

Sir John French arrived in England for a meeting with the Prime Minister and was struck by the contrast having just lived through what he termed as four of the most brutal months of war that the world had ever seen. 'It was one of those mild, balmy days which we very seldom get in the month of December, and the usual English Sunday atmosphere of rest and repose was over every object.'[43] Except for the odd man he passed wearing khaki, it might have been a surprise to learn that there was even a war going on across the Channel. The reality of the conflict was beginning to sink in, though, certainly in west London. Christmas was fast approaching and the war was anything but over. Though the football season continued, steps had been taken in Fulham to contribute a large-scale new effort to the pursuit of victory, involving both players and fans alike.

6

'Any More Chelseaites for Berlin in the Spring?'

The Home Front

If one was still needed, the struggle for Ypres was a wake-up call that suspended any notions at home that the war would be over by Christmas. As Cecil Dean and his fellow Chelsea fans up and down the front settled in for the reality of spending winter in a hole dug in the ground, at home football clubs were taking their own initiative to try and relieve the game of dogged accusations of shirking and laziness.

On 30 November Chelsea brought together representatives from both Millwall and Clapton Orient to discuss what they could do together to encourage enlistment. The following week they met again. This time, more clubs were represented, along with officials from the FA at their offices in Russell Square, two west London MPs and the Mayor of Fulham. They formed a committee and decided that they would officially approach the War Office with regard to forming a specific battalion for footballers to join. Club officials would be in charge of brainstorming how to clothe, feed and house the men until the War Office took over. It was a variation on a theme already occurring up and down the country, that of the 'Pals' battalion, formed wholly from one local community to play on civic spirit and ostensibly local peer pressure to enlist swathes of recruits to go off to war together with their own kind.

The men at the forefront of the footballers' project were a varied crowd. William Joynson-Hicks, MP for Brentford, had no background in football, being a car buff and chairman of the AA. William Hayes Fisher was on far more familiar ground. In his early 60s, he had been the Member of Parliament for Fulham almost without a break since 1885, had also held notable positions in the Treasury and was a member of the Privy Council. A one-time director of Fulham FC, Hayes Fisher had also been heavily involved in the early history of Chelsea. They were joined by the irrepressible figure of Henry Norris, Mayor of Fulham. A property developer with working-class roots, Norris was simultaneously involved with both Fulham FC and with Arsenal. Desperately trying to turn around the finances of the latter he had at one point been blocked by the Football League from trying to merge the two together and in 1913 had settled for moving the Gunners north to Highbury to expand their potential.

In the programme for a reserve game at Stamford Bridge on 12 December, it was revealed that the War Office had put up no opposition to the idea of a Footballers' Battalion. Surely the prospect of enrolling 1,300 or so men from all clubs to form it would not be such a hard task? It was the sincere hope of all involved, that not only players but fans too would flock to the colours at the prospect of serving together. 'The idea is that the players and followers of each club shall, as far as possible, form companies of their own.'[1] In a perfect world there would be a Millwall company, one for Chelsea, one for Orient and so on. The tone of the *Chronicle* was careful to be upbeat, without casting aspersions on those who had yet to enlist. 'It is fully realised that the large majority of Chelsea followers who are eligible have already answered their country's call, but here is the opportunity for any who have not yet done so. Now, lads!'

At 3.30 p.m. on 15 December 1914 some 500-odd men congregated at Fulham Town Hall, a few yards from Stamford Bridge, to discuss the formation of the 17th Middlesex Regiment, the 'Die Hards'. Officials represented a whole spectrum of London football clubs, including Chelsea, Fulham, Clapton Orient, Tottenham, Arsenal, Millwall and Crystal Palace. Both the President of the FA, Lord Kinnaird, and Frederick Wall, its Secretary, were also present in an unofficial capacity to witness the event and the association was willing to put their offices at Russell Square at the disposal of the battalion to help with recruiting.

Joynson-Hicks fired up the packed room with a dramatic speech urging players to make sure that the Germans did not get the chance to get across the Channel and carry out any of their alleged atrocities against the people of Belgium on their own wives and daughters. Henry Norris was more subdued and expressed his disappointment that no Fulham player had yet enlisted. William Hayes Fisher got up to a rousing reception. He was a sports fan, he began, and as such could be classed as one of these 'wicked individuals' who were happy to watch a game of football (applause and laughter). With a note of seriousness he appealed to footballers, as well as their friends, to join the battalion. He had more than a few words for the press with their tales of crowds full of slackers, particularly at Chelsea where he claimed that actually half were in khaki, 'fully a thousand', more underage. There were about 2,000 players fully earning a living from the game, he stated, 'and some seemed to think that the moment these enlisted they would have been fit to fight as soldiers, and if only they had crossed over those 2000 could have driven the Germans out of France and Belgium! (laughter)'. He wasn't going to have it anymore, London and indeed Fulham was quite adequately doing its bit, despite the continuance of professional football. 'He did not care how unpopular he became, but he felt bound to refute the unjust charges which had been made.'[2] They should ignore the falsehood and the fallacy that dogged the profession and instead prove them wrong 'with conspicuous courage and patriotism'. Should they not feel compelled to fight against 'an evil tyrannical monarch, an evil people'. Across the room he pointed to the example of Lord Kinnaird, President of the FA, whose precious elder son had already done just that and been killed in action at Ypres and whose fourth would also fall.

There were still obstacles to be overcome. Clubs would need to be sympathetic, both for the players wanting to go and in giving up their time and facilities to help gain recruits. Players would have to have Saturdays off too, to fulfil their playing commitments, and Kitchener was willing to agree to it until the end of the season. Train fares would have to be covered, possibly by the government, to get men back to the grounds in time for kick-off at the weekend. Hayes Fisher approached the issue of what would happen if a wound meant the end of a man's career and whether or not there should be some sort of pension in this instance. The representative from Crystal Palace wanted to know if it would be possible for players already enlisted to transfer into the battalion to serve with their friends. Steps to iron out all of this would be taken in due course, but for now all that was required was a show of hands.

Three players got up. Fred 'Spider' Parker, the Clapton Orient captain, a married man with three children, was the first to commit to joining the battalion. Frank Buckley of Bradford City followed, as did another player from Brighton. After gentle prodding and more stirring words more men followed and as the meeting concluded thirty-five players had expressed their intention to serve, including three players on Chelsea's books: Teddy Foord, Dave Girdwood and William Krug. Those present belted out the national anthem and went their separate ways – the 17th Middlesex was now in existence.

If the club authorities thought that this would put any gloss on the sport's image, or lessen the tirade directed at football, then they were mistaken. Supporters of the game in all quarters responded by fighting back. One Blues fan, an Australian doctor who had been resident in Britain for some twenty years, had applied for a commission in either a medical or combatant unit in early September. A surgeon at a large hospital, in addition he had a combined total of six years' experience in territorial units, both cavalry and infantry. 'Yet the war office say I am ineligible,' he complained. 'As a regular Chelsea follower I naturally feel "wild" when the newspapers indiscriminately abuse the football spectators, making an especial "set?" at those of Chelsea.' He went so far as to complain to the *Pall Mall Gazette* about the one-sidedness of the press coverage of football and the war. They declined to acknowledge him and as a result he sent his letter on to Chelsea who printed it in the programme on 12 December as an example of 'one of the many "suppressed" communications which … [had been received] complaining that the press boycotters denounce all spectators as professional matches without permitting them a word in self-defence'. The doctor was indignant at the blatant hypocrisy he perceived as being on display and levelled a challenge at the *Gazette*'s editor. 'I will get one professional footballer to enlist in Kitchener's Army as a private if you yourself enlist,' he declared. He too would join himself, if the editor of *The Observer* would do so with him. 'Finally, if you will give a shilling to some fund for every day of active service I have done as a combatant,' he claimed, referencing his service in the Boer War, 'I will subscribe two for every day's service done by you. Let us see if all of this palaver in your paper,' he challenged, 'is genuine or mere hypocrisy and sham.'[3]

Another letter reprinted in the *Chronicle* made similar remarks. 'Would some of those daily and weekly papers which are so strongly denouncing the continuance of football and other sports during the war, just consider for a moment whether it may be possible that the country could do with fewer newspapers, and whether amalgamating several of their publications for a time they could not liberate a large number of eligible young fellows for the front?' In conclusion the editor of the *Chronicle* wryly slipped in his own suggestion: 'What about a Press Battalion?'[4]

Frederick Charrington was still relentlessly campaigning against football and on Christmas Day Lord Derby instigated a 'census' at Everton to ascertain just why so many men remained out of uniform. Over 16,000 cards were handed out at their match and unsurprisingly most had been indignantly ignored. He wanted to know whether men were willing to enlist, unwilling and if so why? A meagre 1,031 cards came back, a handful of them abusive ('mind your own business or something rather stronger'[5]). Of those that graciously gave him a proper response, 335 men claimed that they had been rejected as unfit, 145 were above or below age, thirty-one were waiting for uniforms having enlisted, 200 were willing to sign up, and 144 said that they couldn't because they were on government or railway work. That left potentially 176 men of those that answered who simply didn't want to go to war.

Christmas at Stamford Bridge was far less inquisitive. The *Chronicle* was touting for fans to follow Dave Girdwood, Teddy Foord and William Krug in joining the 17th Middlesex, under the heading 'Any more Chelseaites for Berlin in the spring?' The club was still hopeful of fielding enough men to form a Chelsea Company in the new Footballers' Battalion. 'They can enlist today and all information can be obtained at our offices on the ground. Very little duty will be required until after Christmas, and pending the completion of barrack accommodation, they will be able to live at home, receiving the increased pay usual under such circumstances.'[6]

The traditional Christmas morning match was subdued. Foord and Girdwood played for the reserves at West Ham. For a time the turnstiles at Stamford Bridge did not even open, as the fog was so heavy that it looked as if the game might have to be abandoned. 'Hundreds must have gone home tired of waiting outside.' Eventually, though, 'the fog fiend lifted his skirts and disclosed the sun shining with almost spring-like brilliancy'. Both Chelsea and Manchester City hit the underside of the crossbar or the angle of the upright, but a hawker selling nougat was the only one who found the target. Working on the cinder track and throwing packages onto the terraces he managed to hit a well-known cricketer in the face, but for the 15,000 fans assembled they witnessed no more than a 0–0 draw on the pitch.

The non-result matched the general mood in the stands. 'The festive season leaves us in little mood for junketing,' remarked the *Chronicle*. So many were absent, some of them quite obviously never to return from the front. 'Our thoughts will all be with our dear ones who are doing their best to exterminate the Mad Beast of Europe.' The editor was at pains to keep people's spirits up. When Kitchener's millions were unleashed 'then, why the German baby-killers will be crumpled up like a cigarette paper in a child's fist!' This was no time for being down in the dumps – that did the troops no favours:

> Keep smiling … moping helps nobody. Long faces don't pay long bills and whining never wins wars … if we cannot all be as joyful this Yule-tide as of yore, let us at least keep smiling, even if it be through our tears for lost loved ones. Business as usual; and it is the business, the duty in fact of everyone to turn his face to the sun.[7]

As 1915 dawned Chelsea were fourth from bottom of the league with only Spurs, Manchester United and Notts County below. Troops being entertained as guests at Stamford Bridge seemed to care little for what the result was, or indeed whether they watched the first team one Saturday or the reserves the next. At one match the Queen's Westminster Rifles were visitors and came in to march round the track singing 'Here We Go Again',[8] but some of those who arrived in uniform were sadly less able. At the end of January a number of wounded men who had been released from internment in Germany seemingly conspired to pay a visit to Stamford Bridge. A Mrs Waldron had taken it upon herself to see to their comfort and secure the loan of cars to run them out into the countryside at the weekends but they had other ideas. They manipulated the route and lo and behold the convoy passed down the Fulham Road 'either by accident or design'. It was 'only' a reserve game in progress but they did not appear to be fazed and insisted on watching the football:

> The poor fellows, some of whom had lost both legs, were carried up to the director's stand and thoroughly enjoyed the game, the tea and cake at half time and their 'fags'. It was a pathetic sight for the onlookers, but it was pleasant to witness the cheerfulness of these gallant fellows crippled for life.[9]

These visits became something of a habit and a couple of weeks later the same occurred again against Southampton. Once again the club's officials gave their seats up for the wounded soldiers. Mrs Waldron was mystified by their enthusiasm for the game. 'It is all football with them, they want to see a football match before anything else!'[10]

The club had also been thinking of those soldiers still at the front. Ever since the commencement of the war they had been inundated with requests from fans abroad for donations of footballs to occupy them in their leisure time. Despite the fact that resources at the club meant that the team were often training with one ball – they had been dispensing them to the front. They were all of matchday quality, as the club did not want them to get kicked to pieces inside a week. In that case they would have been 'a poor sort of "gift" to our gallant lads who are so freely offering their lives and limbs for England, home and beauty'. One ball had gone to James Broadbridge and the 3rd Division's artillery HQ; more to Arthur Timoney and the 5th Divisional Train, Henry Jarvis with the 2nd Division Ammunition Column and Albert Ponman and Lawrence Catchpole with their respective supply parks. One had also gone to Fred Brooks, now back at the Base Depot at Le Havre, which had been begun again properly at the beginning of November. He wrote a note of thanks to the club: 'I have the opportunity of writing on behalf of the company to thank you for your kindness in sending us the ball. It arrived on Saturday and to celebrate the occasion we all participated in a game, quite an unusual occurrence after being without a kick for months.'[11] It was not only front-line troops thinking of football at Christmas. Even if none of the Chelsea balls went to those in the fighting lines, the rest, if not with support units or sent to the rear or prisoner-of-war camps, had gone to troops stationed in Britain at the beginning of 1915, waiting to go abroad.

Volunteers for the Footballers' Battalion arrived at White City in January to begin their training, their first parade conducted in front of a large crowd of spectators. As part of the FA's drive to assist recruitment in the 17th Middlesex, its secretary Frederick Wall had sent encouraging letters out to clubs south of the River Trent. On 9 January the *Chelsea FC Chronicle* reported that some 100 players had enlisted in the Footballers' Battalion although it also pointed out that if this was deemed somewhat insufficient, it had to be considered that players (and fans) enthusiastic to join up would have done so long before mid-December when it was formed.

At Chelsea plenty of space was dedicated to sales pitches in the *Chronicle* in order to drive men into the club office to see Assistant Secretary Bert Palmer and commit to enlisting. 'The ranks are fast filling,' proclaimed the editor. 'There is no time to lose. Those of you who are still "thinking" about joining must make up your minds quickly or you will be left out in the cold.' The battalion was full of players ready and willing to serve alongside the ordinary man. 'If you want to be a comrade of these men famous in football, seize the opportunity at once. The Enlistment office is West Africa House, Kingsway, or you can go to the White City and "sign on" like an international footballer.' Posters appeared at Stamford Bridge and generated a steady trickle of fans popping in to see Mr Palmer, patiently waiting to take names. 'Chelsea has already obtained more recruits for the 17th Middlesex than any other league club,' it was proclaimed.[12] The response of both Chelsea and Clapton Orient fans was conspicuous in the early stages of recruitment. Even if players were holding off from joining:

no one can say that Chelsea followers have not contributed their full quota to Kitchener's army … Since the formation of the footballer's battalions our Mr A

J Palmer has found time amid his multifarious secretarial duties to act as an honorary recruiting officer for the battalion. He has already enrolled between 60 and 70 men at Stamford Bridge and hopes to reach the century by the end of the present week.

It was not surprising that the 17th Middlesex, despite its broad mandate for recruiting professional footballers, should be at least initially rather London-centric in its make-up. Travelling to and from White City and maintaining matchday commitments was difficult for anyone too far from the capital, although in February a trip to Grimsby Town yielded another platoon's worth of players and fans. The *Chronicle*'s claims that the ranks of the Footballers' Battalion were 'fast filling up' were a little over optimistic, particularly as far as players themselves were concerned. There had been rumours of clubs blocking their men from enlisting, and even docking their wages or dropping them if they dared join the army while under contract. In command of the 17th Middlesex, Colonel Grantham was a 'dug-out' (as in from retirement), as was his second in command, an Old Etonian named Fenwick with a DSO from South Africa. In his late 50s, Grantham had strong Indian Army connections which his son had followed. Twenty-eight-year-old Charles was killed in the very early stages of the Mesopotamian campaign just as his father began to lose patience with enlistment in his new battalion. At the end of March he wrote to the Football League to condemn the response of players. 'Only 122 professionals have joined. I understand that there are 40 league clubs and 20 in the southern league, with an average of some 30 players fit to join the colours, namely 1800. These figures speak for themselves.'[13] The strength of the battalion though was now up to some 1,200 men and 'nearly 100' had apparently come through Chelsea. Significant measures had been put into place to try and fill the ranks. Henry Norris commented that he, Joynson-Hicks and Hayes Fisher had offered financial incentives to the recruiting sergeant for getting people in to the battalion, Joynson-Hicks a shilling per man, Hayes Fisher and Norris himself sixpence. In addition, for every company that was raised Norris would pay it £20.

Grantham's complaints found little sympathy in the footballing community. ('Et Tu Brute!' was the *Chronicle*'s response.) As it was pointed out, northern players had joined local regiments. Twenty-six London-based players from top clubs had already joined other battalions. Millwall alone claimed to have put 400 players and fans elsewhere before the creation of the Footballers' Battalion. It had also been noted that only 600 professional players with top clubs (some of whom were already in the army) were unmarried and still, as yet the pressing, moral or official of married men into service had not commenced. Considering the London emphasis of the battalion, it then was also significant that so few of the professional clubs were based even in the south, let alone the metropolis. Recruitment, though, was becoming an ever pressing issue across the board. The number of men volunteering to join the services was in decline. After the record high of nearly a quarter of a million recruits in a single month in September 1914, in February 1915 the return was just 87,896, which would not be nearly enough to keep up with the casualty rate abroad.

Football was no longer willing to accept the brunt of the animosity aimed at the sporting world. 'When Lord D[urham]'s … zeppelin arrives,' the *Chronicle* stated, with reference to his desire to see Sunderland bombed, 'will the Germans kindly reserve a little ammunition for the racecourses?'[14] As soon as it became apparent that the racing season would progress as normal it became a bone of contention for those within football taking constant criticism.

It probably went a long way to explaining both the curtness and the lack of responses for Lord Derby on Christmas Day at Everton:

> Probably the large majority of the card recipients were of the opinion that neither Lord Derby nor anyone else had a mandate for this rather inquisitorial proceeding. That would be quite natural … probably, too they remembered that his Lordship's interests were, so far as sport is concerned, entirely bound up in horse racing; that he has a very successful owner, and holds a high position in the racing world, and therefore that he had a far greater right to take the census of the race goers, especially as (in contrast to greatly diminished crowds at football matches) the attendance at race meetings showed little or no falling off as compared with last season. That would also be a very natural feeling.[15]

One MP highlighted the class issue that coloured the debate between the two sports in the House of Commons:

> It seems to me that the two are on exactly the same footing … If you are going to make a great demand, as you ought to make a demand, upon the whole people to devote the whole of their energies to meeting this great national crisis, that demand ought to be made equally on all classes, whether they are rich or they are poor.[16]

The Grand Stand at Epsom Downs had been utilised as a hospital for wounded soldiers over the winter but spring was approaching. The MP for Brixton raised the issue in the House in February: 'were the wounded now going to be kicked out so that racing could begin again or was the government going to take steps to extend this tenancy?' One of the most vehement opponents of football said that all of the men were well enough to be moved so that racing could commence. He was badgered by another who had actually researched the issue and gave a figure of forty-two 'dangerously' wounded men currently at Epsom. His opponent quietly conceded that he would have enquiries made on the subject.

Some dubious-sounding arguments were raised in favour of racing, namely that jockeys were too small to fight and that it must be continued to keep the standard of horses up for the cavalry, but the wily editor of the *Chronicle* did not miss a trick.

'The utterances of Lord Durham on the subject of the continuance of football and of racing respectively take a deal of reconciling,' he wrote in April. 'It would be very illuminating to publish in parallel columns that widely quoted speech of his lordship in which he was reported as having expressed himself as 'almost wishing that a zeppelin would drop to the ground and his speech at the Jockey Club meeting'. He made sure he was able to quote the hypocrisy to the letter: 'There he is credited with saying "What scandal, what injury to the public service, and what detriment to the national service had racing done?" Substitute the word "football" for racing and let the noble lord answer the question himself.'[17] In May racing continued regardless of criticism and a canny Lord Derby claimed that the Jockey Club had indicated that if the government demanded the cessation of the sport it would comply in twenty-four hours. So, he added, 'if racing continued, upon the Government would rest the sole responsibility'.[18] This was a far less subtle stance than that of the Football Association, with equal results.

War had nonetheless been declared between the two sports. 'The same men who consider it of vital importance in the national interest that racing should in no way be interfered with, can reconcile this view with an insistent demand for the total suppression of professional football.' The editor of the *Chronicle* pointed out very deliberately and on multiple occasions that football took up one, perhaps two, afternoons a week, but that racing was a daily occurrence and far more demanding of a man's time to follow. 'So let it go on, by all means, but at the same time let their lordships of the Jockey Club keep their hands off the workman's Saturday afternoon football match or be careful to attack with some other weapon than a boomerang.'[19]

The time was fast approaching though, when it wouldn't matter what an able man's occupation was, that he could well be needed to do his bit abroad. On 19 May 1915 the issue of universal service was touched upon in the House of Commons. Footballers were being enticed to go and pilloried for remaining at home, one MP noted. Racing continued alongside with a fraction of the bad press. Loafers stayed at home while married men went in droves. The Prime Minister became embroiled in the debate and then another man got up and said that the time had come for *every* available resource, both in terms of men and munitions, to be mobilised for the war effort.

Age limits had been raised, height restrictions had been lowered. Married men on the whole were still extremely reluctant to enlist. More locally raised units were encouraged, particularly in London boroughs, but even the numbers coming forward for these were in decline. In line with the creation of the Footballers' Battalion, thirty more units came in November and December 1914. Since the turn of the year, though, the number had dropped to more like five a month. Bantam battalions now welcomed with open arms men 5ft 3in and below and women stalked the streets brandishing white feathers at those not in uniform. But all efforts to encourage enlistment seemed in vain. For now, though, it was the job of those at the front to await the spring so that the fighting could begin again in earnest.

7

'Carry Them Right Off Their Legs'

The Battles of
Neuve Chapelle & Aubers Ridge

The opposing armies on the Western Front spent the winter of 1914–15 digging in, creating ever more elaborate defences, contemplating the coming of action in tandem with warmer, drier weather. In the New Year the hierarchy of the British Army had begun to contemplate how to extricate themselves from the quite unexpected scenario in which it now found itself. The Allies were not progressing anywhere and neither were the Germans. Someone had to take this new concept of warfare, an artillery-dominated, defensive impasse, and try and push the stalemate towards a conclusion. At the end of January the idea of Britain's first independent offensive, in France, was approved and the following month Douglas Haig won the argument as to who would carry it out. On advice from his senior officers he advocated to Sir John French the capture of the village of Neuve Chapelle, some 10 miles south of the border with Belgium. Here it seemed that the Germans might be vulnerable as their trenches bulged into a salient. Its capture would straighten the British line and it was thought to be weakly defended in terms of both troops and artillery, should it have to withstand a concerted attack.

Haig quickly widened the scope of the original plan. His men were languishing in miserable, sodden, shallow trenches, having to build up breastworks to defend themselves as digging down only let more water in on the low-lying ground. Moving forward past Neuve Chapelle resulted in moving towards the high ground of Aubers Ridge. Not only did this get Haig's men off the depressing low terrain that they presently occupied, but strategically speaking, taking it would bring Lille, 16 miles to the north-east, into play beyond. This would threaten the whole German position in the region. Once the enemy line had been broken by his men, Haig intended to send up cavalry to ride victoriously through the gap created and send the Kaiser's men running for home. The importance that this first attempt to transform the British army's fortunes had now taken on was evident in his own words:

> The advance to be made is not a minor operation. It must be understood that we are embarking on a serious offensive movement with the object of breaking the German line and consequently our advance is to be pushed vigorously … The idea is not to capture a trench here, or a trench there, but to carry the operation right through; in a sense of surprise the Germans, carry them right off their legs … Push forward … with as little delay as possible.[1]

Befitting its status as the first attack carried out in a thoroughly new type of stagnant, industrialised warfare, preparation for the Battle of Neuve Chapelle would be groundbreaking in a number of ways. Perhaps most significantly, artillery would be used in larger quantities and in a far higher concentration than ever before. It would be co-ordinated, laying down a short, terrifying barrage, before lifting and jumping further back to form a curtain to stop German reinforcements coming up. Some 340 guns were put in place, one for every six yards of enemy trench, a mind-blowing concentration at this point in the war. As well as sheer numbers of guns, the various types had also been considered when they were allocated their tasks. Lighter calibre pieces were designated for cutting the wire put up in front of the German wire. High explosive shells in particular would attempt to take care of the breastworks and the very toughest guns would be ranged on the ruins of Neuve Chapelle itself and German command positions, as well as on the enemy's guns up on Aubers Ridge.

On 2 March 1915 troops detailed to take part in the BEF's groundbreaking offensive were carefully removed from the lines to prepare for their part in the attack. Two Chelsea fans found themselves marching towards new billets in and around Estaires. With the 2nd Rifle Brigade was 23-year-old William Richards. Having joined the Rifle Brigade as a teenager, abandoning life as a greengrocer, Bill had been serving in the shadow of the Himalayas when war was declared. The diminutive Londoner had sailed from Bombay with his battalion in October 1914 and in turn they departed Southampton for war, landing at Havre as the base re-established there at the beginning of November. Also marching towards Estaires was a reservist who had returned to his old battalion on the outbreak of war. Born in Pimlico, central London, Alf Dorsett had already seen extensive active service with the Yorkshire Regiment in South Africa. By 1914 he was lodging with his brother and his young family right next to Craven Cottage and working as a postman. Having left Guernsey on the outbreak of war, his battalion of the Green Howards had been the second utterly decimated at Ypres in the opening months of the war. Alf was one of the first reinforcements to arrive, stepping off a troop transport in mid-November.

Preparations and rehearsals for the big push were unlike anything that either Pensioners fan had experienced before, despite being seasoned soldiers. Special

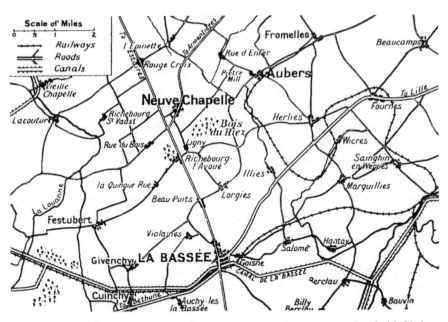

The area around Neuve Chapelle would become familiar to many men associated with Chelsea during the course of the war. *(Authors' collection)*

trenches were dug for practising the initial assault. For now it was estimated that when battle commenced some 12,000 British and Indian troops would face in the region of just 2,000 Germans, but it would not take long for them to summon reinforcements. A huge emphasis was placed on speed and so there was physical drill for men who had largely been sitting idle over the winter. Fitness training was supplemented by bayonet practice, ready for scrapping in close quarters, and the Rifle Brigade were becoming proficient in 'trench blocking', cutting of sections to defend themselves when sharing a semi-captured trench with the enemy. Work was not completed by day either. In the interests of maintaining absolute secrecy, both Bill and Alf were required to set out under cover of darkness in parties hundreds strong to carry out the important task of digging additional trenches to house troops during the battle. As the attack grew nearer, working parties laid out tools, ammunition, made bridges and removed obstructive barbed wire from what would be their path toward the German lines.

On 9 March both the Rifle Brigade and the Green Howards received their orders for the attack, which was to commence the following day barring the interference of the weather. Both battalion commanders promptly convened meetings among the junior officers to give them their instructions. Bill, Alf and their fellow troops were rounded up late that night and bundled onto the road to march towards Neuve Chapelle ready for daybreak, sinking into the cold mud, their breath visible on the frosty night air. Halfway there they were pulled over and issued a hot meal. For many of those present, it would be their last. Before dawn the men were ready and waiting to burst forward and surprise the German Army.

Unsuspecting, like their British counterparts had been, the Kaiser's men sat wet and cold, as they tried to snatch a few hours uncomfortable sleep in shallow, waterlogged trenches, behind thick breastworks. Tangles of barbed wire up to 15 feet thick shielded them from the likes of Bill Richards and Alf Dorsett, waiting to pounce. In Neuve Chapelle itself the church tower was almost the only building still standing. Heaps of rubble were all that remained of the village. Behind their camouflage, British guns prepared to unleash a torrent of shrapnel and high explosive onto the silent defences and smash them to pieces, paving the way for the infantry.

Bill Richards and the 2nd Rifle Brigade were situated in the middle of the line facing Neuve Chapelle itself. When dawn broke a damp, grey, miserable mist gave way to clearer weather and at 7.30 a.m. on 10 March the air was filled with the sound of the monstrous bombardment. A little over half an hour later, men of the Royal Berkshire and the Lincolnshire regiments poured out of ditches and assembly trenches, overrunning the German front lines. Bill clambered up and across the British front line, shells screeching overhead on his way to the German lines as the second phase of the bombardment commenced. Coming up behind the Berkshire men the Rifle Brigade flung themselves to the floor to await their turn to advance through them. At 8.35 a.m. it came.

The artillery lifted its fire to east of the village to form its curtain and Bill and his company heaved themselves up and went forward, still reminded that speed was of the essence. All of the wire had been cleared from in front of the British lines, but as they crossed the battered ground, the men climbed over the remnants of shattered German wire entanglements in little columns. Like the troops before them they met hardly any resistance from the enemy. The muddy ground was a myriad of ditches and dykes and portable little footbridges had been provided to make the attack run smoothly. High explosives had wreaked havoc on the German defences, breastworks built 4 feet high and 6 feet across out of sandbags. When they reached the front line, the Rifle Brigade found it only 3 feet deep at most, swimming with muddy water. They pushed on across the top. Just fifteen minutes after setting out Bill Richards had reached Neuve Chapelle. The front line had been ordered to get through the village as quickly as possible, so in the second he moved slower, more methodically; hauling German soldiers out of cellars as prisoners, mopping up. The attack appeared to have gone well. Bill passed through the village and came out the other side unscathed to find men of the Royal Irish Rifles drawing up on their left, Indian troops on their right.

The advance drew to a halt behind the cascade of artillery fire being laid down to prevent German reinforcements coming up. Orders were given to begin entrenching immediately, and to string up wire. Machine guns raked their front but Bill's commanding officer was most enthusiastic, requesting permission to push the advance forward. After all the Germans had barely put up a fight in front, such was their surprise. When the answer came back, though, it was negative. On the left, things had not gone nearly so well. There was a gap where troops of the 7th Division, such as Alf Dorsett, should have been. On this part of the front the wire hadn't been cut nearly as effectively by the artillery bombardment and German trenches were still largely intact. Only on the extreme right had the first assaulting waves managed to get inside them and at a whole it took them until lunchtime to achieve their objectives, several hours after the Rifle Brigade had already advanced out of the other side of Neuve Chapelle on their right.

Once everybody was in position, all now seemed prime for the second phase of the advance, the attack on Aubers Ridge; but unfortunately poor planning was about to severely hamper attempts to continue the day's work. Orders were issued at 1.10 p.m. and Alf's battalion of the Green Howards was summoned to pass through the original attackers and help assault Aubers Ridge beyond. There was little opposition as they passed over their own new front line, No Man's Land and the original German front, but this was to prove the height of their success for the day.

Mid-afternoon the battalion was ordered to halt near an orchard and wait for more troops due to attack with them. The orders for them to advance fell largely on confused troops, who had already seen action that day and were scattered across the area, and the short notice reorganisation required was proving too much. It was not until 6 p.m. that Alf began to trek forward again. Communications were in total disarray and the result was random, non-cohesive attacks on the ridge. The Green Howards slopped across slick, wet ground, 'intersected by a maze of trenches and drainage ditches'. By now light was failing fast and artillery support had waned. German strongpoints continued to direct a hail of fire at them and attempts to proceed became slower and slower. The divisional commander wanted them to carry on, but the brigadier below him put up a fight. It was clear by now that throwing more men at the enemy defences was achieving little and causing unnecessary casualties. The area was awash with confused troops; senior officers did not know where they were and couldn't control them. At 7 p.m. those in command concurred and Alf and his cohorts were ordered to consolidate their positions, establish communications with troops on their flanks and get themselves ready for a further attack the next morning. The first day of the battle had been satisfactory enough for those at the top. The British and Indian force had broken through and taken up to half a mile of ground on a front longer than 2 miles, including Neuve Chapelle itself. Bill and Alf's corps commander was confident. 'The great point,' he wrote, 'is that we have now proved that a line of trenches can be broken [into] with suitable [artillery] preparation combined with secrecy.'[2] The problem now, though, was that they had to try and break out the other side.

The enemy had already begun to prepare for just that eventuality. During the night the Germans returned to the scene of the battle and reoccupied trenches that they had fled earlier in the day, just out of reach of British bomb throwers, who in Bill Richards' battalion particularly had been effective throughout the day. They began fortifying their new positions, even digging a new trench in order to steel themselves for a further attack. More men had been packed into their trenches overnight, more artillery dragged up and in Aubers itself more reserves were being concentrated. They might have been surprised and thrown into disarray that day, but it certainly wouldn't happen again. When the British attacked on 11 March, the Germans would be waiting.

The enemy began pre-emptively shelling the village early in the morning. Bill Richards and his battalion had been ordered to respond to any German attack in kind and pursue them backwards. To the north, however, Alf Dorsett was to help provide support for the main advance on Aubers Ridge itself. He and his cohorts were somewhat scattered after the previous day's fighting, open on their flanks and suffering fire from all directions. Yet their attack was to commence at 7 a.m. after a fifteen-minute bombardment. It proved to be a complete disaster. The assaulting troops could not even get out of their trenches in the face of overwhelming enemy fire. The new artillery bombardment had achieved nothing and now as battle raged the gunners didn't even know what they were shelling. A lack of observation officers meant that the artillery could not range their guns on any appreciable targets. A multitude of telephone lines that had been strung out to maintain communications were ripped to shreds by German shells. Alf's commanding officer spent much of the day attempting to get the guns pointed where they would be of assistance to his men, but almost a dozen Yorkshiremen alone were put out of action by one mislaid British shell that came crashing down on its own troops.

Some diligent bomb throwing yielded dozens of German prisoners, but that was all that was achieved on 11 March on the Green Howards' front. Alf was close to the enemy, but the battalion was not strong enough in numbers to get through their defences. By mid-morning any hope of further advance had dissipated. Unfortunately General Rawlinson, in charge of both British divisions, wanted attempts to continue. 'The Divisional commanders, in contrast, were becoming concerned that lives were being thrown away without prospect of result.'[3] At battalion level senior officers were in agreement and discussed it with a nearby Scottish unit. The commanding officers concurred 'and reported that an advance on the above places so strongly held would be impossible without artillery fire and an attack by another force from the north'.

The impetus had fully gone out of the British attack towards Aubers Ridge. On 11 March the line hardly advanced at all. The enemy was firmly entrenched now and determined not to give way. The offensive had not succeeded when the Germans were greatly outnumbered and surprised. Continuing to try now that they had been significantly reinforced was flogging a dead horse. Unfortunately, though, those in command failed to acknowledge this point and were resolved to carry on.

At dusk the Germans reinforced their front with six more battalions. Regardless of the difficulties that they had experienced, Bill Richards was ordered to form up with the rest of the 2nd Rifle Brigade and be ready to attack at 7 a.m. They were still waiting to do so when the Germans began a fierce preliminary bombardment ready for a pre-dawn counter-attack. Luckily for the likes of Bill and Alf it was badly ranged and the front lines were left intact, but the infantry were to follow. Day was beginning to break as the enemy advanced towards the Green Howards. Luck was with the enemy and they were masked in the thick mist until they were almost on top of the Yorkshiremen's positions. They found themselves, however, running into a wall of machine-gun and rifle fire put up by the battalion. The attack was repulsed with relative ease, leaving the ground in front of Alf Dorsett strewn with German casualties.

The British attack was still to go ahead. Mid-morning their guns began plugging away again. On the left of Alf Dorsett a gap had opened up as the Border Regiment pushed forward on an enemy strongpoint. Crossfire ripped into the Green Howards as they occupied their new trench and then the shelling began. Despite capturing 129 German prisoners the 2nd Yorkshire Regiment lost double that number of men. Ninety-three had been killed since the Battle of Neuve Chapelle had been launched two days earlier and at the last, Chelsea fan Alfred Dorsett was among their number on 12 March when he fell during the doomed British attack.

On the following day the British and Indian troops were ordered to consolidate their positions. Neuve Chapelle had been captured, but hopes of conquering the rest of their wider objectives were in tatters. Senior officers began squabbling among themselves as to whose fault it was and, for a time, British attempts to take the offensive on the Western Front seemed like they might grind to a halt. The lull, though, was only to last for a few weeks. A second battle for Ypres began in the third week of April at the instigation of the enemy, incorporating their introduction of gas warfare. It would continue until 25 May, but would not hamper the idea of a joint British/French attack further south. Douglas Haig had wanted to continue the impetus begun at Neuve Chapelle immediately, but Sir John French put the breakers on. Although initially enthusiastic about it, ammunition stock was worryingly low as the battle wound down. Now that the French Army were requesting assistance, though, such concerns were quickly forgotten.

Things appeared to be going very well for the Germans and their Austro-Hungarian allies in the east and Allied planning was underway for a huge offensive which would draw their men away from the Western Front. It seemed like the perfect opportunity for the Allies in this theatre of war to strike, not only for the immediate benefit of Russia, to alleviate pressure on the Tsar's army, but because France and Britain were better off if that front stayed open and the enemy remained divided on two sides of the Continent. Joint operations were what the BEF had initially wanted with the French when the idea of the assault on Neuve Chapelle was first suggested. On 24 March, General Joffre enquired as to whether the British would be ready to proceed with something in this vein in little over a month's time. On 6 April, two weeks before fighting flared up at Ypres, the BEF received a plan from the French outlining a large offensive north of Arras, which would require British troops resuming their move on Aubers Ridge in tandem. Joffre's men would carry out several attacks, but the BEF would pick up the front north of the La Bassée Canal and push forward the day after the main advance.

The British plan was refined. All was dictated by the lack of shells available for the guns. As far as was possible, everything that Haig could have made available to him on that score was to be directed at punching two breaches in the German line, rushing men through the gap as quickly as possible, pouring cavalry through after them and restoring open warfare on the Western Front and attempting to reduce an overwhelming dependency on artillery. Although a main attack would take place between Festubert and Neuve Chapelle, troops including Bill Richards would carry out a secondary attack towards Fromelles, rushing the main road where it cut through the German lines, before supporting troops came through and assaulted Le Plouich and Aubers itself, trying to reach the ridge from the north. The French set the date of 7 May for beginning their offensive, meaning that Bill would go back into action the following day. A 200-yard stretch of the German line on either side of Fromelles road, where the road itself ran into the enemy breastworks, was selected for the left-hand breach of line. It was on one side of the road that Bill would be required to attack with the 2nd Rifle Brigade.

The final plan for the offensive had been explained to corps and divisional commanders before 6 May by Haig. Despite the ammunition situation, they were relying on artillery to forge a path across, to smash the German positions prior to the advance. The battle would begin with a forty-minute preliminary bombardment. As the guns lifted and Bill Richards advanced, all of the guns had precise targets in the way of buildings or strongpoints to help the infantry get across as unmolested as possible. Artillery would also be following up after the infantry to continue supporting their advance. Having been held up at random strongpoints in the move on Neuve Chapelle, trench mortars and small mountain guns would go up with the infantry this time too in order to deal with those. Finally, to help weaken the German position further, the Royal Flying Corps were going to bomb buildings they believed to be German billets, bridges, railway junctions and stations and suspected enemy command centres.

Plans were just as detailed for the infantry. Bill and his battalion had precisely ten minutes to accomplish their initial tasks, before the supporting troops of the Royal Berkshire Regiment behind were given fifteen more to pass through and continue on. The Rifle Brigade would then follow them up and each battalion had precise objectives and positions to take care of. The success of the assault on Aubers Ridge up and down the line depended on precision and co-ordination, carrying out the plan to the letter. 'Indeed everything was planned with such nicety,' wrote one assessor:

> that there was a danger of losing sight of the fact that the success of the operation depended on passing a large body of troops through one narrow defile and that the existence even of that narrow passage was contingent upon the effect of fifteen minutes' shell fire upon a well-wired position.[4]

During the course of April Douglas Haig's men reorganised themselves and began to prepare for their new offensive, reclaiming disused trenches, constructing more behind the front parapet, improving communication lines and cutting steps in the breastworks to help men advance quicker. Small bridges were to be carried for crossing German trenches and dykes, while larger ones were also being carried up on limbers to help get the artillery up. Reserves of ammunition were being left near the existing British front line, rations were stuffed into sandbags and canvas sacks were being procured to help take up drinking water. Bill Richards underwent all manner of last-minute training, including cutting wire by hand, and specialist groups were put together specifically to master the art of either bomb throwing or blocking trenches in line with the minute instructions that were to be issued. All the while preparations appeared to have been missed by the enemy opposite, but the somewhat meticulous plans were thrown into disarray on 6 May with heavy rain, which left a thick mist behind the following morning. The French postponed their attack because their lengthy artillery bombardment had been so disrupted. With their delay it was now decided that everyone would go at the same time as opposed to a staggered approach over a number of days. Both the British and French forces would now attack on 9 May.

There was a swagger within some of the British ranks following the initial success at Neuve Chapelle, assuming that this would be a step forward, incorporating lessons learned. But of course the Germans had learnt too and were not about to let themselves be overrun again. Since their rude surprise in March they had been fortifying their position and although the British were not oblivious to this, the extent of just how strong their defences were now was unknown. In spite of this, though, no additional artillery was available owing to events affecting the British Army to the north around Ypres. The guns available were no more in number than had been used on 10 March, when the enemy had no idea they were about to be attacked.

Although they had been subjected to regular bouts of shelling, things had calmed down for Bill Richards and the 2nd Rifle Brigade since Neuve Chapelle as they rotated in and out of the lines. On 8 May the unexpected delay saw them resting up in readiness for when the weather cleared. That night they paraded at 11 p.m. and marched off. Everything went without a hitch and three hours later everybody, including Bill, was in position waiting for dawn.

At 5 a.m. 190 guns let rip at the German lines, but the artillery bombardment left much to be desired. The gun barrels were sustaining damage from overuse and the quality of the ammunition was substandard. A significant number of shells fell short and began to drop into British lines. In the fire trench the Rifle Brigade men suffered casualties and had to fall back slightly to avoid their own guns. The rate of shelling grew to a crescendo in the final ten minutes before zero hour. Bill and his fellow troops moved out towards the breastworks ready to cross at least 100 yards of open ground. German bayonets began to poke out of the top of their own parapet. The enemy was ready.

On their left two mines 70 yards apart, each containing 2,000lbs of explosive, went up and men rushed forward to occupy the crater. The Rifle Brigade advanced together with a contingent of the Royal Irish Rifles into a tempest of machine-gun and rifle fire, picking up casualties immediately. Spread in platoons 30 yards apart they moved swiftly through the maelstrom while the second wave moved up ready to follow. The wire in front had been well cut. According to a Bavarian soldier opposite their sector, the days leading up to the attack had led to no suspicions. 'No special preparations had been noticed, and even the presence of the mines driven under the front trenches of the regiment next to us had not been perceived.'[5]

All around Bill men were being hit from both flanks of the enemy's front, falling to the ground. The first wave of the battalion pressed on and took the German trench opposite, sticking red and yellow flags into the ground to signify their success. They continued the advance 200 yards further on to a bend in the road towards Fromelles. Behind them two more companies, machine guns and battalion headquarters moved across into the enemy's trench amidst a growing storm of German fire, as the men facing them recovered from the strain of the bombardment, gathered themselves and took up defensive positions.

Having swept to their first objective in trying circumstances the battalion might have been forgiven for feeling rather pleased with themselves, but the situation in the midst of battle was about to take a disturbing turn. Looking to their left, then to their right, the Rifle Brigade and a scattering of Royal Irish Rifles, having traversed the German front line trench and penetrated enemy territory, were completely alone. To the right, where men of the East Lancashires should have been, there was nobody. Held up by unbroken enemy wire, 'smashed on their own parapet' by German fire,[6] huge numbers of the fallen now lay scattered across the ground in No Man's Land. On the left, excepting the handful of Irishmen that had joined up with Bill's contingent, the rest of that battalion, likewise, had vanished. Most of their survivors had wriggled through No Man's Land and dropped into a disused fire trench just in front of the British defences. The Kensingtons had flung themselves into the crater formed by the mines but could get no further in the face of the enemy onslaught.

At 6.20 a.m. the brigadier reached the scene to review their progress and found that despite initial success, all forward movement had stopped. Things were categorically not proceeding in line with the rigidly planned timetable. Units were bunching up and becoming mixed as the front men failed to push on. All companies were suffering severe losses and the Rifle Brigade's machine guns were unable to get across the open in front of the British lines. Battalion headquarters had become scattered along with the specially organised bomb and blocking parties that had been trained to smooth the advance. The former were desperately needed to fan out at either end of their new sector and fend off the enemy still in the trenches on either side of them, but the relevant men could not be found. The Germans on either side poured machine-gun fire into their flanks, decimating the Rifle Brigade's numbers, in particular their officers.

At about 8 a.m. the first wave that had advanced past the German front line broke and men began to fall back towards the captured trench. 'Some unauthorised person' had apparently given an order to retire. The sight of Germans coming towards them did nothing to dispel the rumour of a counter-attack but they were in fact enemy prisoners already taken who were fleeing German fire along with the British troops. Confusion reigned. The brigadier jumped on the parapet and began trying to restore order, shouting himself hoarse. He managed to rally his men, but the storm of German fire meant that no further advance was possible and he was mortally wounded for his trouble. As the day wore on Bill's battalion managed to cobble together some form of systematic defence to repel a host of German bomb attacks, also trying to get a trench mortar ranged on what they thought was a machine gun nearby, but their numbers were dwindling. Reinforcements were desperately needed.

Unfortunately it was proving impossible to get men up to support the Rifle Brigade. Their coloured flags could be seen in front, but there were clearly British troops on either side of them, too, so determining where the line ended in the enemy trench and where reinforcements should go was impossible. Between 8 a.m. and 9 a.m. every effort was made to get to Bill and his cohorts, but the route, through trenches already traversed in battle, was littered with broken ladders and bridges, howling men who had already been hit and those that were completely at a loss as to what to do having become mixed up and separated from their officers. The Royal Engineers were even called up to try and dig through into the German trench system so that they could get men up, but it was not a viable plan. Bill Richards's battalion was cut off. The only route up to the firing line was now across open ground. At about 12.15 p.m. an officer scraped forty or so men together and tried to get across to support those in the trench. By the time he arrived he had little more than a dozen of his reinforcements in tow, the rest having been killed or wounded.

On the right of the line, the attack was a total failure. Further to the left, 250 yards of German trench was being doggedly clung to by the Rifle Brigade and the Royal Irish Rifles and beyond that men of the Lincolnshire Regiment had snatched another isolated piece of trench. At the far end, the Kensingtons still languished in their mine crater. In between all of these pockets of British troops the Germans still occupied the line and emptied endless bullets into the invaders from both flanks and from in front of them. In the meantime Bill's battalion dug hard. They put up blocks in the trenches to keep from being overrun by the enemy on either side, resisting all German attempts to flush them out.

So diligently put together and trained before the battle, the special bomb parties had been scattered as soon as they advanced that morning. It was barely relevant, for the 200-odd men holding the trench had now run out of them to throw, theirs and the enemy's that had been lying about.

At his headquarters, Douglas Haig was being kept informed of developments as much as was possible, but he had little concept of what was occurring in front of him.

Later, he ordered the attack to be continued, pressed 'vigorously and without delay'. The instructions filtered down, but it made little difference to the outcome of the fighting under the circumstances. Even trying to get further effective artillery support was near impossible because gunners were unsure where to range their weapons, given that the German lines were now partially occupied by their own men and once again, lines of communication had been cut by shells. The congestion in the lines, the artillery situation and the rate of German fire ruled out further forward action. Having originally ordered for an attack to recommence at 8 p.m. Haig cancelled his own instructions and postponed everything till daylight.

In the meantime the enemy had launched a local counter-attack at the Rifle Brigade, but an officer managed to get a nearby enemy machine gun working and began raking the opposition, pinning them back. As many men as possible were dropped into the enemy fire trench to hold it in preparation for a renewal of the attack the next morning. Arrangements were made for the 7th Division to relieve the battalion, but the relieving detachment was unable to arrive in sufficient time for it to be carried out before daylight. At 2.30 a.m. the Germans put in another hefty counter-attack. Hand-to-hand fighting raged in the trench as the enemy burst in on the British occupiers from both sides and their flanks were driven in. Fiercely they attempted to bomb out the Rifle Brigade. A priest serving in the German ranks was astonished by what a difficult task it was. 'You can scarcely have an idea of the work this represented. How these Englishmen in twelve hours dug themselves in!'[7] Only by the most systematic destruction could they force their way through. 'Almost every single man of them had to be put out of action with hand grenades. They were heroes all, brave and true to the end, until death ... men of the ... English Rifle's Brigade.'

Finally the last of the survivors still in the front line were removed. The battalion had lost every single company officer at its disposal that day along with 632 men, including Bill Richards, who was evacuated home having taken machine-gun fire in both legs. Despite the lessons learned at Neuve Chapelle, once again the British Army had tried to force the issue on the Western Front and had fallen short. The hierarchy of Bill's division put it down to the sheer strength of the German defences. They were, it was said, so fully ensconced in their positions and determined to resist that Haig's men were doomed to failure.

8

'A Sterner Battle to Be Fought'

The Home Front

On 5 December 1914 it was decided by the football authorities that internationals would be abandoned. The Scottish FA, however, had called off their cup competition for the season too (on account of 'pawky sentimentalists' was the opinion at Chelsea) by the margin of a single vote. 'By this mean majority they have inflicted hardship upon clubs already hit hard,' the *Chronicle* stated. 'All these things they have done with a self-sacrifice which has cost them – nothing. The sacrifice has to be made by the clubs that a few men may pose as righteous.' The editor even resorted to sarcasm to drive his point home. 'England, Ireland and Wales may play cup ties … but we, the Scottish FA are patriots to the core; we will compel men to take up arms – by declining to play … cup ties! This smug pose is far more likely to fill the dram shops than the army!'[1] There was to be no such conflict in England. The 1914/15 season would host the only FA Cup run in the competition's history played out while the country was embroiled in a world war.

The only team that had actually been drawn at home in London for the first round was Spurs. It was a niggling complaint for Chelsea. They had thus far played 22 matches in the FA Cup and only eight of them, it was grumpily noted, had been at home. Cup form so far had been mediocre, although in just the club's sixth season the Pensioners had managed to reach a semi-final. The first obstacle in Chelsea's pursuit of the trophy this time around was to be Swindon Town on 9 January. 'The Moonrakers' were twenty years old as a club and at the time situated midway down the Southern League, although they were in fact the reigning champions. It was a feat they had achieved twice in seven seasons, having been runners-up a further three times, so they were no pushovers. The two clubs had had a memorable fourth-round encounter in 1911, a 'never-to-be-forgotten' tie at Stamford Bridge that ended 3–1 to the Blues.[2] The ground had been packed with an unprecedented crowd, 78,000 coming through the turnstiles officially, but estimates of those actually inside the ground topping 80,000.

Although Swindon were drawn at home this time, the officials at the club had ultimately decided that Stamford Bridge was the better venue for their tie. Their ground was 'restrictive' and both clubs could presumably make more money from a larger crowd in west London. It was a boost to Chelsea's cup aspirations, as Swindon were highly unpredictable of late and they would now have home advantage. 'We ought to just about pull through with the least bit of luck, seems to be the general view of their prospects adopted by the players.' With such poor league form the cup gave everyone something to be excited about. 'Our lads will have to play strenuously and well from the start,' noted the *Chronicle*, if there was any chance of progressing to the next round.[3]

Rain dogged the thirty-two first-round ties up and down the country. Nearly half a million fans turned out and were rewarded with 111 goals for braving the weather. Of the London sides, Fulham came through an ordeal at South Shields and both West Ham and Spurs managed to come from behind to advance into the next round. At the time there was a superstition that the holders were apt to get knocked out in the first round the following year, but Burnley progressed without too much trouble. The biggest upsets came when Swansea, of the Second Division of the South Eastern League, beat the mighty Blackburn Rovers, and Derby County were overturned by Leeds City. In the wet weather discipline appeared to lapse and there was a spate of red cards, three alone at Everton and two in a punch-up between Millwall and Clapton Orient players.

At Stamford Bridge 23,000 people turned out. Ten players remained from the 1911 tie, most of them in the Swindon side, and together the teams battled out a 1–1 draw. Complacency appeared to have set in among the Chelsea players. 'Four or five to nothing' one guessed prior to kick off. When the Blues went ahead in the 3rd minute the attitude, according to the *Chronicle*, seemed to be along the lines of 'plenty of time yet to beat this lot!',[4] a philosophy that any football-loving soul realises would have doomed the Blues to inevitable failure.

A replay, this time by right at Stamford Bridge, occurred the following Saturday, the day after the meeting at Fulham Town Hall inciting footballers to join the 17th Middlesex. It was a case of 'touch and go – very nearly gone!' On 70 minutes, Swindon led 2–1 and the Blues, though dominating play, 'stared defeat in the face for a full twenty minutes'. Chelsea had a reputation for capitulating in the closing stages of matches, so it did not look promising at all. Then in the 87th minute, Harry Ford, a local lad who had returned to west London after a spell at Tunbridge Wells Rangers, 'gave rise to a scene of such enthusiasm as had not been witnessed' all season at Chelsea when he equalised at the death.[5] Even the trainer came bounding on to congratulate him for pressing the tie into extra time.

Injury and sickness had depleted the team, but ultimately Chelsea's fitness prevailed. There was a fashion at the time for 'training' teams by way of taking them down to the coast and having them relax, with the odd promenade to take in some fresh sea air. Jack Whitley, Chelsea's lead trainer, did not subscribe to it. He preferred 'old fashioned Yorkshire preparation',[6] and it was telling as Swindon tired and Chelsea scored three more to take the tie at a score of 5–2, setting up an encounter with Arsenal in the next round.

'Buns vs. Guns'[7] was the headline a fortnight later when the Gunners arrived in west London to decide who would triumph for a place in the last sixteen. Like Chelsea, Arsenal had a following that transcended their local area and not only because of their relocation to Highbury in 1913. The first team in the capital to turn professional, for a considerable amount of time if a Londoner wanted to watch football at the highest level he would have needed to frequent the Manor Ground in Plumstead. Arsenal had joined the Football League for the 1894/95 season and had spent most recent years 'playing a game of hide and seek'[8] with the First Division. After eleven attempts they finally reached it and had stayed for nine years before being dumped down again in 1912/13, the year that they upped and moved away from south London. They had almost come back up the previous season, after having sat in second for almost the whole duration, but they collapsed with the finishing line in sight and missed out on promotion to Bradford on goal difference. In January 1915 they were once again embroiled in a struggle for second place and again hopeful of going up.

The new north Londoners had never reached the Crystal Palace final but they had made two semi-finals of the FA Cup. At the time Chelsea had a record with Arsenal of close and exciting matches, never more than a goal between them and it proved very hard for them to score against each other. The opposition had retained a certain element of their roots and arrived for the cup tie with three Plumstead boys among their number, one of whom had just enlisted in the Footballers' Battalion. Unsurprisingly the match drew a crowd of 40,000, the largest of the second round, including Micky Myers, 'erstwhile left winger of the Crystal Palace',[9] who was picked out in the crowd wearing the uniform of the East Surrey Regiment.

For Chelsea there was none of the bluster and overconfidence of the Swindon tie. The game was pacy and robust, the most entertaining game of the season so far at the Bridge, with 'never a dull moment in either half'. It was 'as good as wine compared to water up against the first round replay'. Again the Pensioners' fitness levels were telling. 'We must go hell for leather all the way!' was how one player phrased it before the game. 'And did they not?' The final score was 1–0 to the Blues and Chelsea apparently deserved the win. 'None admitted this more ungrudgingly than the Arsenal officials and players.' It could have in fact been a higher margin of victory but for squandered opportunities on the part of the home side. 'This is not a new failing of theirs, as you well know.'

The game was also notable for an appearance by a platoon of the 17th Middlesex who came in smart formation and marched around the cinder track shoulder to shoulder to the tune of 'Hold Your Hand Out Naughty Boy!' At half-time they collected towards musical instruments so that the battalion might form their own band and the *Chronicle* of the day took the opportunity to try and encourage others to join them. 'Surely there are still a few amongst those who cheered the khaki-footballers as they strode round the track on Saturday eligible and free to join the gallant throng?'[10]

Frederick Charrington was heartily protesting to the Prime Minister about the playing of cup matches and imploring action. He was told that the discussions held with the FA and the subsequent abandonment of international matches was deemed sufficient, but his bluster continued. Chelsea fans didn't care. They had drawn an away tie at Manchester City in the third round and supporters were already clamouring for train tickets to get up to the north-west. The Midland Railway was offering a £1 non-stop special including lunch, dinner and a match ticket to enable Londoners to see their team take on the current league leaders. City had just knocked out Aston Villa away in the last round and it was 'just about as difficult an undertaking as could possibly be set us'. If Chelsea were to win at Hyde Road it would be the first away victory of the season. Nevertheless, win they did by a narrow margin of 1–0 on 20 February. The goalscorer Bob Thompson was 'literally smothered by the embraces of his delighted comrades'. 'It came as a surprise to the world of football. Fancy Chelsea beating Manchester City!'[11] was the general consensus. The players had been confident of a win, but they had been largely alone. The *Chronicle* was quick to claim credit: 'Never once have we drawn attention to the long run of success than we go, wallop, the very next match. Having mentioned we hadn't won away at all, the very next game the team went and proved them wrong!'

Chelsea were now the south's last remaining hope in the competition and for the fourth round drew another difficult tie against Newcastle United. It was a grudge match of sorts as the Newcastle United team had knocked out Chelsea with a 3–0 battering in the semi-final in 1911. They were formidable opponents in the cup, lifting the trophy once in 1910. They had also reached five finals in the previous decade, an outstanding recent record in the competition. To compound the task facing the Blues, the Magpies had also been down to west London already in the league in 1914/15 and had beaten Chelsea 3–0. Having knocked out West Ham, Swansea and more significantly Sheffield Wednesday away from home, they boasted a team of internationals including Angus Douglas, who had gone there from Chelsea. The tie could not be settled at Stamford Bridge, ending in a 1–1 draw, and the Pensioners, having already played a league fixture at St James' Park a few days earlier, were forced to return on Saturday 13 March for a replay.

Meanwhile at Stamford Bridge, where the reserves were taking on Southampton, everyone's focus was naturally on events transpiring in the north and who would make the cup semi-final. At the final whistle a multitude of Blues fans began to congregate outside the office to find out what had happened. Not much, it turned out. The game had finished 0–0 and extra time was being played. Nervously they waited until a few minutes later the tape machine began ticking out news. 'Ford has scored for Chelsea.'

Bobbie McNeill had travelled up for the game with a stinking cold, having left behind the notion that 'If I can run as fast on Saturday as ma nose is runnin the noo, they'll never catch me'[12] and, sure enough, it was from a fast run and centre from Bobbie that the all important goal came.'

The strip was ripped from the tape machine and pasted to the window for the crowd outside and they promptly began to celebrate. Then the nail-biting began, noses pressed against the window to watch the officials clustered by the desk. 'And how slowly the minutes seemed to pass. At last!' The machine began to whirr and then to tick out the result ... C-H-E ... Chelsea 1, but what of Newcastle? 'We've won!' some shouted eagerly. 'Wait a bit!' Others were more cautious. N-E-W-C-A-S-T-L-E ... 0. As soon as it was official, 'an impromptu tango'[13] broke out in the club office. Those outside caught on and at Stamford Bridge rampant celebrations broke out. The replay win was Chelsea's second successive away victory, and still only the second of the season. Celebrations were occurring at the front, too, for when the men of the 15th Hussars, the Londoners anyway, heard the score they 'went dotty'.[14] The trouncing in the semi-final at neutral St Andrews in 1911 had been avenged.

This time the semi-final would be played at Villa Park but if there was any hope for an easy tie, it would be far from it. Chelsea's opponents on 27 March were to be Everton, who were weeks away from being crowned as First Division champions. Train fares were huge, with military necessity ruling out the idea of cut-price specials. Despite the fact that some die-hard Blues had expressed an intention to walk to Birmingham if necessary, the crowd was largely made up of locals. The opening half was nearly level, perhaps with Everton slightly on the front foot. With Chelsea playing in white, it was a rough encounter; Harry Ford was knocked out twice 'and received a rib-lauder or two'. The second half was nothing to write home about either but Chelsea turned the screw and one cleverly positioned shot from Jim Croal after a silly mistake from Everton was followed by 'a brilliant and dashing individual effort'[15] from Harold Halse. In fact, they might even have had a third if Croal had not then fallen over in the penalty area and failed to tap in another. Majestic it was not, but it was Chelsea's day nonetheless and the Pensioners had reached their first FA Cup Final.

Congratulations flowed in. With the cavalry, a fan in the Life Guards sent his 'heartiest congratulations' and happy tidings also came from aboard HMS *Sappho*. A frostbitten corporal in a London hospital was at least cheerful in his own debilitated state that Chelsea had made the final. Even the adjutant of a French regiment penned a letter back to a friend in London. 'I was awfully pleased to learn that Chelsea are doing well in the cup. I am still interested in their performances, and it is a pity to think I shall not be able to watch any of their matches this season. If I am still alive next season I trust I shall be able to do so then.'[16]

Since 1895 the outcome of almost every final, excluding replays, had been decided at the Crystal Palace in south London. The event drew huge crowds, 120,000 plus in 1912/13, but the stadium was now at the disposal of the Admiralty and had been closed to the public in February 1915, so a new venue had to be settled upon. Old Trafford had been used for a final replay in 1911. It was almost new, having opened in 1910 with a capacity of 80,000 and first-rate, modern facilities; additionally, crowd congestion would not interfere with the railway routes being utilised in the south for the war effort. The choice was a disappointment for Chelsea and thousands of fans across the capital and the south-east. Again there were no specials being run and it would cost an average man a week's wages to travel to Manchester. 'Rough on the Blues supporters that after it has taken 14 years for a London club to again reach the final it should be played so far from London,' wrote one fan in the navy.[17]

The build-up for the match was understandably subdued in the wartime circumstances. Frederick Charrington was not at all bothered by the inconvenience of the location and was ready to grace the final, having apparently claimed all credit for the tirade against football in the press. Never one to shy from drama on the subject, he was also claiming in one interview that he was 'nearly killed at Fulham'[18] in protesting at the beginning of the war.

Chelsea travelled north in good shape, apart from an injury to one-eyed Bob Thompson. As a contingency, now a newly commissioned officer in the Footballers' Battalion, forward Vivian Woodward travelled too. Having scored 96 goals for Spurs, including their first ever in the league, he had then quit top-level football before suddenly doing a U-turn and signing for Chelsea. Now with over 100 appearances, 'VJ' had also scored 29 goals for England and had captained Great Britain to gold in both the London Olympics in 1908 and in Stockholm in 1912. This amateur player was key for Chelsea, and as such when they inevitably lost him to internationals and the like they missed his prolific goalscoring. He was as good with his head as he was with both feet. Even though he was a 'toff' the fans loved him. 'There must be … thousands,' wrote one, 'who, like myself, have been really entertained [by this] gentleman's delightful football, which he seems to provide each season.'[19] Rather frailly built, but of a good height, he was a commendable example of a two-footed player. 'Rarely have I seen another forward do so much with so little apparent effort,' wrote one team-mate. 'He made the ball do the work, opening up the play and finding his colleagues with beautifully timed passes. He seemed to stroll through the game yet was seldom out of position.'[20] It was not known until the last possible moment which of VJ and Thompson would play. 'It was splendid to see the spirit of self-sacrifice errant by both in desisting to yield to the other the coveted honour of leading the front line of a team in a cup final.'[21] Ultimately Woodward refused to take the field, 'firm in his expressed determination not to play if all of the professional inside men were fit and well, so that none of them might be deprived of the prized final medal'.[22]

The last team standing in between Chelsea and the FA Cup were Sheffield United. It was the third time already in the twentieth century that they had made a final and they had lifted the trophy twice before, most recently in 1902. The two teams had only met once before in the competition and Chelsea had knocked the Blades out in the first round in 1912. Despite this the northerners were huge favourites. Interviewed before the game their captain postulated that Chelsea's 'pretty football', the First World War equivalent of modern *tiki-taka* with its short passes and complicated build up, would be no match for their expansive, hard-hitting game.

The 24 April dawned miserably in the north-west and the final took place under a veil of drizzle in front of 50,000, the crowd huddled under their hats and umbrellas. The amount of uniformed spectators lent it the nickname of the 'Khaki Cup Final', perhaps hundreds of them present from the Sheffield Pals who would be decimated on the opening day of the Battle of the Somme the following year. There was not a lot in it for the first twenty minutes other than an injury scare for Harry Ford, but then Sheffield began to take the upper hand. They might have put one in before they did actually score just past the half-hour mark, the ball cracking in off the back of the far post. More galling for Chelsea, the goal was a gift, for the keeper and his defenders all seemed to stand about and wait for each other to deal with the threat. In the event, nobody did and there were a few frustrated words exchanged between the captain, Jack Harrow and goalkeeper, Jim Molyneux. Then Sheffield were 'all over 'em'.[23] The Pensioners almost equalised before the end of the first half, but went into the break deservedly behind.

At half-time the band played 'Tipperary' and a collection was made for the Red Cross, sheets held out for fans to toss pennies onto. A thick, yellow fog had descended and it was hard to follow the play from the stands, hard too, in fact for the referee. Chelsea managed to hold off from conceding again for most of the remaining time, but were well and truly under the cosh. The Blues looked down in the dumps and heavy-legged. For the travelling London fans, Sheffield's dominance was hard to watch. The light was fading fast when the Blades scored twice more in the dying minutes, once with an effort that rebounded down off of the crossbar and again with a run all the way from the halfway line. Defeat was hard for the Blues to take, especially when they had hoped for so much and the loss had been so resounding. 'Wait until we reach the final again!,' proclaimed the *Chronicle*.[24] 'In the meantime, hearty congratulations to our conquerors on a thoroughly well earned victory.' The wait would not be easy. Chelsea would have to battle until the 1960s to reach another FA Cup Final and not until the memorable encounter with Leeds in 1970 would the club get its hands on the trophy.

Lord Derby presented the trophy and in front of a dripping wet crowd at Old Trafford gave a speech. The time, he said, for games was now at an end. There was a more significant game to be resolved now. He was right, and not only on the Western Front. At that moment Allied troops were steaming east towards Gallipoli and within a few hours war would have commenced in the Dardanelles.

Cup aside, the league campaign had turned into a bitter struggle against possible relegation. By mid-April Chelsea sat third from bottom, with only Notts County and Manchester United below them. Newcastle and Tottenham were placed just above but only four points separated all five, with two to go down. Notts County had been marked as favourites for the drop, but at Chelsea they were not so quick to condemn them as their last four games would be at home. Chelsea on the other hand were suffering the effects of fixture congestion and by the time the two of them met on 28 April, Chelsea would be playing their sixth game in fourteen days, one of them a cup final. It would be 'a rather dark prospect' if the Blues were not safe before their trip to the Midlands.

'The sun is setting red on the 1914–15 season,' stated the *Chronicle*. 'Blood-red. Before another season is due to begin the grim reality of the world war will have to be brought home in its full hideousness to many who have scarcely yet realised all that it means.' As usual, there was no hint of doubt, no scaremongering as to the outcome. 'That Germany will eventually be beaten and compelled to sue for peace is certain, absolutely, but the cost to all of Europe will be a terribly heavy one – in men, money and material.'[25] There was no doubt in anyone's mind. Pending seismic international events there would be no football season of 1915/16.

Recruitment into the Footballers' Battalion continued and it was thought that perhaps at the end of the season an influx of players might flood to the colours. 'Many have expressed their determination to refuse to do so simply because of the manner in which they have been, and are being "hounded" on all hands.' Others were adamant that when, and not until then, the government decided that every man was required and instigated conscription would they then cheerfully go off to serve. 'Why, they ask, should the married footballer (and the majority of them are married) be expected to go when there are hundreds of thousands of single young men who have no possible excuse, still hanging back?' There was, the *Chronicle* claimed, only one solution to the argument. If there were not enough men in the army, then conscript everybody. Don't 'bully, shame and cajole' a man into enlisting. 'Whether he be a footballer or a "my-sweetheart-doesn't-want-me-to" cinema haunter, if the voluntary system is insufficient to supply the nations needs, why let sentimental notions … bar the way?' The editor hoped that those unmarried men who had been pilloried for not yet enlisting would rise above it 'and, sinking the feelings of natural resentment, place the country before all else'.[26]

The 19 April saw the last home game of the season against fellow relegation strugglers Manchester United, but Chelsea were defeated 3–1. Chelsea were not safe by the time of the visit to Notts County, despite a draw at Everton. The Blues needed a point to stay up and condemn United to the Second Division, but all they could muster was a 2–0 defeat at Meadow Lane. The expansion of the Football League would see to it that in fact, the Pensioners stayed up, but just when that would be, nobody knew.

Amateur football was largely petering out of its own accord, certainly in the south where teams were struggling to raise sides. Professional players had seen the writing on the wall early on as regards their year-by-year contracts. By late April still no decision had been taken and in fact it would not be until July that it was ordained that there would be no more competitive matches. No more contracts employing men to play for a living were to be drawn up. Everything was to be suspended until 'normal service' resumed. There had also been more than one veiled reference to the span covered by the Southern League and financial and other wartime complaints were exacerbating the issue. Back at the beginning of April it was pointed out in the *Chronicle* that despite the name of the league, the spread of clubs geographically covered a wide area, between Cardiff and Norwich, London and Portsmouth. 'It seems fairly certain that several of the leading clubs (Chelsea included) will disappear from the SEL at the close of the season.'[27] Local leagues in Lancashire, the Midlands and a special London League, which would also include a handful of teams from near the capital, would comprise a course of recreational football for the rest of the war. Professional football was now on indefinite hiatus.

Coinciding with the end of the 1914/15 season, the day after the FA Cup Final a Coalition Cabinet was announced. The Ministry of Munitions came into being to take care of the issue of ammunition supply. In terms of recruitment there was a need to get a proper grasp on maximising the potential manpower available to fight the war. As the summer months passed, Britain began the perhaps inevitable swing towards conscription.

'Farewell until the next football season,' wrote the editor of the *Chronicle*:

Shall we again foregather when sweet September arrives – who can say? In the meantime there is the sterner battle to be fought. The whole nation has to struggle for its literal existence and every day from now on will bring the terrible reality of the world war more and more "home" to those who have been slow to grasp all that it means ... Victory must be ours at any cost and every man must do his bit to the best of his ability. If we hope to carry on next season as usual it is from no selfish motive, but the knowledge that it will mean the allied forces of civilisation have crushed into the dust the foul beast which has deluged Europe with her richest blood.[28]

He had already signed off with a final message: 'Good luck to all our gallant lads in khaki and navy blue, and Der Teufel strafe Deutschland.'

9

'Clinging by Our Eyelids'

Gallipoli

On the outbreak of war, in excess of 20,000 additional men were available to report for duty with the Royal Navy. Three different branches of reserves, the Fleet Reserve, the Royal Naval Reserve and the Royal Naval Volunteer Reserve, provided far more than there were space for aboard His Majesty's ships or in his dockyards. It was decided by the Admiralty that some of this excess manpower would be siphoned off and used to create a land force, despite the fact that all of the initial men in question had volunteered themselves for service at sea and comprised a vast array of potential soldiers with no experience of wielding rifle and bayonet. To form this new Royal Naval Division almost 3,500 came from the RNVR, made up of yachtsmen, sailors and others with enthusiasm for the sea. Some 2,000 were former Royal Navy stokers still obliged to come forward in time of need and a further 1,500 were merchant mariners. To lead them came seventeen retired naval officers, some Guards officers, nearly 600 various petty officers from the Fleet Reserve and army officer stock that had offered their services to Kitchener, in particular for northern regiments, and found themselves surplus to requirements. These men were divided into two brigades of eight battalions which would be named after famous naval heroes: Nelson, Drake, Hood and the like.

The War Office was stretched to breaking point already so the Royal Naval Division, as it would be called, would be administered by the Admiralty and overseen by the First Sea Lord, Winston Churchill. For such a hastily assembled force there was much to be done. Some of the officers were as ignorant in land warfare as one of Kitchener's newest boy recruits. Nonetheless they and their men had to be trained first to operate as part of a platoon or a company and then in conjunction with the rest of a brigade or the division as a whole. As well as preparing fighting troops for a life at war there needed to be an administrative framework and the introduction of divisional troops such as engineers and artillery.

Unfortunately, the RND got almost no chance to address any of these issues. With the BEF still not entrained on the Aisne for the north and Ypres, at the beginning of October 1914 this mostly untrained, incomplete contingent of men was launched at the Belgian coastline to help the tiny native army cling to Antwerp and prevent the Germans from crashing towards the Channel coast. Camps still boasted men wandering about in various states of mufti and random naval attire. The appearance of the Royal Naval Division, such as it was at that point, led to all kinds of press coverage claiming silliness such as the men tying their bayonets to their rifles with bits of string. Unsurprisingly the result of their excursion was a disaster for the fledgling division when huge numbers of men became prisoners of war, including one Chelsea fan with the Benbow Battalion who stumbled into the Netherlands with thousands of his fellow recruits, where they would now be interred at Groningen until 1918. There was public outcry when the wasteful losses at Antwerp became known. Following their Belgian nightmare the RND needed to replace Hawke, Benbow and Collingwood battalions almost in their entirety as they were sitting in Dutch captivity. They also needed divisional troops and a base from which to train and distribute reserves when the division went overseas again. The plan for properly preparing the Royal Naval Division for its second attempt at overseas service was then to culminate with the whole formation assembling near Bournemouth to practise large-scale manoeuvres in the New Year.

The third brigade of the RND comprised the only regular troops in the division, a battalion each of the Portsmouth, Chatham, Deal and Plymouth Royal Marine Light Infantry. Although the units had an infrastructure already in place, like the two naval brigades, they too were absorbing a daunting number of new recruits who had volunteered at the outbreak of war. One Chelsea fan had a six-month head start on those who rushed to the colours in the late summer of 1914. Just before Christmas, Harry Trusler found himself at the commandeered Crystal Palace where the Admiralty's new depot was taking shape. One of four sons born near Woking, three of the Trusler brothers left their widowed mother and their land-locked farm on the Surrey–Hampshire borders before the war to join up. Albert was the first to enlist in 1908, before Edwin followed in 1911. Harry, having worked first as a milkman and latterly as a labourer, followed his two elder brothers by going to Portsmouth to enlist in February 1914. The Marine Brigade would draw on their own depots for both recruits and reserves of all ranks until late 1915 and it was at one of these at Deal where Harry resided after six months in the service when war began. Employed on coastal duties and in the Channel, he was spared the debacle at Antwerp and, thankfully, the beginning of another misplaced enterprise that was soon to follow.

Much of the RND made it to Dorset for the intended divisional rendezvous at the beginning of 1915, but any hopes of thorough training were quickly dashed. In fact, in its entire lifetime, the Royal Naval Division would only be in one place together while it was being shot at. Another summons had arrived for the service of the Royal Marines. The Plymouth and Chatham battalions hurried off at the end of January taking the brigade staff with them. The departure was no less frantic than it had been for Antwerp the previous autumn and the men had no idea of their destination as the transports backed away from the quays. Perhaps they were on the way to East Africa? The first two battalions were indeed heading east, but their speculation was off. The Royal Marines in question were on their way to the Dardanelles.

The Gallipoli peninsula is a narrow slither of land sticking out into the Aegean and masking the entrance to the Sea of Marmara. The Dardanelles Straits lay on its eastern side, forming a gateway to the East and Constantinople and as such it was no stranger to conflict. Homer's *Iliad* had documented the Trojan War just to the south; Alexander the Great passed by to invade Persia almost a millennium later. Since then the vital waterway had been crucial to the defence of both the Byzantine and Ottoman empires and more recently had acted as a route to carry British troops to the Crimean War in the 1850s.

Turkey had entered the war in November 1914 on the side of Germany. By the spring of 1915 the Allies were seeking to end the deadlock that had set in on the Western Front. Conquering the Gallipoli peninsula and the Dardanelles provided a route to the Sea of Marmara and the jewel of Constantinople. A first batch of Royal Marines had been sent as a limited landing enterprise to help break through the straits using a naval force. Attempts by both the British and French to force the straits using sea power alone had failed though, and they remained firmly under the control of the Central Powers.

Despite the pressure on both the French and British forces on the Western Front at this time, it was then decided that the issue in the east should be forced by way of a full-scale land assault. Its aim would be to force a surrender from the Turkish garrison at Gallipoli itself at the mouth of the Sea of Marmara. Command of this ambitious endeavour was handed to Sir Ian Hamilton in March and he began concocting a plan for multiple landings aimed at sweeping across the peninsula.

Since Christmas, Harry Trusler had been operating out of Ramsgate aboard a yacht hunting for contraband and on a torpedo boat. As Hamilton began finalising his plans for assaulting the Gallipoli peninsula, Harry was bundled aboard a ship and joined thousands of troops assembling off the volcanic island of Lemnos. The expansive harbour at Mudros was packed to the brim with ships of all descriptions, from HMS *Queen Elizabeth*, her decks packed with menacing guns, to sweaty troopships packed with bored soldiers, smaller warships and the lowliest little tramp steamers requisitioned from the likes of Grimsby and pressed into service. The *Arcadian* bobbed up and down among the multinational collection of vessels, Hamilton and his staff busily planning on board.

Preparations were nearly complete. Following some tactical exercises off the coast of Skyros to the south-west, with the Portsmouth Battalion of the RMLI, Harry Trusler watched the port at Mudros begin to empty rapidly as transports went their separate ways and made off to land their men on Turkish soil. The Royal Naval Division, led by three warships, accompanied by supply vessels and a hospital ship, glided out into the open water and sailed east. On the evening of 24 April 1915, the day of the FA Cup Final at Old Trafford, aboard the *Gloucester Castle*, Harry Trusler passed the beautiful spectacle of Mount Athos 'rising out of the deep blue of a calm sea and sharply outlined against the red glow of the setting sun' as the Royal Marines left mainland Greece in their wake.

The Gallipoli landings commenced at dawn on the 25th. While Allied troops were being catapulted at multiple sides of the peninsula, the Royal Naval Division had been given a less bloodthirsty task. Harry Trusler bobbed up and down on the now claustrophobic *Gloucester Castle*, which was becoming evermore ripe an environment with the Portsmouth Battalion crammed inside. That and the other nine transports of the division had steamed up into the Gulf of Saros to the vicinity of Bulair, not to land themselves but to pretend to, in hope that they may draw Turkish troops off in their direction and ease the pressure on the men trying to gain a foothold further south.

Officers on board thought the whole thing rather a waste of time. Boats were dropped into the water and some of Harry's fellow men feigned a landing. 'It seems rather doubtful whether we really deceived the Turks or not; our gun fire was of such a desultory character that it appears we would have been much better employed at one of the principal landing places,' said one. Having played a bit part in this operation the *Gloucester Castle* then picked up and sailed towards the far end of the Gallipoli peninsula. At V, W, X and Y beaches five landings were taking place by British troops who were by and large being slaughtered as they attempted to get ashore.

Cape Helles at the southern tip of the peninsular came into view at dawn on 27 April, where guns bombarded the shoreline, the *River Clyde* sat rammed into the beach where she had deposited troops and the bodies of those that had failed to make landfall rose and fell in the bloodstained surf. The journey, however, had been in vain. Harry Trusler was not to be thrown into the attempts to seize Krithia and beyond it the heights of Achi Baba in an attempt to push the Turks northward towards Gallipoli itself. At 8 p.m. the *Gloucester Castle*, alongside another ship bearing the Chatham Battalion, was ordered north along the western side of the peninsula towards a headland named Gaba Tepe. In this area, two divisions of Australians and New Zealanders were, as one officer put it, clinging by their eyelids to hold onto the limited ground they had gained since stumbling ashore on the 25th.

The plan for the Anzac Corps had been to send the inexperienced troops ashore at night and ambitiously strike out across the peninsula. By then, the British at Cape Helles were to have forged their way up to meet them so that together the advance northeastwards could be continued. Unfortunately, by 28 April the Anzac troops were still trying to withstand a fierce Turkish assault that threatened to have them fleeing back to their transports and pushed back into the sea. In the preceding days the Australians and New Zealanders had become ensconced in a line a mile and a half long but only up to half a mile deep. Cramped was an understatement for two divisions' worth of men. Thousands had already been killed and wounded in exhausting fighting and yet they had still not managed to establish a position that could be effectively defended. The Anzac troops faced the very real possibility of having to evacuate immediately. The only other option was to crouch under fire and fashion some kind of shelter to withstand being besieged by everything the Turkish troops opposite could throw at them, until help arrived or the enemy was distracted by events elsewhere on the peninsula.

Now into the third day of relentless fighting, the troops were hopelessly mixed and in need of not only rest but complete reorganisation. So it was that General Hamilton had decided to send elements of the Royal Marine Light Infantry north to relieve them. The Royal Marine Brigade's HQ was ordered ashore immediately with both Chatham and Harry's Portsmouth Battalion to come under the control of the 1st Australian Division. Their commander, General Birdwood, promptly decided that the limited Royal Marines he had been lent would go straight up into the lines to relieve as many of his exhausted men as possible.

A ship had darted in between the RMLI transports ordering them to be ready to move imminently. It was by now early evening, but a threatening grey sky prematurely darkened the coastline as 18-year-old Harry Trusler dropped into a boat to make his journey to shore. Visible through the murk were little bivouac fires. The sounds of the battle raging inland grew louder as the Portsmouth Battalion made for land; shrapnel shells screeched towards the beach and showered its occupants with metal and then the crackle of rifle fire became audible. For the raw young recruits like Harry about to enter the mayhem, war was immediately real. Stray bullets peppered the decks of their boats as they made their final approach. In the water some Australians desperate for a bath bobbed up and down among the waves, regardless of metal that came splashing into the water around them.

The narrow ribbon of shingle beach that the landing Anzac force had been confined to was in a total state of claustrophobic disarray. Men from all units were scattered, 'strolling about with their mess tins and conversing without so much as turning to look at the occasional shell-burst whose pellets fell among them'. There was barely enough room to form up a platoon to get it marching let alone the whole of the Portsmouth Battalion.

Assaulting inland from the beach, General Birdwood's colonial troops had taken a line from the sea that traversed along a ridge to a plateau opposite a spot dubbed Lone Pine. The centre of the line then ran to Quinn's Post before defences bent back in a north-westerly direction.

The idea of British relief thrilled the Anzac troops. They were ready to drop:

> Bearded, ragged at knees and elbows, their putties often left in the scrub, dull-eyed, many with blood on cheeks and clothes, and with a dirty field-dressing round arm or wrist ... officers were often indistinguishable from men; buttons were gone ... Many wandered in a half-sleep, like tired children.[1]

Yet there was alarm at the sight of Harry and his cohorts, wide-eyed, young, clearly inexperienced soldiers, gawping up at the heights that contained the menacing Turks and their filthy allies going about their business in the failing light.

Finally, at nightfall, they were ready to move. Harry and his fellow Royal Marines began the steep climb upwards in the rain towards Shrapnel Gully, which comprised one of the only routes up to the fighting line over the rugged ground, scrambling on all fours, tripping over men who had dropped to the floor on any piece of level ground and fallen asleep. In the totally alien terrain, in pitch blackness it was impossible to determine whether or not they were exposed to Turkish fire:

> The sides of the gully were rocky, and what, in the wet season, was the bed of a mountain stream, was now the only path which the landscape offered. On the upper slopes, thickly covered with arbutus, dwarf oaks, and other shrubs, the passage of men had … worn narrow tracks.[2]

The threatening storm broke soon after dark. Then a veil of drizzle soaked the Portsmouth battalion to the skin as they took to their sector. Laden with blanket, waterproof sheet, ammunition, rations and his rifle, Harry Trusler tripped over bodies and men crying in agony in the darkness as he passed along. The term 'baptism of fire' was an understatement for the teenager. The exhausting relief continued throughout the cold, wet night. Wind howled through the lines 'as if it came through snowy gorges'.[3] They might have expected to find trenches like the well-prepared defences taking shape up and down the Western Front, but what the raw young troops found were hasty pits, 'nothing but a series of hastily dug posts, untraversed, unwired, broken with the wreckage of battle, scarred with the marks of intensive bombardment, just a series of foot holds on the edge of the plateau'.[4] In total, terrifying blackness they had no idea what was in front of them, or on their flanks. The continuous noise of a fierce battle raged somewhere to the left; in front flashes revealed the presence of enemy snipers as they let off their rifles, machine-gun bullets thudded into the parapet and the surrounding scrub. Conflicting orders, panicked rumours flew up and down the front. By dawn the original Anzac troops still partly occupied the lines. There were simply not enough Royal Marines in the Chatham and Portsmouth Battalions to replace all of the spent Anzac troops. They remained scattered in isolated holes across the hilltops, starved of relief.

The Portsmouth Battalion now held the perilous centre of the line that had been established by the Australians and New Zealanders. Dominating their sector was Wire Gully, overlooked by multiple steep ravines, covered in tangled undergrowth and rock. The Marines and the Anzac troops lay within yards of the enemy. The two sides were well within the range of throwing bombs at each other. For the Portsmouth's officers going about the troops and seeing to their defences, hopping in and out of the various pits to see their men was death-defying work. It was a far cry from Surrey for young

Harry Trusler. In the damp beds of the ravines and gullies frogs continually croaked away. Wondrous creepy crawlies and lizards were everywhere. One Royal Marine was stunned by the snakes. 'I have seen [one] as big as four feet in length [and] as thick as my wrist.' In among the scrub was heather and wild sage, 'giving off an odour which reminds one of Christmas dinner'.[5]

The day after Harry's arrival, both the Deal Battalion of the RMLI and the Nelson contingent of the naval battalions arrived to contribute to efforts on this front. The Anzac men and the Royal Naval Division components got to work, desperately trying to link up all of the isolated holes that had been frantically dug for cover into continuous trench lines that would run down one side of the gully and up the other. Enemy activity had reduced in terms of attacks, but still the Turks kept up a murderous volley from their rifles night and day. In charge of the force, General Birdwood ordered that his men should refrain from shooting back. Let them waste their ammunition on futile fire.

Opposite, the Turks had far from given up the idea of fully pushing the invaders back into the sea. Towards the end of the week small, isolated attacks were carried out but they were all a precursor for a larger assault being planned by Mustafa Kemal. With plentiful reserves arriving he intended to send a well disciplined force over the heights to crush the Anzac men and their reinforcements. They would, he said, by the help of God, deal the enemy a final blow before further reinforcements could get to them.

'Sniping squads of ten, twenty, or even fifty men were pushed forward by every unit. Strong efforts were made on Thursday to establish a trench line everywhere close to the Australian front.'[6] On the afternoon of Friday 30 April, Harry and his fellow Royal Marines were subjected to a severe shrapnel bombardment. As darkness fell a large amount of activity was noticed going on opposite the Chatham Battalion, too. The Turks appeared to be massing about Wire Gully ready for action. The following day Kemal launched his attack. The Portsmouth Battalion was showered with shrapnel at daybreak before the enemy came up the gully and overran some of the RMLI's forward posts. The bulk of the assault fell on the Chatham Battalion though and spared Harry. 'The din was terrific: shouting and blowing of bugles and the whole place was lit up with fires that were raging in the scrub ...'[7] Despite the fierce intentions of the enemy, it was partly the Royal Marines that managed to hold off Mustafa Kemal and his men, who by early evening had retired.

General Birdwood had been overseeing plans of his own. Fighting had now devolved onto the head of Monash Valley, named after the brigadier who had defended it on landing. After delays and restructuring of the plan, an assault was finally launched on 2 May to try and seize the high ground from the Turks overlooking the gully, where they could menace the Anzac and Royal Naval Division troops below. At the centre of their objectives was the newly christened Pope's Hill and the heights on either side. Because of the difficulty in approaching the firing line narrowly through gullies, the assaulting Australian and New Zealand troops were formed into columns.

The Otago Battalion would take the left side and the 16th Battalion of the Australian Infantry two ridges on the right. More troops of the 13th Battalion were to follow and already at Pope's Hill the 15th too would push forward with the New Zealanders.

The attack was to take place in the dark and for the first time on this part of the front it would be helped by a fierce artillery bombardment beginning at 7 p.m., assisted by ship's guns off the coast to try and crush Turkish resistance at positions all the way up to the heights of Chunuk Bair before the assaulting waves moved up the valley. It was planned that all of the columns would then reach Pope's Hill for 8 p.m. before pouring over and attacking the Turks dug in on the forward slopes. Unfortunately, the columns were approaching half a mile apart and by the time they reached a position to attack the enemy they were completely isolated from each other. The clash that followed was chaos. Surging from a rugged hilltop, 'thickly covered with scrub and dotted with rock',[8] an all-out melee commenced. It did not appear that either the Australians or the New Zealanders reached the Turkish lines. By midnight they were teetering on the edge of the plateau, illuminated in glowing red by a huge bonfire lit by the enemy, revealing baffled officers and men milling to the right of Pope's Hill in total confusion.

Work had begun on a support line about 200 yards from the edge of the gully. A hundred yards or so nearer to the Turkish lines, troops lay pinned to the floor, 'beaten to the ground by a murderous fire', trying to provide cover for the men behind. In between these two makeshift lines there was nothing coherent going on at all. Men tripped over each other with no idea what to do next; 'men from the firing line driven back, reinforcements coming up from the gully, stragglers looking for their units, perhaps a Turk or two caught up in the confusion of the night battle, officers looking for orders ...'[9]

While the chaos at Pope's Hill was playing itself out, Harry Trusler had finally been relieved the previous night, before the attack commenced. The Chatham and Portsmouth Battalions of the RMLI had retired down the hill and although they had had to spend the day digging in, they hoped to get a wash, some decent food and their first cup of tea since arriving on the peninsula. Much to their despair, though, their reprieve was going to be short-lived. Up on the heights, the three assaulting Anzac battalions were completely isolated in their sketchy positions and unable to form a coherent defensive line. The Turks still held the better ground and at 2 a.m. both Harry's battalion and the Chathams were summoned to help.

The Portsmouth Marines arrived on site just as the sun began to light up the eastern site of the battlefield. It had already been a nightmare of a journey for Harry. As he forced his way through the dark towards Pope's Hill and the heights above Monash Valley, the limited routes to and from the fighting were choked with wounded men staggering in the opposite direction. There were Australian reinforcements, ordered up before the Marines who had not been able to make any headway through the crowd. As Harry reached the fighting he and his fellow men, trying to follow conflicting orders, were overrun with men of the 16th Australian Battalion streaming down the steep hill in confusion. It was a terrifying spectacle: 'In the half light of dawn, amid a hail of bullets coming from every direction (for the trenches in the gully itself were under fire from both flanks, from the front, and in places even from the rear) with an uncertain battle raging on the very edge of the plateau above.'[10]

There was absolutely no chance in the confusion that the Royal Marines would reach the head of the gully in adequate formation. The Portsmouth Battalion were simply a straggled line of bewildered young men, told that they were to go straight up into the fight and support the Australians on the other side of the ridge in the frantically scraped cover they had established in the dark. Their route was near vertical and even after taking the time to reassemble the men properly, there was little information about what was going on in front when they began the struggle upwards. When they arrived, Harry and the rest of his battalion found exhausted Australians crammed into their pitiable defences. They simply lay down on the floor shoulder to shoulder next to whoever they found and faced the Turks, now less than 200 yards away. They began firing off their rifles, desperately trying to hold back the enemy. The rumours that Turks were pouring into the gully almost broke the will of the men to resist the enemy onslaught, but Royal Marine staff officers rallied their men and settled them down. The heat was unbearable, the men's thirst completely unquenchable and the flies that descended on the dead and wounded a persistent menace. Nothing General Birdwood could throw at it was going to help hold the ridge in such precarious circumstances. Machine guns were turned on the high ground and it was now littered with hundreds of bodies representing both sides' mounting losses.

The Anzac attempt to push the Turks off the lofty perch they had first occupied following the landing had failed. Having sat in the new front, hasty pits scraped in the ground, having been subjected to heavy enfilading fire for much of the morning, Harry and his fellow men were ordered back along with everyone else to the original Anzac line. By nightfall they had reoccupied the original position and Ian Hamilton's intent on this part of the peninsula in terms of major offensives was at an end. All British reinforcements were already being directed to Cape Helles as the commander prioritised the southern assault towards Gallipoli. Dangerously perched in front of the enemy, the monumental effort expended by the Australians and New Zealanders, with the support of the Royal Naval Division, was for negligible gains. Within a week the 1st Australian Division had lost about half its infantry. Now they were boxed in:

> The end of the great assault left the Australians and New Zealanders hanging on to the slopes above the sea, with scarcely a square half-mile to live on, in an impossible position almost everywhere overlooked at point-blank range by the Turks. The only value of their effort for the time being was that it diverted about an equal portion of the Turkish Army.[11]

That, and if Hamilton changed his mind, they were in a position to attempt to try again to strike across 4 miles of rugged terrain towards the narrows.

Life settled down for Harry. Their hair, eyes and mouths full of dust, the Royal Marines took shifts of twenty-four hours at the head of the valley followed by twenty-four more out, much of it in support lines as the Portsmouth and Chatham numbers had dwindled so much that it was questionable whether they would be able to hold the front line if attacked. Troops were working hard to establish proper defences and establish lines of communication from the beach inland. The stench of death filled their nostrils. Aside from unfortunate dead mules, the bodies on the ridge became quickly repulsive, their stink unbearable. Decomposing faster in the heat than on the Western Front they turned black, 'like ants shrivelled by a fire'. One Royal Marine managed to get up to what would become known as Dead Man's Ridge to knock some down for burial, but hundreds remained. In full view of snipers neither side would risk scaling the heights to remove their dead. On the other side of the slope there were so many fallen Turks that they were impossible to count.

Even when Harry and his battalion were relieved, rest was impossible, as Turkish rifle bullets had a tendency to follow them all down the hill and the noise of the enemy artillery was ceaseless. The beach that would now become known as Anzac Cove was filled to capacity. Crowded with troops, native interpreters and servants, 'scallywag officers, and officers that still manage to keep a shadow of dandyism between their disreputable selves and immaculate past'.[12]

It was becoming impossible not to trip over the maze of telephone wires being rigged up and down. Wireless stations quickly went up commandeering more precious space. At night, absolutely every bit of food, every piece of equipment and all stores had to come through the beach. 'Piles of cheeses, sugar-bags, biscuit-boxes, bales of fodder, cases of ammunition, wood, wire, and stores rose in growing stacks all down the shingle.' Supply depots were far from the comparable luxury that Fred Brooks was experiencing at Havre. In terms of the Anzac troops and the Royal Naval Division finding refuge, the beach was forever under fire. Nobody, regardless of rank, was safe from it. Men were becoming indifferent to shrapnel showers continuing to plague them and metal pattered down among the clutter. As they bathed in the sea, howitzers missing their targets sent up columns of water in the surf nearby. 'The beach produced a profound impression on almost all of us, and has in some cases made the seaside distasteful for the rest of our lives.'[13]

Harry queued for water and food as mules slogged up and down the cove. Little groups came to collect rations or ammunition and clustered together under boxes, sometimes around small fires chatting. 'Spy mania'[14] was rampant, tales springing from 'on the beach', the source of all information. They were supposed to be everywhere, hiding among the stores, dispatching pigeons to the Turkish lines with information. If it was all to be believed, 'there were enough spies to have made an opera'.[15] One intelligence officer did not have to utilise much of said intelligence to smell a rat. 'The first convincing proof of treachery which we had was the story of a Turkish girl who had painted her face green in order to look like a tree, and had shot several people at Helles from the boughs of an oak.'[16]

With the winding down of the Anzac offensive, the Royal Marines' stay with the colonial troops would not last long. They were removed from their trenches for good on 13 May. 'We got a hot meal … after being worked to death and on rations for a fortnight. You cannot imagine the restful time we had for one night; the chief thing of all was the beer and ginger ale which was a little different from the incessant water.' All that was left of young Harry Trusler's unit were thirteen officers and a little over 400 men. The Portsmouth Battalion had lost ten officers killed and seven wounded, along with ninety-three men dead, twenty-three missing and a further 305 wounded. In total, more than 1,200 men were gone from the strength of the RMLI contingent thrown in to assist the Australians and New Zealanders at Anzac Cove. It was significant that so many men had been killed or evacuated westwards wounded, that it only now took one transport to house both battalions. That night they embarked for the southern end of the peninsula and the Royal Marines blissfully slept in hammocks aboard their ship. It was likely to be Harry's last restful night for months to come, for his Gallipoli ordeal was far from over. Southwards the battle for Krithia was still being stubbornly waged, by British and French troops combined and at Cape Helles just eight weeks later a Turkish soldier would fire off a rifle bullet with frightening consequences for the young Chelsea fan.

10

'I Really Wonder We Had Any Left At All'

Festubert

After the relentless fighting at Ypres at the end of 1914, Cecil Dean and the Irish Guards had settled down for a well earned rest in reserve. The battalion sorely needed it. At the beginning of December, despite nearly a hundred stragglers finding their way back to replenish their ranks, they still numbered just three regular officers, a few inexperienced ones from the Special Reserve and 430 Guardsmen. The whole battalion was reorganised back into four companies and the men had to be shuffled among them to spread evenly those with battle experience. It would be some time before they would be ready to fight again. At Meteren, Cecil, who was to be promoted to the rank of lance sergeant, found himself well and truly embroiled in the 'fog of war'. He could not hear any guns, and the only news from the front came in the shape of veiled, nonsensical rumours. The tired Irish Guards were gawped at by plenty of exalted personages. Their commander was in the act of going round his new companies, inspecting the men and trying to get familiar with the new NCOs, telling them all what he expected of them, when Douglas Haig arrived and asked how they were getting on. Two days later the King appeared for a visit and the men were drawn up for noon on the Bailleul–Meteren road. His Majesty walked down the line approvingly. 'I am very proud of my Guards,' he told them:

> and I am full of my admiration of their bravery and endurance and fine spirit ... You are fighting a brave and determined enemy, but if you go on as you have been doing, and show the same spirit as I am sure you will, there can be one end, please God, and that is victory. I wish you good luck.[1]

When not posing for dignitaries, there was the business of preparing the men for winter to attend to. There were new mess tins, one for cooking and the other to use as a miniature brazier in the trenches. There were comforters, socks, blankets, new greatcoats, but oddest of all were the short fur coats. A patchwork of goat and sheepskins, they came in all different colours to keep Cecil and his cohorts warm over Christmas, along with 'other innumerable presents' being sent by families and well-wishers back home. They began to look like a battalion again and began to act like one too. The men received lectures on defensive warfare, viewed experimental trenches dug nearby by the Royal Engineers and took watches at the far end of the town, keeping a lookout for aeroplanes.

On 22 December the Irish Guards marched 17 miles up to Bethune and late on Christmas Eve they went into the trenches, which already looked far more elaborate than the kind they had occupied at Ypres. There was no merriment and exchange of gifts on their front. 'Over two feet deep in mud and slush', they were in a precarious position. The whole area was a myriad of old, disused trenches into which men of both sides could crawl to terrorise each other. The weather was a trial too. First, a hard frost set in, before on 29 December they were hit by a violent thunderstorm which dumped rain on them all for three hours. Some of the communication trenches fell in and had to be scraped out again. 'The water is just soaking through the ground to the trenches,' complained their commanding officer.[2] The men were coated in clay from head to foot and in some places Cecil and the rest of them stood miserably in water up to their knees.

At New Year the battalion lost the last company officer who had marched to Nine Elms in August when a stray bullet claimed him. January was spent in the brickfields at La Bassée, surrounded by stacks of them 30 feet high. 'Not very wet but otherwise damnable,' was one assessment of their position. The enemy were only 10 yards away from the Irishmen in places and they harassed each other accordingly, leaving everybody in a very nervous, jumpy state. Trench warfare continued to develop. That month some of the men attended a bombing course, 'and all sorts of devilish weapons were produced, most of which seem to be more dangerous to the throwers than the enemy'. Days after that assessment the accidental explosion of a bomb killed a young officer, 'dead-blown to pieces'[3] when he was demonstrating the thing and held on to it for too long.

When the Battle of Neuve Chapelle commenced on 10 March 1915, Cecil was in reserve off to the south and his only indication of a battle going on was the booming guns in the distance. St Patrick's Day a week later was celebrated in a fashion. Shamrocks arrived from the Queen Mother and the men were treated to baths in Bethune. 'I arranged that each man who wanted it, had a beer with his dinner,' wrote their commanding officer, 'which is their height of bliss provided that it is free.'[4]

Warmer weather brought new trials. At the end of April the dead bodies lying about the Irish Guards' front were becoming unbearable. It was almost impossible to get to them so that they might be buried and parts of the trenches were verging on uninhabitable because of the smell. 'Some way of destroying them should be discovered,' one writer commented. 'I should think one might squirt petrol on those nearest which we can't bury and set them alight.' But if the existing casualties of war were repulsive, by far the most horrific introduction to the field of battle adding to their numbers in the spring of 1915 was the use of gas, first unleashed in turn against Russians in January and then in April against French colonial troops as well as Brits.

Cecil and his fellow Guards were understandably agitated by the possibility of having this monstrous new weapon unleashed upon them and false alarms were rampant at the beginning of May. On the 5th some of the men were overcome while digging and the battalion commander thought he had seen enough evidence that gas was to blame. The following night he was dragged out of bed at 1.30 a.m. when a message arrived to say that a 'mist' was rising from the German trenches. The mist, he found, was natural enough, but he thought he smelt something worrying in the odd place. Aware it might be his mind playing tricks on him, he nonetheless checked that Cecil and his fellow Guardsmen were alert and knew what they were to do in case of an emergency. Attempts to save the men from gas were primitive. Tins of lime water had been placed throughout the trenches and when the alarm was raised the men were to dunk cotton pads in and then tie them around their mouth and nose to try and nullify the effects. There was nothing at all to protect the eyes, but they had to put their faith in what was presently available to combat this new horror all the same. In the event of the front line being overcome by fumes, the men in support had orders to dip their masks, strap them on and charge through the offending cloud to replace them.

A few days later the battle for Aubers Ridge commenced in the distance. The Irish Guards heard the intense bombardment occurring to the north. 'One cannot describe it except by saying that it was one continuous roar of guns, occasionally relieved by a deep scrunching sound denoting one of our big howitzers had burst its shell somewhere. The whole horizon was thick with smoke, and occasionally one saw the flashes of the bursting shrapnel.'[5] Then came the pounding of the French guns to the south. The battalion's only job that day was to keep the enemy occupied enough so as to ensure he did not siphon off troops and send them towards Aubers. Cecil and his fellow men orchestrated bursts of rapid fire throughout the day. Occasionally they received reports that aeroplanes or artillery observers had seen German troops on the move, but three observation stations spread out through the battalion's lines indicated that there was little going on on their front. A quiet night followed, 'the enemy contenting himself with using many flares and searchlights'.[6] In fact, while the likes of Bill Richards struggled on at Aubers Ridge with the Rifle Brigade, the Irish Guards enjoyed one of the most peaceful days they could remember for a long while. 'I sat out on my rustic chair the whole day,' wrote their commander, 'reading books and papers, at intervals going round various parts of the trenches.'[7]

The failure of the offensive further north, though, meant that soon his men would be required to enter the battle. Before the initial fighting had even died down, the BEF was under pressure to continue pushing forward. It was a particularly trying time for relations with the French to the south. General Joffre didn't think the British were pulling their weight. The situation was made worse by ammunition shortages and the delay in arrival of the first Kitchener divisions, which Sir John French had been relying on to keep up his commitment to his allies. He had a meeting with Joffre on 12 May and was pilloried for the lack of progress on Haig's front at Aubers Ridge. Douglas Haig had in fact already been planning a continuation of the push forward on his front and had changed tack markedly. The Germans were so well dug in that rushing towards distant objectives after a frantic preliminary artillery storm seemed purposeless. The French had launched their attack further south with a relentless bombardment over a period of days, spread out to gradually grind down German resistance and ensure that wire was broken and defences battered before the infantry attacked. Haig now saw this as the way forward. His men would attack again on 15 May towards objectives spread out over 3 miles between Festubert and Richebourg-l'Avoué.

The commander of the Irish Guards was aware that something was afoot on 11 May when he was informed that other troops would be taking over their positions near Givenchy to make way for their departure north towards Festubert. During training the men bivouacked in open fields in the pouring rain while he attended a conference with the brigadier. Lessons learned from the failed assault on Aubers Ridge were shared along with plans for the new attack, while reconnaissance was made of the surrounding countryside ready for their going into action. On the night of 14 May he toured their muddy field, explaining the lay of the land to his company commanders and chatting to the men. Despite the weather, they seemed cheery enough, waterproof sheets stuck on poles to shelter them while they sat in the mire and played cards or sang late into the night.

A preliminary bombardment had begun the day before. Over 101,000 shells were to be fired in preparation for the attack, but unfortunately the rain that soaked Cecil Dean in his field also prevented the artillery from effectively monitoring where their shells were falling. Many of them failed to explode and 'so sodden and sticky'[8] was the ground that it reduced the impact of high explosive ones. After consulting the divisions involved about how effective they thought the cascade of metal had been on their various fronts, it was decided to extend the bombardment and postpone the attack by a day.

The Irish Guards were not required on 15 May to launch the offensive, which was a scaled down version of the attack on the 9th. The main principle was, again, that two breaches would be shelled, one of them for 7th Division and another for the 2nd, Cecil's. This time, though, instead of a massive 3½ miles between the two openings that the artillery was trying to force in the German defences, they would be divided by 500 metres. Instead of advancing nearly 2 miles, troops would be aiming for objectives just half a mile distant.

The first wave of troops went forward under cover of darkness, an early attempt at a night attack during the war. The element of surprise had been ruled out thanks to the lengthy bombardment, although efforts had been made to trick the Germans with false attacks leading up to the 15th, with sudden bursts of gun and rifle fire that came to nothing, men cheering as it stopped to indicate they were about to attack. Results were mixed when the real advance commenced. Some troops faced little opposition, surging forward and turning on two motor headlights on the enemy parapet to signal their success. Others fared less well. They were bludgeoned with machine-gun fire, lit up by a searchlight and flares. A further attack was ordered for 3.15 a.m. after another half an hour bombardment but they had had little chance to reorganise. In all 10,000 men attacked just over 2,000 Germans who, although outnumbered, were well equipped with machine guns and caused merciless damage to the advancing British ranks. At a huge cost, a stretch of something like half a mile of trenches had been wrested out of German hands by the beginning of 16 May.

The priority for the second day of the offensive was to get the two separate attacking forces linked up on the other side of the German front line. The troops that had done so well in the initial night attack, however, were completely held up by machine-gun fire and despite repeated attempts remained pinned down. To the rear, Cecil Dean and the rest of the Irish Guards had been waiting on tenterhooks for an order to join the battle. Some of them were kept busy organising a depot for processing enemy prisoners, but just before dawn they were summoned to help push the attack on through the fierce German resistance. The shellfire on both sides as the Guardsmen waited behind the breastworks was relentless. 'I think it was heavier than at any time since Ypres,' wrote one of their number.[9] There they sat all day, listening to a cacophony of guns and howitzers until they were summoned back to their field for nightfall. Their action-less sortie towards the battle had cost the battalion thirty-one men.

They were anxious hours for the likes of Cecil as 17 May dawned, waiting for a call to battle, sitting ready to move at a moment's notice, hearing snippets of news and endless rumours. It began to rain and the area became enveloped in a thick mist. Assessing the situation the afternoon before, Haig had resolved to abandon part of the attack and concentrate wholly on linking up his two attacking divisions. On either side of them all other troops were to remain on a defensive footing. The infantry received sudden orders to go forward and work their way towards each other at 8 a.m., leaving almost no time to prepare.

The trenches opposite were destroyed by 7 a.m. by an effective bombardment. Rain came down in torrents, filling shell holes and trenches with water and turning the ground to liquid mud. The Germans had staged a withdrawal overnight and the attacking troops found them hard to run down, although a large number of the enemy soldiers that remained surrendered. Things looked to be going well, but when the offensive resumed in the afternoon the momentum vanished and work ground to a halt. The troops belonging to the Irish Guards' division were so disorganised that it was decided to leave them where they were until Cecil and the rest of his battalion could be brought up to help.

At 3 p.m. the Guardsmen got the order to march. Following up a battalion of Grenadiers, as dusk fell Cecil filed into trenches that they had occupied in December, but with the enemy a good deal further off than they remembered. One hundred yards in front had, until recently, been the German front line. The trenches were narrow, deep with a sandbag parapet piled up for protection. Planks lined the floor so that men might get a leg up and see over the top. Wooden boxes were stacked to form dugouts with yet more sandbags to create roofs. Thanks to the weather and the clayey soil the trenches were 'beastly'. There would be no further attack on the 17th. It had taken the battalion so long to manoeuvre their way over 3 miles of swamp-like terrain, that by the time the Guardsmen arrived dusk was already imminent. Mercifully, the Germans left them to it. Cecil had to be content with helping to secure their positions as darkness fell and the rain cascaded down.

Action was due to recommence at first light with yet more shells being flung at the Germans. When daylight came, though, the weather was disgusting, with 'wreaths of driving rain and mist that wrapped the flats'.[10] The battalion received orders to attack a farm named Cour d'Avoine that just about appeared as a dim silhouette through the fog. They had almost no time to get ready. Their commander reviewed it: 700 yards off and apparently strongly defended with a moat around it. A general who had already tried to capture it came up to impart some wisdom. It was lucky he did, bringing another officer who pointed out that the Irish Guards were setting their sights on the wrong objective, 'a bad piece of map reading on my part,' admitted the man in charge.[11] 'Saved from a bad blunder', they began to rethink their attack 300 yards further south. A vigorous bombardment would attempt to level the position and its defenders prior to the battalion's attack, before they went forward over dead flat ground pitted with shell holes that they could dive in and use for cover if necessary. Thankfully, considering the wholly insufficient time that the battalion was given to prepare, the weather caused a delay of several hours and it was decided to postpone the action until early evening. At 2 p.m. the Irish Guards were informed that they would attack at 4.30 p.m. after a heavy artillery bombardment of some two hours. In the interim scouts were sent out to reconnoitre the ground leading up to the farm and officers busied themselves by inspecting the German trench system.

The afternoon began ominously for the Irish Guards. Orders for the bombardment were delayed and the artillery did not actually begin shelling the enemy until after 3 p.m. To make things worse, in addition to losing more than half an hour from their programme, the gunners were not ranging on the most effective targets. Unbeknown to them, although they were smashing what they thought was the German front line to pieces, the enemy had backed off and established themselves further to the rear. There they sat as the bombardment wore on, firing red flares for the benefit of their own artillery so that they were aware an infantry attack was coming. At 4 p.m. the artillery began to rise to a crescendo, pounding the farm in front of Cecil Dean and the surrounding buildings into rubble. The German artillery answered in kind, shells skimming off the rear positions and shaking battalion headquarters with the concussion. The Irish Guards' commander watched in disbelief. Surely nothing could still be alive in front of them?

Unfortunately for Cecil and those with him, plenty of enemy troops had survived the misplaced bombardment. At 4.30 p.m. they stumbled out of their shallow trenches and forward through long, wet grass into a hail of shell and machine-gun fire. Pinned down, they began flinging themselves into shell holes to escape the enemy storm. The leading companies, including Cecil's, lost nearly half of their men in just a few minutes all for the sake of 100 yards gained. More men were gradually fed forward to thicken the line, but at 7 p.m. Lord Cavan, the brigadier, reviewed the situation, and decided that the likelihood of making it to the farm was zero and ordered the Guards to dig in where they stood. At no point had the Irish Guards advanced any more than 300 yards, and their left flank was completely in the air save for an enthusiastic officer wielding a machine gun.

Darkness was rapidly coming on and it was imperative that the battalion secure their position overnight. Men were pulled back to stabilise the line and with the help of men of the Hertfordshire Regiment and some East Anglian sappers they began digging in. All up and down the line the attacks of 18 May had been a failure. To one side, Indian troops had aborted their advance. The ground in front of them was so heavily shelled that they could not get forward. As for the Canadian troops who were to have provided the bulk of the attack, their orders took so long to reach them that they were still coming into the line when Cecil and the rest of the Irish Guards were flailing in No Man's Land.

Ultimately, the joint assault at Festubert came to very little. On 25 May Sir John French broke the news to Douglas Haig that he thought it highly improbable they could win this particular fight. More German reserves had been brought up to defend a position that was already well established. To add insult to injury, the BEF was running absurdly low on ammunition. The only thing Sir John now asked was that Haig's men held the enemy in front of them so as to stop him transferring off men south to oppose the French at Vimy Ridge, where their allies were planning another offensive which would go ahead in June. The Battle of Festubert had been another miserable failure.

Over 1,000 men of Cecil's division alone would be classed as 'missing' and excruciatingly for William Dean and his family, as the Irish Guards began to dig in at 7 p.m. on 18 May, his eldest son was among them. In the aftermath of a scrap it was exceedingly difficult to take stock of a battalion and ascertain just what had become of the men in the heat of a fight. As night fell there were 'heaps' of Irish Guards lying wounded in No Man's Land and in both the British and German trenches. Work immediately began to collect them. To orchestrate this gruesome task, the battalion was extremely light on officers. Of all of those not killed or missing themselves, or seriously wounded, almost every other was carrying some kind of injury. Even their commanding officer had had a piece of shrapnel go flying through the peak of his cap and scratch his forehead. Those that were still able rounded up the men that were left in order to record the cost of the battle in the dark, in pouring rain with no shelter at all. Nearly half the Irish Guards at first were believed to be casualties and at first glance, it looked as if 120 of them were missing. 'Some of these are undoubtedly killed I am afraid,' wrote their leader, 'but others who are wounded have gone to some other aid posts, and so their names are not on the roll of those who were dressed in my regimental aid post, and it may take some time to trace them.' The best way of getting some concrete answers as to the fate of his men would be to get out into No Man's Land and retrieve identity tags from the fallen. 'Missing' might meant that the man might have been seized as a prisoner, but this was highly unlikely to be the case on this occasion as they had got nowhere near the enemy. At 2 a.m. the battalion was relieved and thus moved away from the scene; making it even more difficult to keep tabs on wounded that may come trickling in. Aside from those who had bypassed the regimental aid post and avoided detection that way, by going straight to a field ambulance further back for treatment, efforts would be made to enquire at nearby hospitals. Some men might even still be lying out on the field of battle in isolated shell holes waiting to be found.

It was sincerely hoped that 'missing' in most cases that day would not mean killed. Throughout the Great War some families had to wait for months, years even to learn their fate of their loved ones, but in Cecil Dean's case his family received the answers they were looking for almost immediately. Of the filthy men tramping back towards a collection of barns and leaving the Hertfordshire Regiment to hold the new line, covered in thick clay-like mud and soaking wet, several had a story to tell about the young Chelsea fan's fate. One of the other NCOs had known Cecil for some seven years and so was understandably upset by the day's events. Commanding their platoon at the onset of the attack, Michael Grogan humped his way out of the shallow trench and had only got some 15 yards when he heard Cecil calling his name. He ran back to him and immediately saw blood coming from the young lance sergeant's mouth. 'Where are you hit?' he asked.[12] The answer was not reassuring, for Cecil revealed that he had been hit in the stomach, which might be extremely complicated. 'Go on,' he told his friend, for there was no sense in him being hit too. Grogan glanced back over his shoulder to see Cecil smiling at him as he took his friend's advice and moved off with his platoon.

Another NCO of the battalion, Jack Halligan, was able to confirm that Cecil had not been dragged in wounded via the Irish Guards' own regimental aid post. 'I was in the front line trench that day, where the attack started from and I took the names of nearly all the wounded.' Cecil's was not among them. He was sure, too, that he could not have been taken prisoner. He had been hit so close to their own lines that it was impossible to think he might have been grabbed by the enemy. 'I am only sad to know I cannot give you any hope. I am sorry to say that I have no doubt that he was killed.'[13]

Final confirmation came from a Lance Corporal Borgin, who had been part of the section led by Cecil. Moments after Grogan left his side, he saw the Blues fan struck again, this time in the neck. 'I went on then,' he wrote. 'I am sure he was dead. I never saw him again.' At that, Halligan sat down to write a lengthy letter to Elsie, Cecil's sister, to try and give her some solace. 'The battalion suffered very heavily that day,' he told her, 'but fought magnificently. Platoon after platoon went forward steadily in face of almost certain death without the slightest waver.' He tried to explain the circumstances in which her brother's body might be unaccounted for. 'The grass was very long where the attack was made and the ground very open – hence we have many killed whose bodies have not yet been found.' He did not, though, want to give her any false hope:

> To be kind I am sorry I must be cruel and tell you that I am confident Cecil was killed by the second wound and that it must have saved him endless and useless suffering, for 90 out of every 100 hit in the stomach die eventually. Convey my deepest regret to your dad, mother and Reg … We lost 17 officers and about 350 other ranks practically all in one afternoon, and I really wonder we had any left at all.[14]

It was thought afterwards that if there had only been more gun support that Aubers Ridge might have been conquered. The commanding officers of both the Irish Guards and the battalion of Grenadiers with them were convinced that had the attack been made at night, then they might have succeeded without such grievous losses. It was becoming abundantly clear that if the Great War was to be won, then victory would have to be seized by the tens of thousands of men yet to arrive that had answered Kitchener's call. As 1915 wore on, the average British man would begin appearing in the trenches, those with no experience of military life at all. They were arriving at a worrying time, for as Cecil Dean fell the Germans appeared to be superior in everything, both in attacks such as that at Ypres where they had gained ground, and in defence on Haig's front.

11

'For King, Country and Chelsea!'

The Boar's Head

To try to administer the force created by Kitchener's vast array of volunteers, it was grouped into blocks of new divisions before shipping off to war in their thousands. 'K1' and 'K2' began moving overseas in mid-1915 and K3 followed towards the end of the year. By the end of 1915 a Fifth New Army had been formed, largely of local pals' units. Among them were a group of Chelsea fans that had made an effort to enlist together before the Footballers' Battalion had even been thought of. When Oldham Athletic visited the Bridge at the end of October 1914, a letter appeared in the matchday programme entitled 'Commandeering the Chelsea Chronicle, Cooden Camp, Bexhill.'[1] It came from where a new battalion had been raised for local Sussex men. Formed by a Member of Parliament, Claude Lowther, at the height of the recruiting boom in September, his 'Lambs', as they were to become known, were about to be joined by two more battalions and although they would officially be designated as the 11th, 12th and 13th Battalions of the Royal Sussex Regiment, they were collectively referred to as the South Downs battalions.

By what seemed to be sheer accident, a number of Blues fans had found their way to Sussex and were scrambling for Chelsea reading material. The letter in question was written by a clerk named Clifford Whitley, employed in the offices of the *Daily Mail*. Twenty years old when war was declared, he lived in Hammersmith with his widowed mother. 'Just a little incident that should give the supporters of the "stop football" campaign food for thought,' he wrote to Stamford Bridge in October:

I am a Chelsea enthusiast in camp down here endeavouring to do my little bit for the old country, and I always have the Chelsea Chronicle sent to me. While walking through the line of tents, some of our boys caught sight of the familiar blue printing. There was a miniature stampede, and under penalty of terrible threats I was made to promise to pass it round each week after I had finished with it.

He was happy to oblige, as the enthusiasm for football at Bexhill was not insignificant. 'After the weary monotony of a week's hard drill, and living in an atmosphere of war, it is one of the finest tomes we can have to read and talk about the latest doings of our favourite clubs.'[2]

Impressed with the sentiment, in return for Clifford's letter Chelsea sent a match ball to Sussex for the men to enjoy. A relationship of sorts now struck up between club and regiment, in line with the increasingly strained call for recruits as the autumn wore on. Whitley began to think that, ignoring the geographical irrelevance of Sussex, it would be rather a good idea to attempt to expand the number of Chelsea fans joining the South Downs battalions enough to form a complete company of supporters dedicated to the Blues. Three weeks after his initial letter, at the home win over Bolton Wanderers, a last-minute notice was issued to attempt to gain recruits at Stamford Bridge. Whitley jumped on a train and arrived at the ground with another Pensioners fan of a similar age. Ernest Wenden had actually added a couple of years to his application to join the army. Nineteen years old and an east Londoner, he had grown up in Leyton. Like Clifford Whitley, Ernest was a clerk and worked for a local provision merchant. When war was declared, the first of the South Downs battalions had only been formed a week when he enlisted in the ranks.

The response to Whitley and Wenden's improvised recruitment drive, however, was far from overwhelming and put down to the fact that it had all been rather ad hoc. Several men did pop into the club office the following Monday, but the day felt like a disappointing waste of time to the two Royal Sussex Regiment officers who had made the trip. Two weeks later the editor of the *Chronicle* attempted to rally more fans to their cause at an easy victory over Notts County:

> The two comrades … are both regular and enthusiastic supporters of Chelsea and until answering their country's call some two months back, never missed a match. They are still endeavouring to fulfil their mission, and any of you stalwart lads who are still considering the matter had better make up your minds without delay.

The club would do all they could to help guide men towards the regiment. 'A postcard to the editor, at these grounds, and he will put you on to the right road to joining one of the best battalions in the country.' Rumour had it that these particular Sussex volunteers had it better than any other:

> The 'nothing but Irish stew' yarns do not apply to the 'South Downs'. They have the best of fare! 'A jolly sight better grub than we used to get in town!' Men need not worry about whether or not they would be looked after when they got home either; Colonel Lowther is untiring in his efforts to see to the comfort of his 'lambs' in every way.

He was, they claimed, working tirelessly to raise a guarantee fund 'which will ensure every man who enlists under him a situation at the conclusion of the war'. He also, it seemed, had ensured that if 100 or so unmarried Blues fans enlisted that they would be kept together. 'There really ought to be no difficulty in getting a hundred men to form the "Chelsea Company." Now lads! Roll up, for King, Country and Chelsea!'[3]

They fell short in those sorts of numbers, but by Christmas parts of the Sussex countryside were being touted as a Chelsea stronghold. 'All sorts of conditions of men are included, from the couple of regular habitués of our director's stand to "Ginger" the erstwhile newsboy at Walham Green.' Among their number too was a fan in his early 20s named Fred Russell. The son of a policeman and an electrician himself, although he had grown up by Eel Brook Common, Fred's parents both originated from Salehurst in East Sussex. Life wasn't too unpleasant for him and his fellow Blues fans, so it seemed. 'They are "fed up with Tipperary" and anyone starting the refrain is promptly given the bird. Their popular marching song is now a parody on "Sussex by the Sea" and [they are] appreciative of the good "fare" they receive.'[4]

At the beginning of July 1915 the 11th, 12th and 13th Royal Sussex battalions were rounded up and moved to Maidstone to continue their preparations for life at the front, at that time finally coming under War Office control. Chelsea fan Ernest Wenden would never actually see active service with the regiment whose numbers he had made so much effort to bolster, and in the oddest of circumstances. At 4.20 a.m. on 2 July the South Downs men were due to parade before leaving for Kent. The hour arrived and when the officers and men of the battalions turned out, Ernest was not among them. Despite still being 19, Ernest had married just before Christmas. His wife was a little lost as to what to do, but a senior officer told her to accompany the South Downs men to Maidstone, after all, surely he would turn up eventually. The now 20-year-old subaltern, promoted to officer status along with Clifford Whitley before the turn of the year, had though, so it seemed, vanished into thin air. No amount of enquiries could find any trace of him. In east London his family and his employer claimed not to have heard a thing of him and in August Ernest Wenden was struck off the Army List and a notice was placed in the *London Gazette*. After a month or so, his young wife, a Fulham girl, presumably gave up and she returned home. To add even more to the mystery, the only other clue that ever surfaced was a letter sent to the regiment by the Grand Hotel in Manchester. It alleged that an Ernest Wenden had checked in, but then run away without paying his bill, leaving behind only a uniform adorned with Royal Sussex Regiment insignia. Were Ernest's responsibilities too much for this very young newlywed officer? Or was it simply that the reality of the war became suddenly apparent as the South Downs battalions made their way on to advanced training and proved too terrifying? Whatever his thinking, Wenden took drastic action.

The 39th Division was not to have any specific regional allegiance, but would be drawn heavily from recruits from the South and the Midlands. Units started arriving at Winchester at the beginning of August, with a horse-drawn company of the Army Service

Corps that would eventually make up part of the divisional train. The first battalion arrived on the 13th, pioneers from the Gloucestershire Regiment and by the end of the month a divisional HQ had been established on Jewry Street, albeit it with the officers paying for the rental of their offices out of their own pockets. More units began to arrive: an eclectic mix of Argyll and Sutherland Highlanders, East Surreys, the first of two battalions of Sherwood Foresters. Along with a company of signallers, the three South Downs battalions joined the formation in the last three days of September, just as the burgeoning division was relocating to Aldershot. Immediately following them, new artillery units formed in London began to arrive, including one from Greenwich which had been based on a site of the Thames ironworks, whose employee football team had evolved into West Ham United.

Waiting for them all was an experienced administrator in General Nathanial Barnardiston, a former Assistant Director of Military Training. He had lofty ideas as far as the spirit of his division was concerned:

> The importance of the development of the soldierly qualities of cheerfulness in fatigue, danger and privation; of courage – the result of a man's confidence in himself, his superiors and his comrades; of self-sacrifice, discipline and cohesion, the possession of which, added to a thorough training, will enable us to defeat the enemy.

He had a vast organisational job ahead of him to bring together some 20,000 men, largely amateurs, into a productive fighting unit. To begin with, a number of recruits ended up being passed as unfit for service. As it was throughout Kitchener's new army too, finding competent, experienced officers to lead them was also a problem and when Barnardiston reviewed those in front of him, he resolved to send them off on as many courses as possible to raise the standard.

Now artillery, infantry, engineers, supply troops, staff would all have to be taught not only how to carry out their own roles, but to do so in conjunction with each other in the heat of battle. As far as the South Downs men were concerned, they were in better shape than much of the infantry. They were to form the 116th Infantry Brigade, along with a Hampshire battalion, and found that they were farther along the road to being war-ready than many men comprising the division's other two new brigades. The 13th East Surreys and two new battalions of the Middlesex Regiment had been in existence only a matter of weeks and were still actively recruiting when the move to Aldershot came. While some of the South Down men had volunteered as long ago as 1914, though, others had developed little beyond elementary recruit training. Therefore, despite the fact that the units were told to expect to be pushed for time as far as preparations for departure were concerned, trying to organise a standard level of training was extremely difficult when the division first came together. 'Whilst some units which have existed for a longer period must not be kept back more than may be essential by battalions which have a shorter existence, yet the whole must be trained collectively from a certain basis,'[5] ordained Barnardiston.

The 11th, 12th and 13th Royal Sussex battalions were to begin with two weeks training in small sections and platoons, before graduating upwards. Company training, a number of platoons together, would then be followed several weeks later by full battalion work, when all four companies would assemble. Next, all of the South Downs men would come together with their contingent of Hampshires and train as their allotted brigade, the 116th, before finally full divisional preparation would commence. As so many officers were new, or had been away from the army for a considerable amount of time, the three brigadiers led planning for initial training at the beginning of October 1915 asopposed to the company officers themselves. As well as instilling his penchant for immaculate discipline into his new division, Barnardiston believed that if the South Downs battalions and the rest of his troops at Aldershot were to function as an exemplary unit, that this initial portion of their training was imperative to help the lowest ranked officers build their confidence and belief in the power of their command with their men. 'Platoon training,' he pontificated, afforded 'the opportunity to commanders of all ranks to study the characters and capabilities of every man of their commands, and of incorporating this soldierly spirit. The opportunity should not be neglected.'[6]

Long days began with physical exercise and bayonet fighting before breakfast and were drawn out with 10-mile route marches and copious amounts of drill. Rifles were thin on the ground but it was hoped more would be forthcoming soon. Even without one for each man it was considered imperative that training in their use should commence immediately. No time was to be lost as nobody yet knew when orders would come to proceed overseas.

In mid-October the platoons of Sussex recruits, Chelsea fans scattered among them, came together into companies to continue their training. General Barnardiston saw this as a pivotal moment in the development of the division at ground level. Commanding officers would now learn to work with their subordinates. He quoted his favourite doctrine on the subject:

> Here officers and NCOs learn to make practical application of the knowledge they have acquired, and become the instructors in collective training of men already prepared by their work as recruits to profit by such tuition. Here by degrees, the Captain, Subaltern, Sergeant or Corporal becomes, each in his own sphere, the recognised leader, guider and enlightener of his men.

Eventually they would work as a succinct unit capable of enduring hardship together:

> Gradually mutual esteem, and very probably affection are evolved out of the relations of eager master and willing pupil. The rank and file learn to trust their instructors, and the instructors learn to trust them. When this point has been reached, the unit will bear the strain of discomfort and danger without any loss of cohesion or courage.[7]

Training intensified. During the short winter days, the South Downs men worked hard on their drill and physical fitness. Each evening there were daily musketry exercises and miniature range practices. Rapid loading and firing was to be practised intensely. Recruits were to hand the available rifles around as much as possible so that each might get a feel for them. When sufficient numbers of them arrived, every man was ordered to fire at least one series of fifteen dummy rounds, rapid loading and firing each day. Work was still not then done for the day, as Barnardiston ordained that as much time as possible be dedicated to training for night operations. On top of everything else, 116th Brigade was ordered to assemble three Sussex battalions and their Hampshire neighbours for lectures whenever possible, especially before fledgling tactical operations so that they were fully briefed as to what was about to occur. Route marches went up to 12 miles, sometimes 15, and drill was expanded. Officers were adamant that the absolute necessity for keeping arms and ammunition in perfect condition must be ingrained in all ranks. Negligence on this point must result in punishment, as must any infringements on matters of discipline and smartness. 'Cleanliness and smartness of turnout, even under adverse conditions, are signs of a good and well disciplined unit. Slovenliness and un-cleanliness under any circumstances must never be permitted.'[8]

The South Downs men marched to Witley Camp, which was to be a longer-term home, and the four companies of each battalion came together to begin battalion training in the run up to Christmas. They had now begun to concern themselves with the issue of how to co-operate with various arms. The Sussex men were put into a training group with a brigade of artillery, a company of Royal Engineers, some signallers, medical men and a contingent of the Army Service Corps. Despite the fact that his men would have to be rigorously drilled in the art of stagnant trench warfare, Barnardiston was adamant that they all be instilled with the spirit of the offensive. There was still much room for improvement. At this point the general was more than a little concerned about the leadership on display. 'Hitherto much time has been wasted and training has suffered by the lack of careful previous preparation of the day's scheme.' The men didn't appear to have a clue what they were contributing to when they began their tactical operations, what they were supposed to do or where the as yet fictitious enemy was supposed to be. 'It is important that all ranks should clearly understand the nature of this operation on which they are engaged,' he reminded his commanders, 'e.g. in trench work they should have the "trench system" explained to them, and not merely be told to "dig a trench from a to z."' In outposts, again, all ranks should be taught to take an intelligent interest in the proceedings. 'It has been noticed that absurd situations frequently arise owing to the operations not having been clearly explained.'[9]

The structure of training in ever expanding numbers was abandoned in January 1916 so that the men of the South Downs battalions could complete their General Musketry Course. They began on the first week of the New Year, but the weather was terrible and impacted the training greatly. Time was of the essence however and the Sussex men fired on, despite the fact that they had been issued with their rifles a few days before. The 116th Brigade gave Barnardiston the least to worry about, being the most effective shots in his division by quite some margin. The South Downs battalions produced 494 first-class marksmen before their return to Witley.

On the return to camp, various divisional troops began to take more responsibility for their full duties. The artillery were practising immediate co-operation on request from infantry and retaliation requests; the Royal Engineers were becoming adept at sapping and mining, filling and laying sandbags, assisting the infantry with construction and the repair of trenches and training of infantry 'wiring-parties' as well as helping the artillery with construction of frames, gun and machine-gun emplacements. Signallers rehearsed the laying of cables to maintain communications in battle and RAMC men practised how to keep their facilities as sanitary as possible and rescue wounded men from the field. The divisional train had taken over supply almost exclusively at Witley, but were becoming versed in how the chain now worked at the static front. Things had evolved greatly since the retreat of 1914. Supply sections refilled from the Divisional Refilling Point, taking the supplies up to the regimental points. Here goods were divided up by company and loaded onto first line transport, 'by which the supplies are carried to the limit of safety for animals and vehicles', a 'trench refilling point'.[10] Here supplies were often taken to the communication trenches by improvised hand-carts and carried up the communication trenches on makeshift stretchers made of poles and old sacks.

Settling back into the routine of battalion training having been away was difficult, and General Barnardiston decided to set his men a second course running into the middle of February. Getting to grips with trench warfare was imperative for the Chelsea men and their fellow recruits. The commander did not want it to be detrimental to preparing for the eventuality of open warfare, but they had begun constructing their own systems and he wanted them completed rapidly. All tasks were to be practised by both day and night: 'Trench assaults, repairing trenches, making revetments, laying sandbags, training wiring parties for erection and placing wire entanglements' were just some of the areas he identified as being below par. His demands did not stop there. Trench storming parties, tactical employment of machine guns in co-operation with infantry and bombers, sniper employment, signalling in both trench and open warfare, conversion of captured trenches for own use, establishment and repair of communications, training of patrols, arrangements for and practice of signals as regards 'gas', etc., formation and training of wiring parties for laying and repair of wire entanglements and trip wires, ammunition and grenade supply, food supply, medical and sanitary arrangements: 'all the above mentioned items need particular attention and training'. As ever, Barnardiston had a separate treatise on all manner of discipline and scruffiness, down to how the men carried their rifles – never on a slope while marching and forbidding outright the carrying of them butt up. He was tired of hearing the excuse of 'sore-feet' on the move and, it appeared, tired of sloppy singing:

If singing is permitted on the march (and then only when tactical considerations allow) it will be properly organised and carried out. Under no circumstances will singing be permitted to degenerate into uncontrolled and undisciplined shouting. Cases have occurred recently of troops singing whilst marching through the camp. This contravenes divisional routine order No. 438 (a) of 15th December 1915, to which attention is drawn.[11]

All of this attention to detail meant that for the Sussex men, brigade training, which should have commenced at the very end of 1915, was heavily delayed. This two-week stint was to have prepared the troops for the divisional training which followed and would have them practise co-operating as a complete formation, but time was against them. In February, with work still occurring at battalion level the 39th Division was ordered overseas. Having ruled out higher level training because he thought his men were not ready for it, General Barnardiston was now expected to send them off to war. The South Downs men had still seen no sign of any divisional cavalry and a squadron of South Irish Horse was to join them abroad. Likewise the Field Ambulance men were in a training camp elsewhere in Surrey and went straight to the embarkation point from there. The Royal Engineers at the division's disposal were deemed 'moderately' advanced.

Barnardiston was adamant that any time remaining to them before their departure was to be utilised in getting ready for the trench warfare that he was sure would occupy them on their initial arrival at the front. There were points that the Blues fans with the Sussex battalions had not yet even touched upon. 'In trench warfare, a ceaseless and vigilant watch throughout the 24 hours from specially constructed observation posts throughout the length of the line is always maintained by trained observers. The training of these observers must commence at once.' He also didn't want to see morale plummet through the inevitable inaction:

> All ranks must be imbued with a high spirit of spirit de corps and must consider it a point of honour that the enemy does not gain a footing in their trenches, and, should that occur, they must immediately counter attack and drive the enemy out. The offensive spirit must be very strongly indoctrinated. To give back far more than they receive, to harass, destroy, and 'strafe' with vigour, in fact to be, and to feel, at all times, 'top dog'.

He still thought his officers too weak, but boosting their confidence 'must not lead to blind recklessness and foolish and unnecessary exposure'. Finally, the general did not want all the men's fitness work to go to waste. 'The best methods of carrying out physical training during trench life must be thought out and practised by all arms.'[12]

After more than one false start, the South Downs battalions began entraining on 2 March 1916 and departed for France. On arrival, by chance, the Blues fans present soon found themselves following in the footsteps of their fellow Chelsea supporters

Alf Dorsett, Bill Richards and Cecil Dean, towards the area around Festubert and Neuve Chapelle. South-east of the latter village, Whitley, Russell and the others found keeps, 'as they were called, roughly constructed in and about ruined buildings, and very numerous'. Richebourg St Vaast was nice enough, but utterly deserted. The houses were heavily sandbagged, artillery observation ladders were nailed to sturdy trees. 'The large church,' wrote Edmund Blunden, himself an officer with the South Downs contingent, 'had been bombarded into that state of demi-ruin ... At the foot of the monolithlike steeple stood a fine and great bell, and against that, a rusty shell of almost the same size.'[13] Tombs lay open to the elements thanks to ceaseless artillery bombardments. 'Greenish water stood in some of these pits; bones and skulls and decayed cerements there attracted frequent soldiers past the "No Loitering" notice board.' The trenches that the Sussex men found were thinly defended, with a single line of sandbags, 'with scraps of dugouts like toolhouses leaning against it' and a useful but naked duckboard walk running along behind them past graves, shell holes and ditches. The weather was awful, 'everything was mud and moisture'.

At the end of spring the men found themselves to the south of Festubert when orders came for a move back towards Neuve Chapelle to replace another division going into reserve. They arrived in mid-June and commanders were immediately informed that two battalions were expected to assault, capture and retain part of the network of German trenches almost straightaway at a position referred to as the Boar's Head in front of them. The division vacating the area had made fair progress with preparing for such an action, including accumulating stores of ammunition, bombs and engineers' material nearby and they handed everything over to grateful staff officers who had almost no time to prepare. Two of the South Downs battalions were selected for the task; the 12th, including Fred Russell, and the 13th, with Whitley. They were thrown into the lines to become used to the surroundings for a little under a week before they were withdrawn again to train and were joined by detachments from the Royal Engineers and Gloucestershire Pioneers.

Whitley and the 13th Battalion had carried out some successful trench raids already, but the attack on the Boar's Head on 30 June 1916 was to be the most elaborate undertaking so far by any of the South Downs men. The principle was to stop the enemy from withdrawing troops and guns from this area of the British lines to withstand the battering the Allies were about to unleash on them to the South. On the opening day of the Battle of the Somme on 1 July, the Sussex battalions were to launch themselves forward on a front of about 500 yards and seize the German front line, turning it into a British support line. They would then surge forward and seize the enemy's second line, turning that into the new British front line. Ambitiously, while all of this was being consolidated, pioneers and an Australian mining company would be rapidly creating new saps to begin connecting it all up into a working trench system that joined up to the one that the British were already using.

On a muggy, stormy afternoon, Whitley and the other officers were informed as to what they would be expected to do. In wheat fields to the rear, the departing division had hacked into the ground a replica of the trench system at the Boar's Head to practise in. Unfinished, the centre section consisted of canvas outlines in among the crops and No Man's Land had been noticeably reduced in order to avoid damaging the surrounding wheat. Men were withdrawn to practise throwing bombs in another facility dug by the previous residents, but all preparations were hampered by rainfall that reduced the whole area to liquid mud. During the afternoon of 28 June, Whitley, Fred Russell and the two chosen battalions of the South Downs, the Chelsea fans among them, returned to the trenches. That night gas was discharged slowly towards the enemy. It was more a feint, to imply that this resource was fully at their disposal on this front, than an attack. Four cylinders gently hissed away, the only sound on an otherwise silent night, designed to look like an 'accidental discharge'[14] with no artillery, machine-gun or rifle fire to support it.

The following morning it seemed very much business as usual for the Germans, who were observed crawling about on their parapet, baling out their sodden trenches with buckets on sticks, putting up wire and going about some presumably nefarious business behind a canvas screen beyond one of the isolated outposts on the Sussex front. At 2 p.m., however, their serenity was shattered by a ruthless, three-hour long bombardment by the British artillery preparing for the attack the next day. A flurry of gunfire, not only from 39th Division, but two others in support, pummelled the narrow front, howitzers smashing down their shells on the parapets and support lines. As well as baffling the enemy, by carrying out the preliminary bombardment the day before it was hoped that their efforts at cutting their barbed wire would yield better results and there was the added advantage that any retaliation would not hit dense collections of men massed in forward trenches ready to attack. So as not to reveal where an attack might take place, the artillery had previously only been allowed to register their guns on the Boar's Head, but now they revealed their hand in brutal fashion and pelted shells at it. Several breaches were made and kept open with the help of rampant machine-gun fire in enfilade. To the rear, Edmund Blunden, with the 11th Royal Sussex Regiment, listened to the racket overhead. 'Our heavy artillery thundered away for hours at the German line; no answer came. How could we lose?' That night under cover of darkness the enemy was forced to bring fresh troops into the line, struggling past piles of wounded and dead being carried away.

Across No Man's Land a staff officer was touring the various headquarters with a part to play in the upcoming battle, synchronising everyone's watches. The men of the South Downs battalions had spent the day in last-minute preparations. The Chelsea fans present had been collecting extra bandoliers of ammunition, rounding up bombs, strapping rolled waterproof sheets onto the back of their belts. In addition, each man was expected to carry up to four sandbags forward to assist with consolidating the German trenches into the British system. Some would also have picks and shovels in addition to gas helmets and iron rations which were to be carefully inspected before departure.

In silent darkness, Clifford Whitley led his men through the thick mud past battalion headquarters on their way into battle. The 13th were in position by 1.30 a.m. and an hour later Fred Russell and the men of the 12th had joined them on the other side of a prolific ditch. Owing to the state of the ground, the brigadier had instructed them to assemble as far forward as possible. Men crawled out through the mire to cut the British wire in front. Then there was nothing to do but wait. Blunden and the final South Downs battalion were ready to assist with carrying up material and ammunition and to help bring back the wounded.

At 2.55 a.m. the air was wrought with the screaming of metal, exclusively high explosive shells, in a final ten-minute bombardment before they went into action. Blunden was astounded. 'Mad ideas of British supremacy flared in me as the quiet sky behind us awoke in a crescent of baying flashes, a half-moon of avenging fires.' His hopes were to prove short-lived. 'Those ideas sank instantly, for the sky before us awoke in like fashion, and another equal half-moon of punishing lightnings burst, with the innumerable high voices of machine guns like the spirits of madness in alarm shrilling above the tempest blast of explosion.'[15] He and his men retreated to a cellar for safety. Outside, German shells first rained down on the British support lines, then edged backwards, turning into a fearsome barrage on the British front line, shells and machine-gun fire spraying the parapet. The response had been immediate and strong, 'heavier and more effective than optimists anticipated'.[16]

The British gunners fired on doggedly. The 39th Division's artillery had been given a monumental task, a complicated programme 'entailing at times great accuracy, great rapidity and probing fire over a period of seven hours'. The inexperienced artillerymen were firing as many rounds in a minute as they had previously attempted in a day. 'Moreover, the least failure to keep to the long and complicated timetable would have been disastrous.'[17] Borrowed artillery on either side contributed fire not only to the main bombardment, but to a subsidiary hail of shells as a distraction on nearby targets, including the farm that Cecil Dean had died trying to claim a little over a year before.

On the main front, the guns paused to baffle the enemy as to when the attack was coming. The debut of the South Downs men in fully fledged battle was fast approaching. Both battalions were to pour over the top and towards the German lines at 3.05 a.m. in four waves. It was impossible to rush the whole way, so they would be covering it in quick time. The first two waves, 50 yards apart, were to seize the furthest objective 'at all costs': the enemy support line.[18] On no account was there to be any stopping to ponder anything before this point, for the two waves behind were to make good the German front line which they would have passed over.

The leading men of the 12th and 13th Royal Sussex Regiments scaled the parapet and forming columns in single file, began pushing into No Man's Land. Immediately they were faced with heavy machine-gun fire. The German response to the opening bombardment had been so severe that it could not have come as a surprise. Indeed prisoners confirmed that they had been expecting an attack. As Clifford Whitley, Fred Russell and the rest of the Blues' contingent began flooding forward they were greeted by knowing calls of 'Come on Sussex.'[19]

The British artillery had now refocused their efforts on an intense twenty-minute barrage to be laid down on the enemy as the South Downs battalions began their advance. As the successive waves went over, though, the German artillery fire too became heavier, smashing into the parapets as men attempted to cross specially constructed bridges into No Man's Land. A few gas shells were used by the enemy, raining noxious fumes down on one or two observation posts, valuable telephone lines were being cut and one high explosive shell wiped out almost an entire wave when it smashed into their ranks. In the chaos the rest of the Sussex men advanced on.

As well as contending with enemy shells, the advancing troops were being enfiladed with machine-gun fire. As they approached the German lines they found barbed wire still intact too and obstructing their path, especially on the left in front of Fred Russell and the 12th Battalion. There was no time to be lost, despite their difficulties. Officers had been given explicit instructions to keep the men moving forward and under control. No straggling or 'souvenir' hunting was to be tolerated and the attack was 'to be vigorously pushed on [with] no cessation until it is complete'.[20]

On the right flank of the attack, Cliff Whitley managed to jump down into the waterlogged German trenches with his men. Fierce hand-to-hand fighting broke out as the South Downs men penetrated the enemy system, dominated by glinting bayonets and flying bombs. Heavy casualties were inflicted upon the inhabitants as the 13th Royal Sussex began, in part, to reach their support line, but they were about to be undone by their own devices. The left-hand portion of their advance was breaking down. The direction of the wind pending, it had been planned to release smoke from mortars to obstruct the enemy's view of the battlefield. In spite of meticulous planning, when it was duly released on 30 June the wind changed to the south and began blowing it back across the attacking battalions. Both were hindered and could barely see a few yards in front. Whitley and his men found themselves staggering into Gloucestershire Pioneers attempting to dig new communication trenches across the battlefield. The Sussex men began to lose track of where they were and the attack dissolved into small groups not knowing which way to go. Isolated bodies managed to reach the furthermost objective of the enemy support trench, but consolidating their positions was another matter. They got in each other's way and the smoke made getting through uncut wire even more difficult. Any troops who found their way into the line found themselves subjected to a sudden, intense barrage of high explosives.

At the other end of the line Fred Russell and the flanks of the 12th Battalion were frantically signalling the letter 'Z' to inform headquarters that they were still held up on uncut wire on their left and by a ditch on their right. The two centre companies had managed to get into the enemy front line and some, allegedly, had got as far as the furthest objective, but the fourth wave was having trouble even getting to No Man's Land amidst a storm of German artillery fire. In total no more than forty men reached the enemy support line, blocking and bombing parties frantically working at close quarters to clear them, accompanied by sappers with dynamite. Special dugout parties were there only to flush out German hiding places that other troops had swept past on their way to the main objective, each of them allocated a particular piece of trench. Inside they found troops dazed by the bombardment, squirreled away deep underground.

Right on schedule the artillery dropped to a much lower, sustainable rate of fire. They were, however, fully ready to assist the infantry in putting down shells on any problem spots. All the South Downs battalions had to do was communicate the code word 'mustard' to bring down an intense five-minute firestorm on a point of concern. If the phone went out they could activate the same support by way of a star and smoke signal from a captured trench. To the north, twelve additional guns were ready to bear on any German troops spotted massing for a counter-attack on the code word 'ginger'.[21]

Meanwhile a contingent of Australian miners was out in No Man's Land attempting their own method of creating a new communication trench, trying to connect up a British line to a captured German one. A hydraulic system pushed lengths of piping horizontally underground towards the enemy trench and then ammonal canisters were forced along it so that when the whole contraption was detonated, it should blow a trench instantly into the ground and save the men having to dig one out. The Australians laboured under heavy shellfire, checking that the pipes were remaining level as they were shunted along, but the sodden nature of the ground undid them. Forty feet from the German trench the pipe angled up and broke the surface, coming to a stop 5 feet from the enemy parapet underneath a tangle of barbed wire. When most of the charge blew, the ground was so soft that although a 60-foot long, 20-foot wide crater was formed, it also blew to a depth of 10 feet, too deep to be practical.

Elsewhere the Gloucestershire Pioneers were attempting to dig out communication trenches the old fashioned way with mixed results. One company found that their area was crammed with so many troops that their task was abandoned and they manned an empty trench instead; one got caught up in a muddle of retiring men and abandoned their task to clear out two communication trenches that had been blown in and another resorted to collecting the wounded and distributing ammunition. Only one company managed actually to dig a trench that could be used to evacuate stricken South Downs men.

1 An aerial view of Stamford Bridge (with West Brompton cemetery above), *c*.1909. *(Authors' collection)*

2 View of the eastbound platform at Walham Green (now Fulham Broadway) station in 1907. *(Authors' collection)*

3 North End Road, from roughly outside where The Cock pub is today, looking away from Stamford Bridge. *(Authors' collection)*

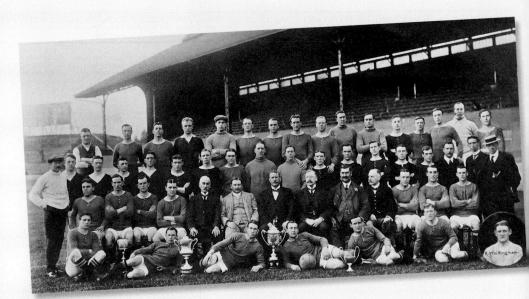

4 Chelsea Football Club 1912/13. *Back row:* Moir (Assistant Trainer), Hawkes, Crews, Brown, Waight, Johnson, Steer, Turnbull, Hewitt, Denoon, Harris, Bull, Tickle, Norman Wood, Brebner, Vivian Woodward. *Third row:* Ransom (Trainer), David Calderhead Jr, Charlie Freeman, Fairgray, Jack Harrow, Harry Ford, Buchanan, Goodlad, Whitley, Jim Molyneux, Horn, Cartwright, Wilkie, Teddy Foord, Thomson, Bert Palmer (Club Secretary), Palmer, Calderhead (Manager). *Second row:* Dolby, Harwood, McLeod, Harding, Messrs J.T. Mears, W. Claude Kirby (Chairman), J.H. Maltby, H. Boyer, G. Schomberg, (Directors) Downing, Bridgeman, Read. *Front row:* Taylor, Angus Douglas, Ormiston, Cameron, Walter Bettridge, Dodd. *(Authors' collection)*

5 James Broadbridge at about the time Chelsea was formed. *(Private collection)*

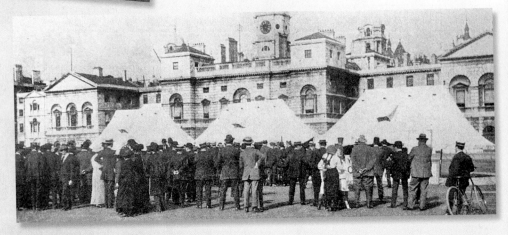

6 Crowds flock to Horse Guards Parade to enlist in the opening days of the war. *(Authors' collection)*

7 Hangar aux cotons and the
Quai de la Garonne at Havre.
(Authors' collection)

8 Thomas Bason. *(Private collection)*

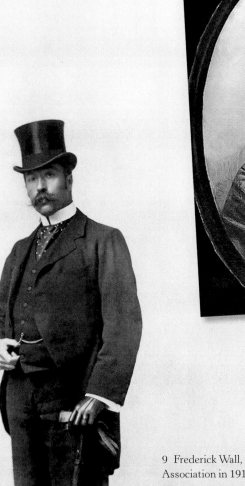

9 Frederick Wall, Secretary of the Football
Association in 1914. *(Authors' collection)*

10 William Hayes-Fisher, MP for Hammersmith & Fulham. *(Authors' collection)*

11 Fulham Town Hall (left), yards from Stamford Bridge with recruitment posters displayed. *(Authors' collection)*

12 William Alfred Dean. *(Private collection)*

13 Elsie, Cecil and Reg Dean. *(Private collection)*

14 Cecil Dean as a drummer in the Irish Guards, c.1908. *(Private collection)*

15 Bob Whiting (far right) undergoes rifle drill with Brighton & Hove Albion. *(B&HA)*

16 Men of the 17th Middlesex in camp prior to departure. Sid Jerram stands far right, Herbert Jerram sits far right. *(Private collection)*

17 Bert Palmer, Chelsea's club secretary who collected names of Blues fans wishing to enlist.
(Private collection)

18 The 17th Middlesex on a route march. *(Paul Reed)*

19 The Stamford Bridge crowd at the match against Sheffield United is dominated by men in uniform and those too young to join the colours. *(Authors' collection)*

20 The crowd at Old Trafford on 24 April 1915 was so dominated by soldiers that the match earned the nickname of the 'Khaki FA Cup Final'. *(Authors' collection)*

21 Jack Harrow (left) shakes hands with the Sheffield United captain before kick-off. *(Authors' collection)*

22 Men of the Royal Naval Division in training at Crystal Palace at the end of 1914. *(Authors' collection)*

23 Example of the crowded scenes on Anzac Beach that followed the Gallipoli landings. (Australian National War Memorial (ANWM))

24 Harry Trusler. *(Authors' collection)*

25 Cecil Dean during his time in the trenches, 1915. *(Private collection)*

26 Men hidden in the undergrowth at Wire Gully. (ANWM)

27 Soldiers of the 11th Royal Sussex Regiment enjoy Christmas dinner, 1914. (Paul Reed)

28 Men of the South Downs battalions queue for baths at Cooden Camp, Bexhill. (Paul Reed)

29 Vivian Woodward. *(Authors' collection)*

30 Men of the 17th Middlesex on church parade in west London, February 1915. *(Authors' collection)*

31 George Collison (far right) with family. *(Private collection)*

32 The devastating effects of the 1916 fighting on Guillemont are evident from this photograph of the 'High Street'. *(Authors' collection)*

33 Patrick Ronan.
(Private collection)

34 Pat's wife Annie with one of their children. *(Private collection)*

35 Sid Jerram. *(Private collection)*

36 A pioneer battalion at work building roads at Messines, 1917. *(1/2-012772-G, Alexander Turnbull Library, Wellington, New Zealand)*

37 The rate of shellfire at the Third Battle of Ypres rendered the terrain a moonscape, void of all features. *(Authors' collection)*

38 Bob Whiting. *(B&HA)*

39 Arthur Wileman. (Luton Town Football Club)

40 Billy Brawn, one player
associated with Chelsea FC
who exercised his right to
appeal against military service.
(Authors' collection)

41 Angus Douglas.
(Authors' collection)

42 Edwin Siveyer.
(Private collection)

43 Chelsea 1919/20. *Back row:* Dickie, Harold Halse, Calderhead (Manager), Walter Bettridge, Harry Wilding, Colin Hampton, Logan, Whitley (Trainer), Jack Harrow. *Front row:* Harry Ford, Dale, Cock, Croal, McNeil. *(Authors' collection)*

To the rear, Edmund Blunden had heard the rate of shelling decline but no news arrived. He expected that someone would call them forward as reinforcements, but nobody came. At last a few stragglers from the battle 'blundered dazedly round the trench corner' and dropped to the floor. Blunden was bursting to know what the battle was like and asked excitedly a man in little mood to elaborate:

In a great and angry groan he broke out, 'Don't ask me – it's terrible, O God.' Then, after a moment, talking loud and fast: 'We were in the third line. I came to a traverse, got out of the trench, and peeped; there was a Fritz creeping round the next traverse. I threw a bomb in; it hit the trench side and rolled just under his head; he looked down to see what it was.'[22]

The South Downs battalions were feeling the heat crammed into the enemy support line, their casualties mounting quickly under a barrage of shells and machine-gun fire. On several occasions they invoked 'mustard' from the artillery and watched the rate of shells increase to three per minute from each gun in short blasts, but the German bombardment was too much. Things had reached a dire state and men of both battalions began falling back to the original German front line. The enemy then focused all of their energy on laying down fire on top of them and for two and a half hours the Blues fans still present up and down the line underwent a monstrous ordeal as they attempted to cling on to their new positions. Casualties among the officers and NCOs mounted rapidly, leaving the men leaderless. It felt as if the Germans were bringing more and more guns into action. Machine guns poured their fire both from in front and on the Sussex flanks.

Finally, a captain of Clifford Whitley's battalion called time on the mayhem. Seeing that his men had failed to hold their objective, that parties were staggering around with no direction and that they were in danger of being cut off and annihilated, to the chagrin of senior officers at the time he ordered the men back. Along the line, just a few men of the 12th Battalion still held their position. Unable to get hold of any more bombs or ammunition, the sergeant major in command too gave the order to retire. Picking up heavy casualties as they flocked back, the South Downs battalions ended up right back where they had started. The uncut wire, lopsided smoke, a lack of reinforcements, the enemy's stout defence and the narrow front had all conspired against them. It was later acknowledged by the complaining senior officers that 'wise discretion'[23] had been exercised in throwing in the towel.

At 6.45 a.m. divisional HQ ordained that the attack would not be renewed. On reflection any hope of success, it was felt, would depend on orchestrating an entirely new bombardment before the Sussex men went forward again and such a thing would be impossible to organise at such short notice. Instead, plans were now made for the relief of the 12th and 13th Royal Sussex battalions.

The Germans had suffered hundreds of casualties. Such was the ferocity of the hand-to-hand combat in their lines that only four men had been taken prisoner, the rest were slaughtered if they didn't flee. The returning South Downs men told tales of piles of enemy dead littering the lines and, demolished by British artillery, some parts of the trenches becoming impassable because of the amount of bodies obstructing them. From across No Man's Land all manner of unmoving limbs could be seen sticking out at odd angles. The Sussex men themselves were still taking on casualties back in their original positions, as the German artillery continued to pound their parapets. Nearly 150 of the South Downs volunteers were dead and hundreds more wounded. More than 600 inhabited nearby casualty clearing stations alone in the aftermath of their elaborate raid. Hundreds more were unaccounted for and it was hoped that they would begin straggling in as the day wore on and the area became calmer. They were eventually relieved by battalions of the South Staffordshire and Cambridgeshire regiments. The brigadier tried to see the positive in such a costly and ineffective action: 'I consider that though the attack failed to retain and consolidate the enemy's position, the main objectives of the operation were successfully carried out.'[24] Heavy casualties had been inflicted upon the Germans opposite, not only by the raid itself but by the preliminary bombardment the day before. Both the German front and support trenches, as well as numerous communication lines, had been decimated and the enemy had been obliged to hurriedly and inconveniently carry out reliefs in the area on account of the British action. It had, however, been a rude introduction to war for the Chelsea contingent of the two attacking battalions, who lost Fred Russell during the assault. Despite their incomplete training and the fact that they had only been at the front a matter of weeks, the commander of 116th Brigade was impressed with what he had seen, not only from the 12th and 13th battalions but from the 11th and the contingents of pioneers, engineers and artillery that had contributed to the day's events.

At ground level the men saw things a little differently. Edmund Blunden was listening to one survivor, 'already exhibiting his twice-perforated mess tin with his usual dejected wit'. Word filtered down that all of their efforts had been secondary in importance to much larger events:

Our affair had been a cat's-paw, a 'holding attack' to keep German guns and troops from [elsewhere]. This purpose, previously concealed from us with success, was unachieved, for just as our main artillery pulled out southward after the battle, so did the German; and only a battalion or two of reserve infantry was needed by them to secure their harmless little salient.

The men were angry:

The explanations were almost as infuriating to the troops as the attack itself … and deep down in the survivors there grew a bitterness of waste; one of the battalions indeed seemed never to recover from its immense laceration, though reinforcements, and good ones, made up its numbers.

The area around Festubert had once again claimed the lives of Chelsea fans, although this time it was not those of regular or experienced soldiers, but men who had flocked to the colours on the outbreak of war. What the brigade felt was summed up by some sentry who, asked by the general next morning what he thought of the attack, answered in the roundest fashion, 'Like a butcher's shop.'

All of the efforts of the South Downs battalions on 30 June 1916 had been carried out with one aim, to divert the enemy from what was to happen the following day. The 'Boar's Head Massacre', which was to have bitten off a chunk of the line, 'no doubt to render the maps in the chateaux of the mighty more symmetrical',[25] was about to become a forgotten footnote in the history of the Great War. 'In the far and as yet strange-seeming south a holocaust was roaring': on 1 July the Battle of the Somme began, and with it came the blackest day that had ever befallen the British army.

12

'Merely Murder
If You Show Your Head'

The Battle of the Somme

By January 1916 the BEF had grown to nearly forty divisions on the Western Front, nearly a million men comprising regulars, territorials, Kitchener's troops, as well as a wealth of volunteers from throughout the Empire. This huge influx enabled the British to extend south and take some of the pressure off of France's army, which had some 100 divisions deployed along the front. With such huge numbers of Frenchmen present, it stood to reason that any planning for a large-scale offensive in 1916 would defer to this ally's thinking, so although the British hierarchy at least in part favoured action closer to Ypres and the Channel, it had long since been decided by the advent of summer that the season's campaigning would be done on the Somme, where the two nations' armies joined at the river itself.

Though planning began, the Germans would not be content to let their enemies dictate events on the Western Front. They threw a monumentally sized spanner into the works when they launched a huge, bloody and fierce assault against the French at Verdun in February. Destined to cause hundreds of thousands of casualties, the battle immediately reduced the potential contribution that the French would be able to make further north on the Somme. At the end of spring, as Britain's allies were at their wits' end, they were pushing Douglas Haig to begin the BEF's huge undertaking as soon as possible. By the time the battle actually came about, the objective of the campaign on the Somme was, strategically speaking, to relieve the pressure on the French at Verdun, to stop the Germans from siphoning men off and diverting them to other theatres such as Eastern Europe where they might trouble other allies and to wear down the enemy on the Western Front.

The French and the British had picked a formidable place to attack, for although the Somme had previously been a reasonably quiet sector, the Germans had certainly not been idle. Far from it, in fact; for nearly two years they had been digging in and their defences were stout: deep trenches, reinforced shelters, wire entanglements in thick belts. Woods and villages along the line had been turned into fortresses, deep cellars had been extended and connected up and some tunnels and dugouts ran as deep as 30 feet below ground. A first line system of multiple trenches ran along the front, incorporating the villages. A second system lay further back and a third had been started, so that in places the depth of the German positions ran to thousands of yards. They were fiercely bedded in and ready to sit on their portion of occupied French soil for as long as necessary.

The summer would be a huge undertaking for the British army, who were untested in a fight on this scale. The plan was for the Fourth Army to make the attack, puncture the enemy line and for a reserve army to then come up and make the breakthrough. Haig had advocated a plan to take the first two systems in their entirety at the onset and the Fourth Army's commander, Sir Henry Rawlinson, had bent accordingly. Haig had also placed a significant emphasis on the idea of exploitation, namely by the cavalry, through any gap created. It was ambitious in the extreme.

The British had taken over their Somme sector in 1915, but preparations for the offensive were epic in scale and had to be carried out in addition to the job of holding the line presently occupied, often in foul weather. The area was rural and new railways and tramlines had to be laid to bring equipment and supplies in for the huge number of troops massing nearby. Roads were improved and constructed from scratch, shelter had to be provided for troops, dressing stations had to be built to cater for the wounded, food and ammunition stores needed to be built up, miles and miles of telephone cables had to be dug in, new trenches needed to be constructed, mines had to be laid, even wells had to be dug and pumping plants constructed to make sure that there would be enough drinking water for thousands upon thousands of men.

The amount of work undertaken had, of course, not gone unnoticed by the German army, but the weight of the massive bombardment that was unleashed upon them in the days prior to zero hour was a shock. With more than 1,500 guns, in some places crammed together and firing over the top of each other, it was like nothing on earth ever heard before, furious violence as over a million shells were flung at the enemy. Huge mines were detonated and as the last, frantic storm of shells went over it became clear that battle was about to commence. The German artillery opened up in response, far from silenced by their British counterparts as had been hoped. The Battle of the Somme commenced on 1 July 1916, a bright summer's day. Thousands of assaulting troops swept forward at a steady walking pace. Although the bombardment had been monstrous and had left some of the Germans facing it on the verge of mental collapse, they had not necessarily been in physical danger as might have been thought, thanks to their deep dugouts. Bad weather had also stopped artillery co-operation with the Royal Flying Corps throughout and the impact of their shells was not as effective as one might have hoped with the aid of aerial direction. This was to have horrific consequences when so much hope had been placed on the success of the barrage. The British Army suffered the blackest day in its history, accumulating almost 60,000 casualties. Nearly 20,000 of those were dead and whole battalions all but ceased to exist for the time being.

Quick gains had been made at the southern end of the British front, but further north the opening of the offensive had been a disaster. However, there was no possibility of giving up and going home. Casualties mounted in their thousands during the opening days of July as commanders incoherently pursued local objectives to try and prepare for another large-scale advance. Haig favoured the idea of capitalising on what had been successful so far: continuing to push on in the south. This advance began on 14 July and by the end of it the German Army had lost their second line of defence on a front of 3 miles, but the army had still not seized all of the objectives set for 1 July, even in this area. The army's latest efforts had not been without gains, but fighting degenerated into disorganised scrapping, expensive in men and resources, despite efforts to cull this trend.

One surprising addition to the ranks of the BEF was involved in trying to scrap on to the initial objectives. When Cecil Dean fell at Festubert, his father had already rejoined the army. Despite having retired after almost thirty years of service, as casualties mounted at the front the need for experienced, competent NCOs was a constant issue. Age limits shifted accordingly, so that by December 1914, as his young son was recovering from his ordeal at Ypres, in his mid-40s William Dean had managed to find himself military employment with an unlikely regiment. In October the South Wales Borderers began actively trying to recruit for three new battalions, including a bantam one of men who were too short to join a normal unit. The first new formation, the 10th Battalion, began drawing volunteers from locations such as Abercarn, Newport and Tredegar. By the time William joined them at Colwyn Bay just before Christmas, the battalion numbered some 600 men. William was still involved in the unit's early development in north Wales when he learned of his eldest son's death, before the battalion then moved on to Hampshire in July 1915. A year after rejoining the army, William Dean arrived in France, the same port as his lost son, ready to become embroiled in a conflict the likes of which he could never have imagined when he enlisted as a 14-year-old in 1884. As fate was to have it, he was destined for the very same trenches as his son, for the same sector where Cecil's body still lay unidentified on the battlefield.

Part of the 38th (Welsh) Division, William was not involved in the opening throes of the Battle of the Somme, who were almost immediately summoned south. When the 10th South Wales Borderers arrived, they found themselves near Fricourt looking at an imposing obstruction. A dense collection of massive oaks, beech, birch and willow trees and thick undergrowth, so far Mametz Wood, set in a dip in the landscape, had escaped the wrath of the artillery. Firmly held by the enemy, Mametz was to become a haunting memory for Wales.

The assault for the wood was underway on 7 July. When the initial attackers were held up by machine guns and two assaults failed, William Dean's battalion were sent for. The 10th South Wales Borderers advanced through a maze of trenches that had been pummelled out of recognition as the guns were turned on the wood. Rain poured down and the men waded through thick mud until they were held up by machine guns. The troops were ambitiously ordered up again, but with his men scattered, soaked to the skin and exhausted, the brigadier cancelled the attack.

On 10 July attempts to seize the wood were launched on a grander scale. After two days resting in Mametz itself, William's battalion were sent in again. They reached the eastern end of Mametz Wood without too many casualties and began their advance 'with great vigour and dash', but as they continued to work on, resistance stiffened. Little groups of men tried to make progress despite 'savage opposition', but it was a lost cause. All that the brigade was able to do was organise a sketchy looking line running at a somewhat awkward angle. Mametz Wood was a baptism of fire to say the least. By 12 July it was ostensibly cleared of German troops, but at a huge cost. William Dean's battalion had never before suffered a major assault in such awful weather. Neither had they attacked such a strongly held, wooded position let alone attempted both of these feats at the same time. The 10th South Wales Borderers came away from its first large-scale action less 200 of its men. The Welsh Division has suffered a crushing 4,000 casualties. Having barely been at the front six months, the rebuilding now necessary would mean that it would not be ready to take part in another battle for over a year.

Nearby another wood was becoming synonymous with the wasteful attrition that seemed to have begun enveloping the battlefield. The ruined village of Longueval ran up to the fringes of Delville Wood, 156 acres of now battered foliage and tree stumps. Troops had reached the outskirts of the wood on the morning of 14 July, but not in sufficient enough numbers to try and take it from the enemy and it now formed a salient in the British line. Despite no longer having the element of surprise, the 9th Division, which included Chelsea player and the current manager's son, David Calderhead, advanced on the wood itself on the following day. Going in shortly after dawn a number of hours later they had managed to take all except the wood's north-west corner, which was strongly held by the enemy. But it quickly transpired that the problem was not seizing Longueval or Delville Wood, it was hanging on to them tooth and nail while the enemy flung every possible thing he had at them trying to drive them out again. The division was repeatedly bludgeoned as it attempted to hold onto the wood. The unfortunate South African Brigade bore much of the brunt, ordered to stay put 'at all costs'.[1]

Thousands of shells rained indiscriminately down on this single spot, at times at a rate of up to seven per second. Men became victims of their own artillery. The inside of the wood was so monstrous an environment that it had earned a nickname of the 'Devil's Wood'. A ferocious German counter-attack on 18 July was flung at exhausted troops. The enemy, although hammered for more than two weeks, had managed to get reinforcements up and by sheer weight of numbers they began with a fierce bombardment, forced their way back in the remains of the wood, into the village of Longueval beyond, until they were checked in the south-eastern corner of what remained of the trees and held back. By 19 July the South African Brigade was a mere shadow of what had been sent in four days earlier. Of over 3,000 men, fewer than 800 came out again. Another brigade was sent in to replace them with almost no time to prepare. A German unit opposite that had been 2,700 strong had now been reduced to less than 300 men. It became clear that to seize and hold Delville Wood was impossible on this scale. It needed to be a partial objective as part of a wider advance with support on either side. Another big push was being planned and the men of the Footballers' Battalion had been marked to take part.

The 17th Middlesex had been hard at work since its inception in Fulham in December 1914. Just after Christmas the battalion was about halfway to a full number of recruits and by 12 January some 600 men had assembled at White City, the site of much of the 1908 Olympics for training. Their high profile perhaps explained why they did not have to wait as long as some other units for their khaki uniforms, which arrived within a matter of days. At least nine players with connections to Chelsea were destined to be part of the battalion early on, but there were men representing a whole myriad of professional clubs including Arsenal, Aston Villa, Bristol Rovers, Cardiff City, Crystal Palace, Fulham, Luton Town, Manchester United, Millwall, Northampton Town, Nottingham Forest, Oldham Athletic, Plymouth Argyle, Queens Park Rangers, Southampton, Tottenham Hotspur and Watford. Impressively, at least half a dozen current players each from Reading, Brighton, Clapton Orient, Croydon Common and Grimsby Town had responded to the call for recruits. Special posters prompting men to enlist with slogans such as 'Do you want to be a Chelsea Die Hard?' went up at football grounds. Speeches were given in proximity to others, such as at Tottenham and Hackney, and by the middle of February the battalion was getting on for full strength.

Fans far outnumbered the players who could be seen conducting their route marches in and out of London's sights at this stage and Chelsea were contenders for the biggest contributors on this front, along with Orient. The *Chelsea Chronicle* believed at one stage that over 100 men had gone through Stamford Bridge to get into the battalion, volunteering at matches, obtaining the relevant information from the club secretary in the office and reporting to various enlistment locations. Many signed their attestation forms at Chelsea Town Hall or the battalion recruiting office at West Africa House, Kingsway, and Stamford Bridge locals were evident throughout the ranks of those that enlisted in the first six months.

One newspaper remarked that the men had taken to their incessant drilling 'like ducks to water',[2] but White City was far from luxurious accommodation. Neither was the food anything to brag about, such as in the South Downs battalions, if the rumours were to be believed. The adjustment to military life was trying for the volunteers reporting to the site in west London. Attempts were made to entertain the men, such as a cinema trip where they were able to watch footage of themselves on parade, but the tough monotony of their training led to disciplinary issues in the early days, as did the draw of the capital offering much more enjoyable pursuits than drill. Most of the men's transgressions revolved around the loss of freedom. Twenty-four-year-old George Collison was a dental mechanic. The fifth child in a large family, mostly of boys, they had scattered in their joint determination to go to war. As George, 5ft 5in and 'slightly pigeon breasted' popped up to Chelsea Town Hall, a short walk from both his home and Chelsea Football Club, to join the Footballers' Battalion in April 1915 and the other boys went off to the London Regiment, the ASC and the artillery, the family home was all but abandoned. George's disciplinary transgressions were typical of the local men coming into the regiment during their training: late back from leave, absent for parades, missing roll call and variously going walkabout for up to several days. Alfred Andrew, a rugged-looking furniture porter with imaginative tattoos of girls on his arms who also lived just by Stamford Bridge, was missing long enough to be struck off as a deserter before eventually reappearing. Punishments varied, being confined to barracks for example. William Daley, a 30-year-old husband and father, an earthworks excavator for the Underground, was simply 'admonished'[3] for a twenty-four-hour vanishing act, while 21-year-old William Tillbrook, who had enlisted in January 1915, forfeited a promotion for absence in the same month. Neither was the wandering confined to the fans. At least one Chelsea player was guilty too. Reserve goalkeeper William Krug, 21 years old, half a head taller than most of the recruits with a scar across the left side of his face, received field punishment number two for wandering.

If getting the recruits to stay still at White City and in their various camps as training developed was a challenge, the Chelsea men present were not angels even when the authorities could keep tabs on them. Twenty-two-year-old Richard Peters was a mechanic at a sewing machine factory, married with a baby son and living a few yards from George Collison. He had a habit of disregarding orders and not doing as he was told, while 27-year-old Fred Eastwood, a fitter's mate who lived next to Brompton Cemetery, was confined to barracks for eight days for 'unlawfully disobeying an order'.[4] Nineteen-year-old Albert Gilling, a carman who lived off Wandsworth Bridge Road, was reprimanded for urinating in an improper place, but he would have had to go some way to outdo what sounded like one outstanding night out for another recruit who enlisted on the same day. Twenty-eight-year-old William Goddard was a father of three living just along Chelsea Embankment from both Collison and Andrew. He had been absent on occasion, but his crowning glory came on 13 March 1915 when, still confined to barracks after a previous transgression, he committed a string of offences. Beginning with breaking out of barracks, on the same day he was also consecutively charged with drunkenness when he finally returned, urinating in an unauthorised place before finally using foul and abusive language on the sentry that caught him. Still afterwards he would be consistently missing from roll call, as well as being punished for bringing civilians into camp, overstaying his leave and refusing to obey an order.

On the day of the FA Cup Final in April, as Chelsea were preparing to face Sheffield United at Old Trafford and as Harry Trusler was sailing towards Gallipoli, long awaited orders arrived for the 17th Middlesex to leave London for the picturesque surroundings of Holmbury St Mary near Dorking. After further stints near Mansfield, by the beginning of August their shooting had begun on Salisbury Plain along with divisional training that included live exercises. The Footballers' Battalion was originally to be part of the 33rd Division, one element of the 100th Brigade along with a Public Schools Battalion of the Middlesex, a West Ham contingent of the Essex Regiment and a battalion of the King's Royal Rifles.

Orders arrived at the beginning of November to go abroad and the 17th Middlesex arrived in France in the middle of the month, heading towards Hazebrouck and then soon on to Bethune. On 8 December the battalion was transferred into the 6th Brigade, 2nd Division following a reshuffle of available units that took place following the debacle at Loos. William Krug, the goalkeeper, sent a postcard back to Stamford Bridge as the Footballers' Battalion made their way into the trenches for the first time on the 17th of the month, and as Christmas approached he and the rest of the battalion had begun acclimatising to life at the front.

The 17th Middlesex suffered early losses. The first was to meningitis, but it did not take long for the war to begin claiming lives. One of these was a boy soldier. Robert Joseph Harding claimed to be 19 when he enlisted on 4 March 1915 at Chelsea Town Hall. In fact, he was still 16 and appears to have got around the attestation form by listing his absentee father as his next of kin. At the end of January Robert was shot multiple times during a stint in the trenches and the still 17-year-old was buried at Chocques Military Cemetery. The famous amateur player Vivian Woodward's time with the battalion was also to be cut short. The Chelsea man had joined up in early September 1914 as a private in the London Rifle Brigade, an existing Territorial unit. Having also applied for a commission in the regular army, the time when his services were required came none too soon after the bloody first battle of Ypres and the development of the new army battalions. Woodward transferred to the 17th Middlesex at the beginning of February 1915 and was a company commander by the time they departed for the front. He was barely there eight weeks before a German bomb came flying into the Footballers' Battalion's lines and tore into his right thigh. It was originally thought to be a grave injury, but having reached home it was established that it would not necessarily put an end to his athletic career.

Without him, the battalion moved into snowy trenches at Festubert, the Chelsea men among them following in the footsteps of so many other Blues fans already. By the coming of summer the 17th Middlesex had become well versed in the inertia of trench warfare, livened up of course by as much football as their formidable team could get in their spare time. As the Battle of the Somme commenced, their division was raiding trenches and experiencing desultory shelling north-west of Arras, living a quiet existence by comparison, but this was not to last. The Middlesex Regiment would be more heavily engaged, in higher numbers than at any other point in the war on the Somme. Six battalions were in the vicinity of the battlefield on the opening day alone. At midday on 18 July an order arrived at 2nd Division Headquarters urging the Footballers' Battalion to be ready to entrain and join the Fourth Army on the Somme and two days later they did just that.

Delville Wood had by now earned the reputation of a monstrosity from those that had served within it. Bordered by roads, some of the northern part fell away down a reverse slope, giving the enemy the higher ground and a huge advantage, as well as a covered approach into Longueval. Full of lurking snipers, the trees, 'chiefly oak and birch, with dense hazel thickets',[5] were nothing but a mangled mess of remains punctuated by dead stumps:

> torn and blasted by the awful avalanche of shells, which fell on them continuously. Gaping shell holes were everywhere evident; the trenches in many places were shallow, mere excavations, insufficient to protect the troops crouching in them from the lurking snipers who, hidden by the horrible debris thrown about in all directions, crawled to within 20 yards in the hope of finding a target in some incautious officer or man. In parts of the wood, patrols, and even single men, of the opposing forces were hunted or stalked, one by the other. The air was thick with a horrible stench from dead bodies and the pungent odour of gas. 'The Devil's Wood' was indeed a terrible place.[6]

The 24 July was a dull and cloudy day, riddled again with heavy artillery fire on both sides. Whispers of German troops massing for a counter-attack proved accurate and they advanced on the wood again from the north-west. Their efforts were thankfully brought to a halt and at 3.45 p.m. Sir Douglas Haig arrived at Querrieu to see both French and British commanders and insisted on the importance of consolidating the positions already held and of clearing Longueval and Delville Wood of enemy troops. In place of the 3rd Division, the 2nd, including the 17th Middlesex, was called up to take their turn inside the remnants of the wood. Orders arrived at headquarters just before midnight. The 6th Brigade, and with it the Footballers' Battalion, was to settle down in reserve and await their fate.

Destined to see action first, the 99th Brigade moved off immediately to take over Delville Wood, taking up a position early on the morning of 25 July. It was a perilous stance to be assuming and 'the immediate digging of very deep and narrow trenches'[7] was their utmost priority. They were heavily shelled. The 5th Brigade followed them up into the line and at 10.30 p.m. both were informed that the following day, the 27th, they would be expected to attack in conjunction with troops moving on Longueval and the surrounding area and that their part would be to seize back the rest of the wood. After a heavy artillery bombardment lasting an hour, the Brigade prepared on the 26th by pushing forward at 7.10 a.m., investigating their new surroundings and attempting to take prisoners, and also trying to mark the position of any machine guns or trenches among the battered foliage that might be manned by the enemy.

The following morning, four battalions attacked in two waves following a stiff bombardment of over 100,000 shells. The first wave rushed through the shaken Germans occupying Delville Wood and an hour later the second passed through their compatriots on their way further into the bedlam. They began furiously trying to consolidate their position under less opposition than they might have expected and the wood was largely back in British hands when men of the Royal Fusiliers pushed on and cleared the Germans en masse out of its northern section, taking nearly 200 prisoners. The Allies alone had had nearly 400 guns trained on Delville Wood throughout the day in an attempt to clear it, but the enemy was not about to back down. The German artillery too had no qualms about smashing the remains of the trees and undergrowth to pieces with artillery. Troops were being cut down by their own guns. The enemy had been anticipating a renewal of the advance on the wood, excitedly sending up false alarms in the preceding forty-eight hours in their eagerness to check it. German troops massed ready to carry out a bombing counter-attack and decimated the troops in their way. The two sides fought at close range, sniping at each other from shell holes and chucking bombs, the enemy moving up a given trench, bombing them with snipers supporting them on each flank. Pigeons arrived back at headquarters with messages begging for more bombs and they were dispatched with troops of the Royal Berkshire Regiment. All afternoon hundreds of guns continued to punish Delville Wood, Longueval and the surrounding area, including a dressing station attempting to evacuate and treat the wounded. The noise was terrific. The approaches to the area were being heavily shelled by the German artillery and in the frenzy it was proving impossible to get troops up to support those inside the wood.

The Footballers' Battalion, players and fans alike, spent 26 July digging and resting near Bernafay Wood, subjected to gas alarms as the Germans were using the monstrous shells further forward. Almost 900 men of the 17th Middlesex watched more than two dozen aeroplanes buzzing like wasps, crisscrossing, diving upon each other in the evening, under orders to move at short notice should they be needed to support 99th Brigade's attack on Delville. As early as 11 a.m. on the 27th the battalion received both news that that brigade was in need of assistance and orders to reinforce them in trying to drive the Germans out of the wood. Gathering up rifles and equipment, the Chelsea men among their number prepared for their most daunting task yet. Off they marched via Montauban and Trônes Wood towards the hellish bombardment going on in front of them, the crashing of artillery shells becoming louder and louder as they approached the fierce fighting ahead.

As the men of the 17th Middlesex trudged towards the battle, weighed down with bombs and petrol cans full of drinking water to share out with those already inside the wood, they had been given some intimation of what to expect from their brigadier in the shape of a memo earlier in the month. It was designed to try and prepare them for the horror that he knew they were about to face on the Somme and he had ordained that its contents be reiterated down to the last man. 'The fighting in which the Brigade will soon find itself involved has now reached a stage closely assimilated to open warfare,' he began, 'though many features pertaining to trench war such as bombing and trench mortar work still constantly recur.'[8] This was going to be very different to their experience of war so far. 'The long period of trench warfare to which we have grown accustomed has led us to forget, to a great extent, those principles of mutual support (and above all covering fire) which should be restudied by all.'

There was no military sense, however terrifying the prospect, in the likes of Teddy Foord, William Krug and the fans who had followed them to war trying to hang back from the artillery bombardment that would be crashing down about their ears. 'It must be impressed on all ranks that they must be prepared to accept the risk of casualties from our own shell fire and to advance as closely as possible to their objective under our own artillery barrage. Casualties will possibly be caused by our own shells,' he instructed clinically, 'but the general result in nine cases out of ten will be a successful assault and a great saving of life to our own men.'[9] 'There comes a moment,' he continued, 'when the artillery must lift and this is the psychological moment when success or failure hang in the balance. If the infantry are close up and can rush in at once before the enemy has time to man his defences and machines all will be well.' He had gleaned this doctrine, he claimed, through lessons learned by Britain's allies. 'This is the secret of the French successes. The reason why so many of our attacks, in the past, have failed, is that the infantry have been too far from their objective at the moment of the artillery "lift" and in consequence have been caught in the open by concentrating machine gun fire before they could get to grips with the enemy.'

Despite the clear emphasis that had been made in training on the static life of trench warfare that the Footballers' Battalion could expect, more mobile methods of fighting had not been entirely neglected and it was imperative that they now remembered the essence of these as they went into the unpredictable fight for Delville Wood. 'In addition to covering artillery fire, no forward movement against an unbeaten enemy should be undertaken (unless the nature of the ground absolutely prohibits it) without strong covering rifle, machine gun and Lewis [gun] fire.'[10] They must not get overexcited once they arrived on the scene. The battalion must remain clinical in the process of ejecting the enemy from the wood, the brigadier claimed:

All positions captured must be at once put into a state of defence. Battalion commanders must always have pick and shovel supply in mind. Counter attacks are inevitable. If the infantry are well protected and Lewis and Machine guns are well cited, with plenty of ammunition, the more the enemy counter attacks the better. Killing Germans is more useful than occupying ground.

They must also remain alert to all of the dangers that modern warfare could throw at them that their training could simply not prepare them for the real terror of: 'The enemy has been making extensive use of gas shells,' the brigadier reminded them. 'Gas helmets must always be ready for use.'

The men must attempt to keep their heads. 'The adequate supply of ammunition for Lewis guns is likely to present serious difficulties. Their particular value probably lies in repelling counter attacks. Lewis Gun fire in an attack must therefore be carefully regulated and waste of ammunition avoided.' There was one particular sticking point that he was keen to drive home:

> The very large number of officer casualties which occur is apt to seriously prejudice success. It is without doubt that many of these casualties are avoidable. Battalions should go into action with the smallest necessary number of officers – 3 in a company should suffice to start with – the remaining officers and a proportion of NCOs should be held in reserve.

The brigadier drove home his harsh point for the large contingent of professional footballers that were included in the 17th Middlesex's hierarchy:

> Officers must not take unnecessary risks. It is a very glorious thing to die for one's country, but much more useful to live for it and it is the duty of every officer, whilst playing his part to the utmost, to avoid becoming a casualty as long as possible.

He reminded them that they had nothing to prove:

> The British soldier thoroughly appreciates the fact that his officers are prepared to be killed first and it is not, at this stage of the war, desirable for an officer to go out of his way to give further proof of it … The men are well aware of their officers' courage and depend on them. Early casualties in officers mean more casualties in other ranks who become as 'sheep without a shepherd'.[11]

Reinforcements destined for Delville Wood were laden with ammunition and equipment, but the sheer volume of shellfire made it extremely difficult for the likes of the Footballers' Battalion, who were headed for the right-hand side of the wood, to get to those dwindling troops trying to cling on to the position. Finally, at 5.15 p.m. two companies of the 17th Middlesex and two of the 17th Royal Fusiliers managed to get through, though suffering heavily on the way up. At that time an air patrol was reporting that the wood was almost completely destroyed. Chelsea men began to fall as soon as the Middlesex battalion approached the battle, including Edward Stevens who lived off of North End Road. At the outbreak of war he rushed to marry his sweetheart. Within months the 21-year-old milkman had enlisted at Chelsea Town Hall and went off to war with her name tattooed inside a love heart on his arm. Edward survived barely long enough to reach the wood. He fell leaving behind his widow and an 11-month-old son. His body was never recovered.

The sheer ferocity of the shellfire being thrown at the wood was shocking for the new arrivals. Further back a pile of ammunition burned, struck by the German artillery; one gun team watched two men and two of their horses smashed to pulp. Despite the terrifying consequences of an encounter with one single shell of the thousands indiscriminately flying back and forth with no mind for killing their own men, it seemed it took little time for some to acclimatise, or simply give up one's nerves to the screech of imminent death raining overhead. A divisional artillery officer made a note in his diary of an encounter with a German who had already been shaken to hell inside Delville Wood:

> Two Tommies [were] bringing home a Boche prisoner when they ran into a barrage. Both the Tommies jumped at once into a trench, while the Boche sat on top of the parapet smoking his cigar and smiling. One of the Tommies shouted at him, 'Come down, you fool; you'll only get killed.' 'Why?' he asked. 'Well, can't you see your friends are putting up a barrage?' they said. 'Barrage?' said the Boche. 'Barrage! Do you call this a barrage? If you want to know what a barrage is like, go over to the other side'; and he pointed to his lines.[12]

Throughout the night the remaining members of the 17th Middlesex continued to relieve as much of a battalion of the King's Royal Rifles as possible. By midnight almost the entire Footballers' Battalion was occupying a position roughly in the centre of the carnage that was Delville Wood. By morning the vague outlines of what was transpiring as far as commanders were concerned had improved slightly and the 17th Middlesex were surrounded by machine gunners and men of the 2nd South Staffordshire Regiment as attempts continued to relieve the 99th Brigade. The north-east corner of the wood remained unsatisfactory at daybreak as the shelling went on and the situation remained confusing. At 7.40 a.m. a message from the Footballers' Battalion arrived at headquarters reporting German troops massing at the east end of the wood for what might be a counter-attack. The response was to bludgeon that spot with yet more shells. By mid-morning they were advising brigade commanders that the enemy had penetrated far inside the remains of the trees and the South Staffordshire Battalion were coming under increasing pressure on their left from incessant artillery fire from the direction of Guillemont to the south-east.

The 17th Middlesex's brigade had been ordered to plan for an attack on enemy strongpoints that had been established in the east end of the wood, in conjunction with yet another planned heavy artillery bombardment. 'Every endeavour should be made to hold the wood'[13] was the instruction being handed down, but this hardly accounted for any impetus coming from the German side. By midday the brigadier, who had now assumed control of the area completely, was dispatching news up the chain of command of a horrendous barrage coming from the German lines, but no frontal attack. By early evening, though, a German prisoner was reporting that a counter-attack was being prepared for that night. As darkness came on, the South Staffords dispatched a pigeon to say that all was quiet on that point, but almost immediately the heavy enemy shellfire began to grow worse. Inside the wood, they and the 17th Middlesex began to send up distress signals. 'Soon portions of the trenches held in the wood were completely obliterated.'[14] Rapid rifle and machine-gun fire poured into the British ranks, but the artillery pitched in and the troops inside the wood dug their heels in and clung on. In the darkness the scene was one of utter confusion. Colonel Fenwick, the commanding officer of the Footballers' Battalion, their third already in the course of the war, was struck in the head and wounded. Edward Bell, a former Southampton and Crystal Palace player who would ultimately have responsibility for the battalion devolve upon him in Delville Wood, could not even figure out if his own men had been attacked.

By 11 p.m. the incessant noise of rifle and shellfire had died down. In the chaos no return on casualties was ever furnished by the battalion, but those with a Chelsea association had been hit hard. Henry Woolger, a hairdresser whose family were originally from Bishop's Stortford, had enlisted as a 22-year-old and was among those killed, as was Norman Wood. A Stockport player, the 24-year-old had been on Chelsea's books and he too fell at Delville Wood, leaving an illegitimate son less than 2 years old. Some vanished into the mangled remnants of Delville Wood and were never seen or heard from again, such as Percy Polley, a porter at a hat-maker's who left behind a widowed mother who lived less than two minutes walk from Stamford Bridge. She had to wait a year for the 23-year-old to be officially certified as having been killed in action. Charles Colam was a tall 20-year-old, a car examiner on the railways who had walked up North End Road from his large family home to Fulham Town Hall to secure his place in the 17th Middlesex. Charles had already been wounded in May but had stayed on with the battalion. His father had to wait nine months for the crushing news that his boy too had fallen on 28 July. Men were wounded and suffered in agony on the battlefields of the Somme. A fraction older than Charles Colam and in the same company, Cecil Selley lived just yards away from him in Fulham. A pianoforte tuner, he had enlisted comparatively late, at the end of May 1915. Cecil had already been wounded, in a way, suffering the ignominy of a hospital stay at Rouen when some of his fellow soldiers proved that their early rebellious streak was not fully behind them at the front. His eye was lacerated by a flying lump of bread in a food fight. Cecil was hit in the pelvis as the battalion attempted to cling to the remnants of the wood. He was comparably lucky to some who suffered unattended, in that it was possible to evacuate him back to a casualty clearing station, but the 22-year-old did not survive the day.

The struggle for Delville Wood finally abated, at least for the time being, but the reprieve would prove to be short-lived. The South Staffords had been decimated and just before dawn, 2nd Division HQ received a graphic report from the Footballers' Battalion. 'Heavy artillery has smashed our front line. I am holding ... but very [weakly] Enemy putting on terrific barrage.'[15] On 29 July the 17th Middlesex's ordeal was prolonged. It proved to be another hot, clear day of sticking it out, for again both the enemy's guns and those of the British artillery poured an endless stream of shells onto the wood. That night a battalion of the Essex Regiment moved in and relieved the tired-out Middlesex Battalion, who took over a support line further back. More than 200 men had been killed, wounded or were missing. In their place the Essex men, as and when they could manage it, were to patrol the shattered woods with the aim of picking off and bringing in as prisoners any enemy troops they found lurking among it. As much digging as possible should be carried out, in the main a communication trench to make movement easier back towards Trônes Wood.

George Collison had managed to come through almost physically unscathed. 'We were in a place, which no doubt you have read of in the papers, Delville Wood,' he told his mother, 'and the Germans shelled us to Hell for 48 hours and the sights were terrible, after that there was 17 hours bombardment by our artillery ... it is merely murder if you show your head, you are instantly sniped.'[16] He had been involved in brave shenanigans with little regard for his own personal safety. 'I was in a communication trench when a shell dropped in,' George told his mother. 'It killed one and wounded two. I caught the shock of it and my ears and nose bled, and I was properly dazed for a few hours.' Despite this he began pulling numerous wounded men out of harm's way. 'I am not bragging ma, but I know you would like to know what I was recommended for. It was for good work,' he wrote home:

I helped bring an officer in, what was lying wounded in the open. Then myself and [a] pal volunteered to get him to the dressing station through the wood which was being shelled. We got the officer there and started back, when a shell dropped a few yards off us and wounded my pal in head, arm and leg. I got him in a shell hole and cut his equipment off and coat and bound him up and got him into our own trench.

He was pragmatic about his actions:

Anybody would have done the same in the circumstances. I also got a wounded German in and he gave me his cigarette case as a souvenir ... What is London looking like now, I wonder when I shall get the chance of coming home. Au revoir for the present.

His actions were brought to the attention of the divisional commander. 'Your commanding officer and Brigade commander have informed me that you have distinguished yourself by conspicuous bravery in the field on 29th July 1916,' he told George in a note sent down the line. 'I have read their reports and although promotion and decorations cannot be given in every case, I should like you to know that your gallant action is recognised and how greatly it is appreciated.'

Chelsea's players had not fared badly, all things considered. William Krug was lightly wounded at the beginning of August, but otherwise unhurt. Teddy Foord, a local boy who still played in the reserves, had enlisted at 19 despite already being married, raising his hand at the first gathering of what was to become their battalion. He had thus far survived the 17th Middlesex's first encounter on the Somme. The 30 July saw the battalion resting, a welcome relief. George Collison was startled by the lack of familiar faces once they reached relative safety. 'There is only a few of the old battalion left … there are 4 of my pals only in one platoon.'[17] It was, sadly, to prove just the beginning of his ordeal on the Somme. The Footballers' Battalion would get just a few hours rest before they were summoned again.

13

'All Ranks Behaved Magnificently'

The Battle of the Somme

As August approached the situation inside Delville Wood remained precarious. Whilst the Footballers' Battalion was withdrawn from the front lines to try and get some semblance of a break, the 13th Essex in their place were plagued by snipers. On 1 August a report was sent back to General Congreve, in command of their corps, to claim that only one battalion of the brigade was actually fit for any kind of offensive operations. That night the 17th Middlesex were taken even further away from the nerve-wracking confines of the wood, which was now held by just three companies laden with machine guns and lighter Lewis guns to drive off any attack. They were 'advised' that forty-seven reserves precisely would be arriving to reinforce their depleted numbers. The horror of the Devil's Wood had exacted its toll on the Footballers' Battalion. A number of the men were left unable to function. Fulham boy Cyril Dale claimed to be 19 when he enlisted. In fact, the teenager had craftily given his grandmother's address on Fulham Palace Road to muddy the waters as he was just 16 in March 1915 when he attested at Chelsea Town Hall. Joseph Norman, a 19-year-old gardener who lived by the gasworks, had also found the experience too much, as had Fred Brown, who lived with his widowed mother's employer along with the rest of his family. Having been a newsboy, by the time he enlisted Fred had taken a job as a booking clerk. He had carried out his training with the 27th Middlesex, probably on account of his young age, in an attempt to stall his military career and had not arrived to join the 17th until 1916. All three of these very young men had to be withdrawn from the lines with 'shellshock' after their experience in Delville Wood.

By the end of July, politicians in London were becoming nervous about the lack of any seemingly significant progress on the Somme in exchange for the casualty figures emerging. August was to be a depressing month on the battlefield as losses then continued to mount and the pressure to eke out some kind of result from the 1916 summer campaign remained high. Sir Douglas Haig seemed aggravated by the lack of control displayed by his subordinate commanding the Fourth Army on the spot, Sir Henry Rawlinson. The senior man had issued orders for small, ineffective and localised assaults to stop, but the reality was that command had devolved down to a level lower than Rawlinson's, that as much as he might have wanted to oblige Haig, he had lost control somewhat. Haig was adamant that success lay in economically approaching an objective, wearing down the enemy and waiting for a point at which putting in reinforcements when the fighting reached fever pitch would make a decisive break. In this vein, by taking the village of Guillemont, Falfemont Farm to the south-east and Ginchy, the British could not only secure for themselves a better position for beginning a more general advance, but would also be able to help the French situated to the south of the River Somme. Nothing was to happen, he ordained, until 'the responsible commanders on the spot are satisfied that everything possible has been done to ensure success'. At the beginning of August, the French General Foch visited

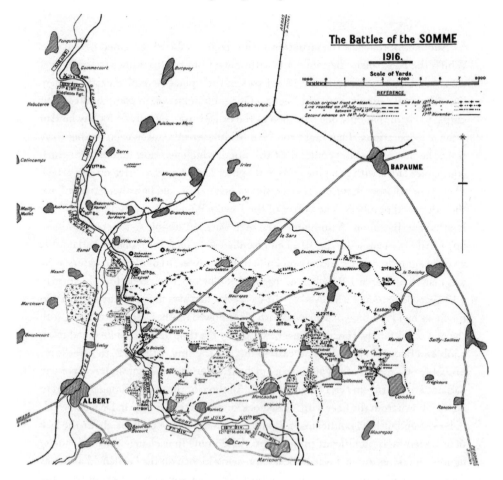

The Somme battlefield of 1916. *(THP)*

Haig and the upshot was that his men would be ready for a combined effort with the British with six days' preparation. Rawlinson worked with the French and they decided that on the 7th the British would attack Guillemont and the French would attack to the south. General Congreve, whose corps would carry out the attack, was never one to sit on his opinion and got on the telephone to say that owing to the weight of the German barrage currently on the area, his troops would not be sufficiently prepared for an advance until 8 August. Bearing in mind Haig's opinions about commanders being satisfied, he eventually concurred with the junior man's judgement.

Just hours after the 2nd Division left Delville Wood, orders arrived from Congreve to say that a new attack was to be undertaken to try and take Guillemont. His corps, comprising five divisions, began to readjust to be able to concentrate their attentions on the village and the surrounding area. Guillemont itself sat on the eastern side of Trônes Wood in between what had been the original German second and third line systems prior to 1 July. The buildings had mostly been flattened and afforded assaulting troops little cover. Reconnaissance had shown that here were few trenches within it as such, so it was more likely that the enemy would be lurking in dugouts and trenches on the outskirts.

Preparations began in force. Men began to dig a new trench specifically towards the village for ease of access, but all along the line battalions attempted to edge their positions forward wherever possible to give the men attacking an advantage when it came to restarting the offensive. Ammunition was gathered and the artillery continued to try and pick away at their counterpart German batteries to the east. In return, the enemy guns 'belched death and destruction'[1] day and night. The situation that the Footballers' Battalion, who would be attacking from a position to the south of Longueval, were facing was not encouraging. The enemy had brought up numerous reinforcements, numerous guns and strengthened their existing positions, so that although they were inevitably tired after the gruelling bombardments that they had been subjected to, the idea that they would be pushovers was far from true. When the attack was launched on 8 August the British were doomed to failure:

> The resources allocated were still not adequate to overcome the deadly combination of enhanced German defences, the open and enfiladed nature of the ground to be crossed by the assaulting troops and the increasing necessity of bombarding the whole of an area.[2]

Nevertheless, work continued for the men unfortunate enough to have been detailed to carry out this assault. The 17th Middlesex arrived on the front on the night of 5 August, taking over lines south of Longueval from the east Londoners in the Essex Battalion. Detailed orders were issued less than forty-eight hours later. Their division was to capture eastwards of Waterlot Farm, which lay about halfway between Delville Wood and Guillemont. They would move across to a road dubbed 'High Holborn' and then south towards the outskirts of the village itself the train station and the railway embankment, as far as a trench running across the northern limits of Guillemont, named, ironically for the Chelsea fans present, Brompton Road. They would be accompanied by men of the Duke of Cornwall's Light Infantry and by a company of sappers. Forming the left half of the attack, while the 1st King's Regiment attacked on their right, the South Staffords would be in support and the Essex Regiment in reserve further to the rear.

The attack was to be preceded by a hefty seventeen-hour bombardment of heavy artillery, which began with a vengeance at 9 a.m. on 7 August. The wrath of their guns was in part directed at the Germans to the east at a position dubbed Z-Z Trench by the British. The weaponry included forty eighteen-pounders and twelve howitzers, firing two or three rounds a minute for twelve hours. The British gunners also made six 'Chinese attacks' which were occasional flurries of increased fire to confuse the Germans about when the inevitable assault would come. They lasted for fifteen minutes, spouting a mixture of shells that jumped backwards and forwards furiously, implying that the infantry were about to burst forward. At 9 p.m. the artillery assault paused while the attacking troops got into position. Straightaway the Footballers' Battalion began sending out patrols to check the German trenches to see how strongly they might be held on the other side of Waterlot Farm. They came back with the worrying news that the lines were indeed full of enemy troops and that the bombardment appeared to have done little damage to their defences. The torrent of artillery then resumed at midnight, other corps guns also targeting the German lines, attempting to draw attention away from the front at Guillemont. The rampant shellfire continued all the way up to zero hour.

Specifically, the 17th Middlesex were to attack Z-Z Trench, east of the road running between Guillemont and Longueval. Once they had seized their portion of trench, they were to establish a defensive flank and then open fire in a south-easterly direction to assist the unit next to them. The Footballers' Battalion were to maintain this fire until twenty minutes after zero, unless they could clearly spot the neighbouring battalion and the situation dictated otherwise. They were to establish there a series of posts along Z-Z Trench and hold them as outposts rather than pack them out so as not to give the German gunners too big a target. Intermediate posts between Z-Z and Waterlot Farm were supposed to act as supports that would hopefully form a proper line that was eventually intended to join up to Delville Wood to the north.

An easterly wind threw dust and smoke from the German artillery's intense fire into the faces of the men waiting to attack. At 4.20 a.m. they climbed out of their jumping off trenches to crawl out in front and shortly after dawn the first troops got to their feet and went forward. Numerous conferences meant that all the way down to the rank and file, the men of the Footballers' Battalion had been vigorously schooled in their tasks for the day. The battlefield was cloaked in thick mist with visibility limited to about 10 yards, meaning that the troops could not actually see their objectives.

On the right of the 17th Middlesex, the King's lost direction coming out of the trench dug especially for the attack and ended up veering off to the south, missing crucial strongpoints that were to have eased the path of their advance once put out of action. Experience of attacking Guillemont and the surrounding area on 30 July had taught the British that it was a dangerous place to assault. On the approach of troops, it appeared that the enemy retreated into deep dugouts in the ruins of the village, with numerous entrances, and that after the initial wave of attack had passed over, they emerged carrying machine guns and caught them from behind. 'Many a hard won position had been lost again owing to neglect in rounding up the enemy out of his dugouts and shelters.'[3] This left the Germans able to shoot their attackers in the back; so much emphasis during preparation for the assault had been placed on the mopping up to be done by troops who followed the first waves.

Two flares went up as signals that the enemy's front line trenches had been taken. Both the Footballers' Battalion and the King's appeared, to officers waiting for news to the rear, to be doing well. Despite impressions, though, the commanding officer of the 17th Middlesex had decided that he wanted to wait for a runner to confirm that they were at their first objective, as so many lights were going up that it was confusing as to whether they were even British or German. He also sent a supporting platoon out to reinforce his troops. The first waves of the King's had sent a pigeon back with a message to confirm that they had reached initial objectives, but their commanding officer wasn't entirely clear as to what had happened. They had entered the nearest German line as planned and then reached the station on the northern outskirts of the village, their first two objectives. He thought his men had taken the third objective, which was the second German line, but he was going forward again himself to ascertain exactly what was going on.

To the south the neighbouring division had failed thus far to claim Guillemont itself. The Footballers' Battalion was in Z-Z Trench as planned, but were under heavy fire too, being mercilessly enfiladed by machine-guns and hit with bombing attacks. The situation was rapidly becoming incomprehensible to those trying to orchestrate it. Having found their portion of the trench empty when they jumped in, the front waves of the battalion had established a bombing post with a Lewis gun at the end of a German sap and had begun to make their way down it to gain touch with the 1st King's.

The 17th Middlesex became lost as to where they were. The green signalling flares that should have been shooting up to let them know that the troops around them had armed were absent from their allotted positions. They were even straining their ears to hear their fellow Brits bombing anywhere in the vicinity, but this bit of ingenuity yielded no results in the mayhem. Communications were dire. 'It is, I hope,' wrote the brigadier afterwards, 'realized that although messages could be sent back by pigeon, all messages sent forward from Brigade Headquarters had to go by hand from Bernafay Wood as all wires were immediately cut and with the constant barrage kept up, we could never be sure how long a message would take.'[4] The men of the Footballers' Battalion failed to get down to their objective and attempted to return to the original bombing post. The lone survivor who later came back said that he had found his fellow troops killed or absent and the trench full of Germans. Their party had simply evaporated.

The heavy enemy firepower was accounting for the Chelsea men of the 17th Middlesex. Young Joseph Norman, whose stint in Delville Wood had earned him a stay in a base hospital with shellshock, left the battlefield with a 'blighty'. The fragment of shell that imbedded itself in his right forearm was significant enough a wound to see him put aboard the SS *Stad Antwerpen* and sent home to London. Patrick Ronan, missed by his wife terribly, was not quite so fortunate. The 30-year-old father of two, a costermonger on the North End Road, had left 9-year-old Alice, 7-year-old William and his cart with his wife Annie in order to go off to war. The first generation of an Irish family to be born in London, it seems likely that the guarantee of a proper income was his biggest incentive for his joining the battalion, as getting anything to sell and thus making a living was becoming more problematic in Fulham as the war went on. Pat had already had a period away from the battalion in June when he was lightly wounded in the back, but at Guillemont he was hit more severely by a bullet to his left arm. Unlike Joseph Norman, though, he would not be seeing his family. Three weeks at a base hospital and Pat would be back at the front.

At 5 a.m. a runner shot into the 17th Middlesex's headquarters to report that the original attacking party had been entirely bombed out of their objective. The commanding officer promptly ordered A Company to send out half a dozen bombers and a handful of men with fixed bayonets. They were to go along an old trench towards an imposing German strongpoint, imaginatively known as Machine-Gun House, to meet up with the King's, who were supposed to have taken it as part of their second objective. Half an hour later his party had reached a corner near the spot, but couldn't get any further, although they were still attempting to bomb their way out of trouble. One single Lewis gun had managed to get back into Z-Z Trench so he sent another up to try and consolidate. In the assault on the village itself, troops had made some progress towards Guillemont before being held up by the rate of German fire. Those who got furthest forwards were stuck in isolated shell holes with no support, their front raked continuously by machine guns. This was to prove the extent of the success experienced in the advance by the division on Guillemont on 8 August 1916.

At 6.10 a.m. the headquarters of the 17th Middlesex received word that the relief party sent up by A Company was being heavily bombed back. It was now evident that all but one man who had entered Z-Z Trench from the Middlesex Battalion was dead or captured. They had tried to get in touch with the battalion next door, but could not raise anybody at all. The enemy were now coming out from behind Machine-Gun House so that the 17th Middlesex had had to settle for garrisoning the furthest point they had reached to attempt to cling on. The day before, their commanding officer was informed that the South Staffordshires in the brigade had been told to keep up with events, so that if the Footballers' Battalion called upon them they could go to their aid of their own accord and just report in later to say they had gone forward to assist them. This extreme step was only to be used if it looked as if speed of communications was compromised and if it looked like following the normal channels through brigade headquarters would endanger the likelihood of success for the battalion. The situation had unfolded in just this sort of manner and the 17th Middlesex now contacted the Staffords immediately to ask for two platoons and one Lewis gun to head to the northern part of the Footballers' Battalion front, just as word arrived that they were being pinned down by machine guns. Their commanding officer also immediately ordered that a machine gun of their own and mortars be directed at the offending weapon.

A Company was to suffer heavy casualties in their endeavours to help their fellow men. Twenty-eight-year-old Fred Eastwood, the fitter's mate from Ifield Road who had been one of those to struggle initially with military discipline, simply vanished on the battlefield and was never seen or heard from again. William Goddard, he of the colourful disciplinary record, was also killed. The 29-year-old father left behind three little girls, Emily, 6, Annie, 3 and 2-year-old Jessie. Edward Horwood was yet another youngster who had lied about his age to get into the battalion at the recruiting office in Kingsway. At the time only 17, the teenage chemist's assistant from near Battersea Park was closely associated with the Salvation Army. When he was killed on 8 August Edward had just turned 19 and left behind an already widowed mother and a host of siblings.

By 7.15 a.m., battalion headquarters was at a total loss as to what was happening in front of them, as no more information had come in and they remained still fixed on last known positions. Despite meticulous preparations to maintain them, communications were shot once again. Contact aeroplanes detailed to monitor progress from above couldn't see anything because of the weather, and flares, mirrors and lamps for relaying movements, along with bright tin discs that the men wore on their backs, likewise couldn't be observed through the mist. Commanders had become overly reliant on runners and pigeons. It took more than an hour and a half for any news at all to get through to the commander of 55th Division, whose men were gunning for the village itself. At 7.25 a.m. an erroneous message was received at one headquarters from an observation officer that stated that the Footballers' Battalion and the King's had met up. This was fed down to 6th Brigade, so at this point it was mistakenly thought that everything was moving along well. Further action was delayed by the isolated snippets of news, much of which contradicted the last message received. Reports came in after long delays, adding to the confusion. Somewhat pointlessly, at nearly 10 a.m. a note arrived to say that everyone that could have originally penetrated Z-Z Trench was gone, by which time the point was completely irrelevant.

Confusion remained rife across the battlefield and the fate of many of the Middlesex men on this date would never be learned. Sergeant Jack Cope was yet another father, a school caretaker by North End Road, born and raised in Fulham. Despite having a wife of ten years, whose name was tattooed in a heart on his arm, and a young son at home, the then 32-year-old had been one of the earliest recruits to make his way to Kingsway in January 1915. He vanished on 8 August and his wife Annie would have to wait, agonisingly, until July 1917 before the army accepted his death as having occurred during this action. Frank Albrecht was young, 22, but had an exemplary record and had worked his way up to the rank of sergeant. The clerk, who lived off the river on the way up to Eel Brook Common, like Jack Cope had joined early in January 1915. Having already spent time in a hospital in Rouen after a wound to the thigh, he had also been injured as recently as 1 August. He remained on duty, though, and for his trouble was another of the men of the Footballers' Battalion who disappeared on the 8th. His father, who worked at the local gasworks, would have to wait until May 1917 to have his youngest son's fate put in writing by the authorities, after a lengthy period of waiting and hoping that he might turn up alive and in captivity.

The 17th Middlesex had been ordered, albeit in a message that had been dispatched at 8.50 a.m. from brigade but only arrived nearly two hours later, to isolate Machine-Gun House to the south of them. They were then to bomb south again towards Brompton Road and Guillemont Station, where their neighbours the King's should have been waiting to greet them. This appears to have been the first occasion that they received the message, although brigade were sending it for the second time. As it was already getting on for 11 a.m. and as the message was again delayed, it was in fact given out a third time. The commanding officer had a bombing party that had already been sent out and he instructed them to carry out this order. They managed to get south of four deep dugouts which were to have been early objectives of the King's and to send some snipers into the ruins further on. The main barrier to their efforts was machine-gun fire coming from around the house itself. If the King's were inside the train station as they should have been, the Footballers' Battalion might have made touch, but they were not. The bombing party of the 17th Middlesex did manage to travel some 300 yards but hours before, at 7.15 a.m., a pigeon had arrived back at the corps loft with a message claiming that a large number of the King's had been annihilated. It appeared from reports that this might have happened as early as 7 a.m.

Three companies of the King's had indeed vanished. Later investigation appeared to reveal that they had been entirely surrounded by machine guns, in similar events to those of 30 July in the same spot, by troops from deep dugouts and tunnels wielding machine guns after they had passed over them. Artillery observation officers reported that the train station which they should have occupied as their second objective was surrounded on two sides by trenches occupied with Germans. What would the divisional commander learn from this grievous loss? That it was absolutely imperative for any attacking force to get across No Man's Land as quickly as possible in order to prevent the enemy bringing their machine guns into action. Very strong mopping up parties needed to follow the initial waves to flush out these dugouts before the enemy could turn them to his advantage. The remaining company of the King's had tried to go forward to do just this, but ended up back where they had started after suffering heavy losses. At Guillemont itself, 55th Division's troops were cut off, confused by a mass of smoke and the mist cloaking the battlefield. When a German counter-attack came, they were in no position to withstand it. Fighting hand-to-hand, clinging on despite a lack of drinking water, many of them carrying wounds and having run out of bombs and ammunition, they were finally overwhelmed.

Family lore has it that the Jerram brothers arrived home from Stamford Bridge one day, where six people lived crammed into two rooms near Eel Brook Common, having been swept up by patriotic fervour. The pair announced to their mother that they had volunteered to join the army at the match. She was apparently none too happy. Twenty-two-year-old Herbert and 19-year-old Sid were earning modest livings, the former as a packer in a wallpaper factory and the other working as a cook having abandoned an apprenticeship in cabinet-making, and it seems that the excitement of the war was too much for the boys to pass up. Despite the chagrin of mother Elizabeth, a widowed charwoman, they dutifully reported to Fulham Town Hall and side by side joined the Footballers' Battalion in April 1915. Elizabeth had already suffered the loss of a child when Herbert and Sid's 17-year-old sister died of tuberculosis while they were in training, and indeed her boys had already been through a fair ordeal at the front thanks to Delville Wood. The brothers went into battle side by side and Sid had a narrow escape, being struck lightly in the back on 28 July. He was evacuated back to a hospital for a short recovery period that ensured that the brothers, who had thus far experienced the whole of their war together, would never see each other again. On 8 August Herbert was fatally wounded and died at a casualty clearing station as the Footballers' Battalion attacked towards Guillemont. Sid was miles away at Rouen and Herbert died without him, but within a few days, the now 20-year-old Sid would have no choice but to get back to the business of war alone.

While Herbert was being evacuated the field of battle began to calm down. 6th Brigade received orders to continue the attack and any time after it got dark to wrap up all of the objectives that they had been given for the morning. The 13th Essex, the brigade's reserves, were to be thrown in the next morning and two companies of the South Staffords attached to the 17th were to help. The Footballers' Battalion were to organise a strong supporting party of bombers to help the Essex men try and isolate Machine-Gun House from the rest of the German defences. The general in charge of their division was not impressed and let his feelings be clearly known when he sent a report up the command structure to corps level:

I would like to point out that it is extremely difficult to organise attacks such as were ordered for and carried out on the morning of the 9th August, owing to the difficulty in relieving exhausted troops, or getting fresh troops up in sufficient time for the officers to know the ground and for the troops to have their objectives pointed out to them.[5]

It seemed to him a ridiculous notion:

> In a situation such as existed on the night 8th/9th August where it was impossible to know definitely what points were held by us and what points were not, the difficulty of arranging artillery bombardment and barrages, especially by night, was immensely increased.

At 2.30 a.m. the dubious attack commenced. An hour later the brigade's first attempt to carry the original objectives had failed. A second endeavour against this very strong position went again at 4.20 a.m. Bolstered by Lewis guns, they attempted to make a strong advance towards the right flank of Z-Z Trench. The enemy immediately layered a barrage on top of them. Thinking that the Germans were massing heavy numbers, twenty bombers and fifty bayonet men of the 17th, under an officer of the South Staffords, were sent forward to occupy a trench to the south-east of Machine-Gun House. He led the gallant party forward, but the Germans were firmly ensconced in their position. Plans were underway for a third attack when it was all abandoned. The 17th Middlesex were relieved that afternoon and marched back the following day to the ironically named Happy Valley. Further attempts to capture Z-Z Trench had cost nearly another 200 men. The 17th Middlesex's war diary recorded the events and stated that on 8 August 'all ranks behaved magnificently'.[6]

Responsibility for the capture of Guillemont passed out of the hands of the Footballers' Battalion and the Chelsea contingent among them. Troops at the southern end of the British Somme front had suffered for their initial success in the first half of July, launching further attacks from less than ideal, squashed conditions and maintaining the British army's difficult link with the French next door who had a different way of operating.

After a day in Happy Valley the 17th Middlesex began a journey that carried them by rail miles and miles from Guillemont, from the German artillery, lurking snipers, mangled trees and out the other side of Amiens. A week after the battle 716 new men arrived to join the surviving initial recruits, taken from almost every other battalion of the Middlesex Regiment, nineteen battalions in total. The Footballers' Battalion resembled less and less the one full of players and fans who originally flocked to west London to serve together. For now, the 17th Middlesex's part in the Battle of the Somme was over, but with campaigning still to do to try and push this massive British enterprise to a conclusion, it was only a matter of time before they would be dragged back into the fray.

14

'A Fair Chance of Success'

The Battle of the Somme

At the conclusion of their time at the southern end of the British sector on the Somme, the 2nd Division was transferred north in the middle of August to just south of Hebuterne, some 15 miles south-west of Arras. It was quiet in comparison to Delville Wood, but hardly danger free. The Footballers' Battalion took over a wide stretch of trenches, plagued by German trench mortars. On 22 August the 17th Middlesex entered them for the first time. The troops found their work varied. There were numerous patrols, one of which ended in a fist fight in No Man's Land for one battalion with their German counterparts. Mining activity was rife on this front too and there were nasty surprises when saps were blown in, in addition to intermittent shelling. At the end of the month the divisional artillery finally arrived having been left to languish to the south a while longer and began registering their guns on local targets. There were also plans to utilise gas in this area and a 'Special Brigade' was assisted by soldiers including the 17th, who carried up the noxious cylinders. There was a lot of improvement work to be carried out too, repairing trenches, reclaiming damaged fire bays and preparing dugouts. For all the efforts to improve their surroundings, though, nothing could be done about the weather. At the beginning of September the rain arrived and the churned-up ground in the trenches and the shell-ravaged surrounding area turned to a muddy swamp, inflicting misery on the men and causing their gas attacks to be abandoned.

The British Army on the Somme had now been underachieving at a huge cost for weeks. It has been said that August and early September was arguably 'the least rewarding and most utterly depressing chapter in the whole tragic epic of the Somme offensive'.[1] To the south, battle still raged for those familiar objectives such as Delville Wood and Guillemont, which were finally seized at the beginning of September, although the weather prevented any large-scale action during much of the beginning of the month. Another big offensive was planned for 15 September to attack part of the original German third line system. By this time, the enemy's unfinished position had been much worked on, but the British would be bolstered by the first use of tanks when they launched an attack near Delville Wood. Ten divisions went over the top, determined to have some effect on this grinding farce. London Territorials took High Wood, Flers fell, and after the misery of what had befallen the men recently, these gains were at least something to cheer about. The Germans were rocking on the Somme, but they had not given in yet. Despite the arguable success encountered to the south of the Footballers' Battalion in mid-September, it did not appear that a collapse was impending on the part of the enemy. And so it went on. Another attack on 25 September had the limited aim of mopping up some objectives that had gone begging on the 15th, the role of tanks evolving so that they now moved behind the advance to deal with problem points rather than leading it. Guedencourt, Les Boeufs, Morval and Combles fell.

The German line in front of the 17th Middlesex now had been attacked on 1 July. Troops made some headway but eventually had to withdraw right to their original positions again. There had been a complete stalemate while the offensive progressed further south. On 28 September, a conference was held and followed up by a visit from Haig with a view to planning for renewed offensives, signifying that despite the coming of autumn, higher command was still not through with the campaign of 1916. In the meantime, at Hebuterne the Footballers' Battalion continued about their daily routine. There was still patrol work, men nearby were mining, counter-mining and there were daring night raids on enemy trenches, all of it punctuated with enemy bombardments of both mortars and shell. Elaborate raids were planned in the middle of the month to take prisoners, ascertain who was opposite and cause as much damage to the German positions as possible. Original plans involved gas, complex bombardments and mines. Wind ruled out the gas, but successive raids were nonetheless effective despite the reaction provoked on the part of the enemy.

The 17th Middlesex went into the trenches near Serre at 11 p.m. on 15 September. The stint started off quietly, with the men attempting to repair trenches, but on the 17th it began to rain again, turning the trenches into a swamp. The battalions were about to send a patrol out when the Germans hit out. At 9.10 p.m. the enemy commenced a bombardment on their front line with 'minnies'. As many as eight mortars were in the air at the same time and in the immediate aftermath it was estimated that seventy trench mortars fell on the Middlesex front lines and on surrounding saps. Sid Jerram was having a hard time coping without his brother Herbert. He had now picked up a wound from a machine gun in his right side, back and arm, but his injuries would not be enough to keep him out of action for long: 17 September with its flurry of shells proved the final straw for the 20-year-old, at least for now. As the Germans continued to harass the battalion he had to be temporarily removed from the lines with shellshock. 'Our trenches were knocked flat ... there was gas too, killing and wounding a number of men.'[2] The battalion attempted to get a retaliatory bombardment to silence the German gunners, but it never materialised. The night calmed down after that and it was all over by 9.40 p.m. 'We immediately sent working parties up to commence re-digging the trenches damaged but the heavy rains made work extremely difficult.'[3]

The following day it was still raining hard and the trenches were in a rotten state. Working parties kept going all day in an attempt to get the trenches into a good enough condition for habitation. They were still hard at it in the early evening as darkness approached and the enemy suddenly began harassing them with trench mortars. They were being showered with gas shells. Newly promoted Lance Corporal John Clements had been an orphan for some years. He lived off of Lillie Road with his brother, sister-in-law and a collection of nephews and worked as a clerk for the Army & Navy Stores. He had missed the ordeal of Delville Wood because of a sprained ankle sustained returning from the trenches two weeks before, but had picked up a wound at the end of August. As the mortars unleashed their fire, eleven men, including John, flung themselves into the rear entrance to a nearby sap. At that precise moment the Germans blew a mine at a nearby tunnel and it filled with gas. All eleven men, including John, were fatally overcome by the fumes. Five more men were missing, six wounded and two more would die later of injuries sustained. Shortly afterwards the 39th Division arrived to relieve the Footballers' Battalion of their occupation in this tumultuous area.

The weather had now begun its inevitable decline towards winter. Still there was a mistaken belief that the Germans were wavering: hit them hard enough now and they might topple over. In this scenario, surely there was no choice but to press on before snow swept the battlefield, and try and push the campaign to a conclusion? Rain in October repeatedly delayed large-scale operations on the Somme, but that did not stop piecemeal scrapping from taking place, wasting both men and equipment for the sake of pitiful gains. Men who had already seen quite enough of the Somme were being dragged back into action, shattered battalions alongside raw new drafts. One young guards officer experiencing the war for the first time described the strategy as picking up a division and repeatedly throwing it into action until there was nobody left. The weather grew colder and wetter as the month progressed. The logistics of moving men and equipment, not to mention cumbersome guns, through liquid mud was a nightmare across this apocalyptic landscape where there was no colour, seemingly no living thing. As the mud got thicker and the rain got heavier the men's suffering escalated. In places there were wounded rotting alive in No Man's Land; the men went about their business at least knee-deep in the mire. Nobody was under the illusion, from Douglas Haig down to the rank and file, that the war would reach its conclusion in 1916. All that remained was to bring about a satisfactory end to the campaigning season and establish a sensible position ready for new attempts to come in 1917.

With the onset of November the state of the weather improved sufficiently in the eyes of those who called the shots to start contemplating a tail-end offensive on either side of the River Ancre, at the northern end of the Somme battlefield and including the area where the Footballers' Battalion was situated. There was, according to Haig, 'a fair chance of success'.[4] But the state of the ground already ravaged by rain remained appalling. After a period of attempted training in the morass, the battalion went back into the lines to the south of Serre on 22 October. Casualties were picked up just in the exhausting march to the line and in the 17th Middlesex's trenches, which they shared with the rest of their brigade, they were up to the waist in muddy water. About the trenches shell holes too were full of stagnant liquid and the relentless moving about had made the communication trenches ghastly. 'Reliefs took hours to accomplish and sometimes had to be completed in daylight, progress to and fro from the lines being painfully slow.'[5]

Any original planning for this front had been subsequently reduced in scale owing to conditions, until the coloured lines etched on a map as objectives were reduced from five to three. The German positions in the region around the Ancre were strong back on 1 July, but in the interceding months they had bolstered them even more, repairing damage and reinforcing them based on the knowledge gleaned from their sufferings further to the south during the summer. St Pierre Divion, Beaucourt-sur-l'Ancre and Beaumont Hamel, which were to be objectives, like the rest of the villages nearby, had been fortified and were fiercely defended by machine guns. In addition, at the end of October a whole division had reinforced the enemy's numbers on part of this front.

The men of the Footballers' Battalion wiled away the early part of the month clearing roads, carrying equipment and attempting to keep their camp remotely clean. On the 5th they entertained themselves with a football match against the South Staffords and unsurprisingly beat them easily. The following day they returned to trenches near Redan Ridge and spent their time cleaning and bringing up equipment for the attack, ladders, bridges and Bangalore Torpedoes for penetrating the enemy wire. By 10 November the 17th Middlesex were out of harm's way again when orders finally arrived for the next push. Even as they were issued, there was still some debate about whether or not the ground was in a fit state to allow any attack, despite dry weather and a cold spell that promised to harden the sodden ground. Additional pressure came about because commanders could not keep preparing the men and then standing them down. They either needed to go ahead, or seriously consider withdrawing them from offensives altogether for the winter and letting them rest. The following morning, in command of the relevant army, General Gough had consulted his subordinates sufficiently to allow his decision to send forth his men on Monday 13 November.

As decisions were being made by senior officers, the 17th Middlesex sent out their normal working parties. Meanwhile, the artillery of eight divisions, plus more from neighbouring corps, was being readied for their part in the attack. There was to be a fierce bombardment beginning at 5 a.m. daily in the run up to the action, which had already begun on the 11th. Siege batteries would pound away at a gradually increasing rate of fire for an hour, when they would suddenly release a flurry of shells and be joined by the lighter calibre guns. Fifteen minutes later they would all stop for one hour and then resume their normal daily programme. Doing this on the days preceding the offensive was intended to deceive the enemy as to when an attack was coming, as well as to damage the German front and cut their wire to pave the way for the infantry. Unfortunately the weather was so foggy on 11 November that it proved impossible to register their guns properly. It all pointed towards another postponement. The Germans answered the morning bombardment tenaciously, but when no attack materialised they stopped firing.

On the 12th the artillery repeated the exercise and the Germans answered with force again. The light was better and it was easier to register targets, concentrating on the three coloured, hypothetical lines that the infantry would be assaulting. Then the Gunners had to register the front line, 'which was no easy matter, especially as all the telephone wires were broken'.[6] Serre was in flames, with a torrent of shells coming down on it. 'All the rear communications, [observation posts] etc. were being shelled to blazes by the big stuff, and in retaliation the Boche put up two quite good barrages on to the White City and Redan Ridge.'[7]

The 17th Middlesex spent the day, 'Y' Day, finalising their preparations for the attack. This would be the first large-scale assault made by the Footballers' Battalion since Guillemont and Delville Wood, and planning was precise. The advance would take them up onto Redan Ridge, with two battalions going forward. Single-file columns, the men three paces apart with a distance of about 100 yards between each group, this phase would be carried out by the 13th Essex on the right and the 2nd South Staffordshire Battalion on the left. Due to follow the latter, the 17th Middlesex's platoon sergeants and junior officers had already walked part of their intended path under cover of darkness. At 11.15 p.m. they collected up their men and marched off. At midnight the men were issued with hot drinks and food before gradually getting into position. The code word 'Smith' was whispered back to divisional headquarters to confirm that everything had gone to plan. Owing to the awkward, wet conditions, the men climbed ladders and crawled out onto the top of the parapet ready to attack, fortunately obscured by mist and suffering no casualties. It was the only favour that the Footballers' Battalion would receive from the weather during the course of the attack. At 5 a.m. the siege batteries began what the Germans were beginning to assume was a routine bombardment of their lines. Forty-five minutes later, the rest of the allotted British artillery roared to life and at 5.51 a.m. the infantry showed their hand, getting up to advance across No Man's Land.

The assaulting companies of the 17th Middlesex followed the South Staffords on the left side of the attack in four waves. Thick fog hung over the battlefield and the Middlesex men couldn't even see No Man's Land. But this would not be allowed to dissuade the British troops from advancing, as they had been told that in this event they were to do so using a compass. 'But,' a senior officer pointed out later, 'marching by compass bearing as a peace manoeuvre is a very different thing to doing so under heavy fire.'[8] Dutifully the junior officers brandished their compasses as they trudged blindly towards Pendant Copse, their objective. So jovial at the thought of action were B and D companies it was alleged, that some of the men went forward playing mouth organs. There was nothing to be cheerful about in No Man's Land, though. Inches of mud greeted them. Constant shelling that the artillery had exchanged with their German counterparts had churned up the ground that they were attempting to advance over. 'Gaping shell holes and mine craters full of water were everywhere, making the crossing dangerous.'[9] The advance moved slowly, men wading through the mire. It was difficult for the troops to maintain their bearings and some of the South Staffords advanced too closely under the artillery barrage and found themselves cut down by British shells.

Towards the southern end of the sector the attack was met with some success, but in the north, where the Footballers' Battalion had been sent forward, things were not going quite so smoothly. Men were either scythed down or forced to cower in shell holes as the bullets rained overhead. Communications were beginning to go awry in the miserable conditions. The Royal Flying Corps was unable to render assistance as intended, not only because they could not operate through the mist, but because they were drawing the wrong conclusions from flares thrown up by the Germans that were the same colour as those being lit by British hands. On the ground, the well-intentioned compasses were proving inadequate to keep the assaulting battalions on track. The first information that 17th Middlesex headquarters received was a long time coming. Then at 7.20 a.m. a company commander arrived wounded and revealed that the attack was confused, and that all manner of units had become mixed up in front of the German lines. Troops had marched across each other in the fog, the 8th Brigade drifting south first across the South Staffords and then across the 17th Middlesex before turning back and retiring. The men could not figure out where they were or what they were supposed to be doing. The Footballers' Battalion began to swerve north-east. During the morning the men were scooped up and formed into two composite battalions, the Middlesex were mashed together with the South Staffords and some of the King's under their own commander and placed on the left of the attack, a total of about 300 men.

While the neighbouring brigade was able to go on with their advance towards a final objective at 7.30 a.m., word did not filter through until half an hour later that the 17th Middlesex and their 6th Brigade compatriots were not in a position to do so. B Company were held up on wire, as was A Company, and both were thoroughly baffled by the mist. D Company had not fared much better. In the meantime the timed artillery barrage was leaving the exhausted men behind as they struggled through the mud and came to a halt. The wire in front of the German line had not been cut at all it seemed, and the enemy's ground was a sticky morass into which men sank, sometimes up to the waist. The whole nightmare scenario was finished off by machine-gun fire that opened up as the barrage vanished into the distance and the Germans rose from their dugouts and enfiladed the wire as the assaulting troops scrambled about looking for a way to drag themselves through. The men ran out of bombs and their rifles became clogged with mud and unusable. All they could hope to do was thrust the bayonet at any man who got too close. Along the Middlesex front, with officers falling, those that remained began to contemplate rounding up the handfuls of men they still had and retiring.

On the Footballers' Battalion's right the 13th Essex, followed by the King's were not doing much better. For two hours brigade headquarters had heard nothing until the former's commander sent out two officers to investigate. They spied a few friendly troops in the German front line and a large group huddled behind a small bank in front of the British wire and pinned down by heavy small arms fire. Other men had fully infiltrated the German lines. Isolated pockets of them were disconnected from each other and finding it impossible to hang on against snipers and bombers. Gradually they began to withdraw. In front of the Middlesex Battalion the Staffords were still held up by wire too. Officers desperately tried to find gaps, but the mist obscured everything and left them vulnerable to machine guns. Some men on the battlefield simply threw themselves into shell holes and stayed there instead of attempting to get forward, hiding from the sight of not only the enemy but their own officers. ('I do not for a moment imply that this is the case to any great extent,' wrote their divisional commander after the battle, 'but it is a difficulty which we have got to face and I am taking steps to see what we can do to overcome it.'[10])

Among the majority who stayed exposed to German fire, casualties within the ranks of the Stamford Bridge locals had been high. Albert Drury was a 34-year-old company sergeant major and a domestic servant in peacetime. Resident near Parsons Green Station, he died of his wounds at a casualty clearing station at Fournès on 14 November leaving behind a wife, Clara. With D Company, who had ground to a halt at the uncut German wire, Pat Ronan had spent two weeks in hospital after sustaining his wounds at Guillemont, rejoining the battalion at the end of August just after they had entered the lines at Hebuterne. He fell on 13 November and was buried at Mailly Wood Cemetery, but not before a blood-stained final letter that he had received from his loving wife Annie was removed from his pocket. It revealed just how sorely she missed him: 'I feel very sorry that the [leave stopped]. Can't you put it to your officer dear about your [leave] … what with the weather out there and being out there all this time with no [leave].' She was having a hard time making ends meet back home, a few yards from Stamford Bridge. 'All the shops shut at 8'o clock and all the barrows [have] to be cleared too, and at 9 o'clock [on] Saturday.' As much as his absence saddened her, she couldn't help but think that the front was the best place for him. 'No wonder you joined the army for this game is too much worry. Ben tries all he can, but don't seem to get any stuff at all. I did hear we are going to be served out tickets for our food.'[11] His enlistment might have been a financial necessity for the sake of their young family, but that didn't alleviate either her loneliness or her concern. 'Well Dear I hope you will keep well as I know you suffer with your chest. [The children] send their best love and all at home. Well Darling I must close with best love to you my love. From your ever loving wife Annie.' The bottom of the letter, returned to her for safekeeping, was smothered in kisses. Other than that, all Annie, who now had two children to try and raise alone, was left with was a card telling her the nearest rail station to Pat's grave if she was ever able to afford to go, his medals and the obligatory death plaque and scroll.

At about 9 a.m. on 13 November the remnants of the brigade were ordered to withdraw to the British front line and reorganise. At that moment only seventy-nine men could be found and a 2nd lieutenant took charge of them. The divisional commander wanted to continue the attack, but Brigadier Daly told his superior that his battalions, including the Footballers' Battalion, were wrecked and could not. He suggested instead to the senior man that it should be fresh reserves sent forward. He also advised that they not advance against the same front, but to the immediate north of it, attacking from the south-west and enlarging a gap that now existed in the enemy wire. As it transpired, all of that would be a job for new troops the following day. Of the original attackers, by midday, although they had captured a swathe of prisoners, the brigade had only made a small dent in the first objective and not on the Middlesex front. Even those troops that had managed to permeate the objective had their flank in the air, exposed to the enemy.

The 2nd Division's commander wrote a report that revealed no small amount of frustration as to the day's events. He attributed the failure mainly to the uncut wire which had held his men up, but this, like the mixing of troops that so confused the advance, was down to the mist. 'I can't help thinking that there were far more gaps than were seen or reported [in the wire], but … fog prevented them from being seen,' he wrote. 'In fair light they could be spotted from a distance. Whenever men could be seen in front getting through others behind would follow but the fog stopped all that.'[12] He recommended in future that if fog or darkness was to be encountered on the battlefield, then the amount of ground to be covered should be reduced accordingly to avoid confusion.

To the south, both divisions had met with success, seizing Beaumont Hamel and hundreds of prisoners and advancing well towards Beaucourt-sur-l'Ancre. In contrast, on the other side of the 2nd Division, beside the 17th Middlesex, men had been compelled to abandon their gains. In command of the whole collection of troops, General Gough was of the opinion that a renewed attack might point towards success. He'd need to reinforce though if it was to carry through, but he, somewhat optimistically, was of the belief that he could make this happen with the same corps on a significant front of 3,300 yards the following day, from Beaucourt to the slope of Redan Ridge facing Serre.

The remaining men of the 17th Middlesex had retired, although they were far from out of danger. Shells fell on them and the trench that they had ended up in was in such a shocking, saturated state that they were forced to climb out and move about on top of it in the open. The overwhelming, depressing characteristic of the battle was the disappearance of so many men, seemingly without a trace. 'Reports of individuals are so conflicting,' wrote the divisional commander, 'that it is impossible to give any accurate information as to what actually took place.'[13] He was disturbed with how much of a sham evacuating the wounded had been. In retrospect he had recommendations to make, 'having special parties left back well in rear to deal with the collection and evacuation of wounded in the forward areas'. He attributed the chaos to the fact that the division was weak in numbers when it went into action, 'and the number of infantry which could be spared to supplement regimental stretcher bearers was insufficient. If a labour, or other battalion could be earmarked for this duty and parties sent up from it after dark, much suffering could be saved.'

As it was, many of his men had simply been left on the battlefield. A and C companies had suffered conspicuously and dozens of men were unaccounted for. Sid Jerram, who had returned to the battalion in time for the battle following his shellshock diagnosis, was among the missing and was later revealed to be in a German prisoner of war camp. He had been wounded for a second time and would be treated in an enemy hospital at Cambrai for multiple gunshot wounds to the back and arm. He later recalled that as he was falling backwards to the ground, wounded, all he felt was an overwhelming sense of relief that this might actually bring about an end to his war. Twenty-one-year-old John Ford, a machine hand from Sands End who had enlisted on Valentine's Day 1915, was found to be taken prisoner, although it would be nearly six months before his father John Sr was reassured that he too was safely in a German camp. Likewise, Peter Haggerty, a labourer who lived with his wife and three sons in a single room off of the King's Road, had been taken into captivity. Others were not so lucky. William Norman, a baker from Harwood Terrace, had been one of the first to enlist in the battalion. He was reported missing on 13 November, but the only confirmation that arrived from the enemy in the aftermath was in the summer of 1917, when they revealed that they had buried him. William Page was a 26-year-old fishmonger from Wandsworth Bridge Road who had a 6-week-old baby son when he enlisted in early 1915. He too was first stated as missing, but later it was revealed that the Germans had also buried him. He left behind wife Mildred, 4-year-old William and 1-year-old Dorothy when he fell.

George Collison, by now a corporal, had come through the engagement at Guillemont physically unscathed. He had been in hospital for most of October suffering from illness and only rejoined the battalion three weeks before their assault at Redon Ridge. He was doing far better than his elder brother Jim, who was about to be discharged and placed in a home where at the age of only 27 he would be destined to spend the rest of his life institutionalised. Shot in the back, with residual damage to a kidney, he was prone to bouts of hysteria and was irrevocably scarred by his experiences in the London Regiment. With shrapnel imbedded permanently in his body, he was housed first at Roehampton and then Chepstow after the beginning of the Second World War. His life wrecked by his experiences on the Western Front as a young man, and after more than half a century in residential homes, Jim eventually passed away at the age of 83.

George's fate was nowhere near as drawn out when he vanished on 13 November, but was still agony for his family. They appealed to a local Chelsea figure, Lady Mellor, for help in finding out what had happened to him. After making enquiries on their behalf she received a sad letter on behalf of Lord Lucan at the Red Cross. 'I regret to say our first news … is terribly sad,' it began. They had managed to locate a private of George's company recovering on a hospital ship and he described the day's events. 'I went over with Corporal Collison and saw him struck by two or three machine gun bullets.'[14] The men were at the time lying along a ridge with a sunken road behind them. Had George stayed down, he might have been saved. But confused and disturbed, the 25-year-old staggered forward seemingly unaware of his actions and found himself in full view of the Germans on the other side of the ridge, heading towards their barbed wire entanglements. He was hit again almost immediately. A Private Crompton crawled out to rescue him and managed to pull George to safety. Then orders to retire came and he left George with two other wounded young men and backed away towards the safety of the sunken road. The Red Cross were not hopeful that he would turn up in captivity, although the Germans had come out to collect the wounded and it wasn't impossible that they might have either cared for him or buried him. No further news came to light and George Collison did not see London again as he had hoped. He was never heard from again and was commemorated on the Thiepval Memorial along with 70,000 other men who vanished on the Somme.

The Footballers' Battalion's contribution to the shattering offensives of 1916 was over. On the morning of 15 November a battalion of the Royal Fusiliers arrived and relieved the 17th Middlesex who withdrew into a support position. By mid-afternoon they were back in Mailly, where the following day they climbed into lorries and turned their backs on a horrific four-month induction into fighting the Great War. In their absence a last attack went forward on 18 November in freezing conditions under a veil of sleet and then, finally, the Somme campaign drew to a close. Britain was now resigned to spending at least another year at war. Across all combatants, the nations involved had accumulated over a million casualties since July, over 400,000 of them British. Some 131,000 of those were dead. Sadly for all those in khaki, this was by no means the end of it:

> The sanguinary struggle which raged from 1st July to the middle of November 1916 was but the prelude to further and bloodier contests, in which the numbers of troops and guns employed on both sides increased beyond the wildest dreams of pre-war strategists – heedless of the terrible cost in lives of men and material.[15]

15

'Fatherless Little Ones'

The Battle of Arras

Born at Canning Town in January 1883, Robert Greenhalf was the first of what would be eight children for Robert Sr, a boilerman, and Margaret, a match-maker. Little Robert's father, however, went by his stepfather's surname, Whiting, and his firstborn would continue the tradition. 'Bob' Whiting's mother died when he was 17, leaving his father with a large family to take care of. Bob was old enough to work and along with his next brother Edward was employed as a dock labourer in the East End. Two years later Bob found a job at the Thames Ironworks & Ship Building Company and became a member of the Ironworks' football team, which had just evolved into West Ham United. At 6 feet and a solid 12 stone it was unsurprising that Bob found himself in goal. Having learnt his trade in the reserves, he moved on to Tunbridge Wells Rangers before being spotted by Chelsea during a FA Cup tie. In the spring of 1906 Bob, now 23, was signed up as a second goalkeeper. As the next league campaign began, the regular first-team keeper, Micky Byrne, was injured in the opening game of the season and Bob, known as 'Pom-Pom' after a rapid firing naval gun on account of his kicking ability and also noted for his fierce punch, worked his way into the first team. He was ever present in goal before transferring to Brighton and Hove Albion. In the meantime he had married Nellie, a Kent laundrywoman, in 1907. A son Robert was born in March 1908 and another, William, followed in September 1909.

Bob was still with Brighton at the outbreak of war, on his way to making over 300 appearances for the club when the Footballers' Battalion was formed in December 1914. Nonetheless he joined at Kingsway on 31 January with a handful of other Brighton players. Travelling up from his home in Hove, the 30-year-old wrote across the top of his attestation form: 'I wish to allot my pay to my wife.' He was among the ranks of the 17th Middlesex when they departed for the Western Front at the end of 1915 and began his introduction to war along with his fellow players and the fans that had rushed to serve with them. In December Bob wrote back to Albion. 'I daresay it has been rotten not having or seeing any football. There is plenty out here and we are receiving challenges every minute of the day but we are too good for them all.'[1] It was going to take quite some team to beat this competitive group of professionals in their leisure time. 'They are trying to pick a team out of the whole army out here to play us, so it will be a big match, though I think we are certain winners.' Meanwhile he was busy becoming used to a soldier's life:

> We are having some exciting times in the 'big match' out here. It is great sport to see our airmen [soaring] … Going great guns in the French language out here, quite a genius at it. I hope this will find you and all old friends at Brighton in the best of health as it leaves me at present. Am looking forward to be playing next season with the old club.

Bob Whiting was not present when the 17th Middlesex went into action during the Battle of the Somme. In the spring of 1916 he contracted scabies thanks to the squalor of the trenches and was evacuated home. On 23 May he was admitted to a military hospital at Brighton for treatment. Released a week later, the thought of returning to the front and leaving his wife and his boys was too much. Bob went absent without

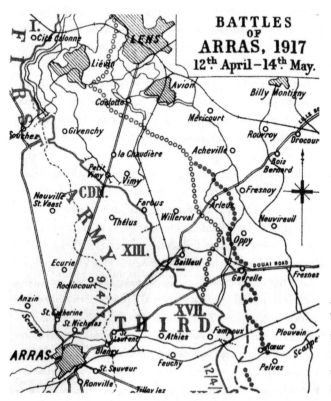

Arras – where Bob Whiting would go into battle with the 17th Middlesex in the spring of 1917. (*Authors' collection*)

leave. As the summer wore on, the situation grew worse as Nellie transpired to be pregnant for a third time. The police finally caught up with Bob in October 1916 and he was arrested after being unaccounted for 133 days, allegedly telling the detective sergeant that he wasn't fit to be at the front and citing his hospitalisation. On 18 November, five days after the Footballers' Battalion fought at Redon Ridge, Bob was shoved back on a transport from a military prison. Docking at Boulogne he was sent on to Étaples for four days before rejoining the battalion for the first time in more than six months. At the end of February 1917 Bob Whiting was finally subjected to a Field General Court Martial at Albert. He was sentenced to nine months' hard labour for absence on active service, but the sentence was suspended shortly afterwards. Bob rejoined the battalion days after Nellie gave birth to their third son, Joseph. Back at the front he was about to witness the horror of battle when the 17th Middlesex were called upon to help try and push the war towards a conclusion in 1917.

Almost as soon as the Footballers' Battalion was pulled out of the Battle of the Ancre in November 1916, plans were underway as to how to carry on the war when spring came. At a conference held at Chantilly in November as the Battle of the Somme wound down, General Joffre was adamant that the Germans not be given time to recover from their ordeals at Verdun and on the Somme in 1916. At this early stage it was ambitiously suggested that the Allies would carry out offensives on multiple fronts, Western, Russian and Italian, delivered strategically so that the Germans would not be able to move reinforcements around the Continent to strengthen themselves elsewhere. With luck, strong, decisive attacks would rock the enemy to the core and cause it to topple to defeat before the end of the year. It was clear from this outline, though, that another year of dogged fighting was expected. Certain French factions were alarmed by the idea of more attritional fighting, in particular after the massacre at Verdun had pushed the nation to the brink. Then General Nivelle came forward with an alternative solution and the authorities were swept away on a tidal wave of misplaced enthusiasm. He had surged forward at the latter end of 1916, regaining significant swathes of territory that had been lost during the fighting at Verdun. Now he thought he could take the exhausted French Army and launch a huge undertaking in the area around Soissons and Reims, while the British fought on a smaller scale to the north at Arras. Not even his own subordinates were convinced and they voiced their consternation, but nevertheless doubts were played down. Joffre was promptly dumped as the French military leader, replaced by Nivelle, and plans gathered pace.

The ground east of Arras had been attacked by the French in 1915 without overwhelming success, but this meant that when the British took over the area facing them in the spring of 1916 their allies were in a position to provide the benefit of their wisdom so far as future action was concerned. Sir Douglas Haig knew it would take an immense amount of artillery preparation, including targeting heavy artillery on strongpoints prior to an assault. There was also the issue of the caves and tunnel networks burrowed under the sector, some of them centuries old and incorporated into the enemy's defensive system. A memo ordered preparations for the capture of the high ground at Vimy Ridge to the north of Arras, to secure observation over the Douai plain and assist the advance on their right. The attack on the ridge was a daunting, crucial task in order to make sure that the Arras operations were successful. The Germans had been holding the imposing ridge since October 1914 and this feature of the Artois countryside was key to their defences in the area. From the British side it gently rose to over 300 feet to give the enemy a commanding view of everything that they were up to, before the ridge then dropped away steeply on the German side down onto the plain below.

Preparations for the offensive of spring 1917 were being hampered by larger events that threatened the Allies' position. The enemy might well be able to soon call on a huge reserve of troops to help defend the Western Front. The Russian Revolution threatened to end the war on the Eastern Front, freeing up immense amounts of men and material. Then, with planning already well underway, on 17 March the Footballers' Battalion received news at dawn that the enemy were simply retiring in front of them. Up and down the line troops, including Bob, were ordered forward, albeit cautiously to see what the Germans were playing at. On the first day alone they crept some 2 miles after the steadily organised, retreating enemy and in the days following, cavalry patrols rode through them to tentatively ascertain where they were going. It emerged that the Germans were picking up and purposefully retreating to a new position, known as the Hindenburg Line. Not only would this strategic withdrawal shorten the length of front that the enemy would be required to defend, but it was monstrously fortified to withstand any new offensive.

The German strategic move had thrown into disarray planning for the British attack east of Arras, which nonetheless would have to go ahead in support of the French to the south. By the end of the month the Footballers' Battalion had completed a long march north to the Arras sector. Training for their part in the offensive began immediately, a demanding array of bombing and Lewis gun courses, punctuated by football games. Bob Whiting was joined by the likes of Fred Brown, who since being shellshocked after Delville Wood had been deemed fit to return to the trenches, but only after an investigation. It had come to light that he was yet another of the Fulham recruits lying about his age. Fred had only just turned 17 when he enlisted in April 1915. It turned out that when he suffered his collapse after Delville Wood he was actually barely 18. Fred had been returned to the battalion, in which now he was actually old enough to be serving, just two weeks before the attack on the Somme. His only physical hardship so far had been laryngitis caused by the miserable winter. It was among the coldest that the men could remember and the conditions were also telling when Fred was admitted to a Field Ambulance with severe trenchfoot. He rejoined the battalion on 3 April, just as another heavy snowfall arrived, interrupting training and then causing more problems when the ground thawed again and was left a slushy mess.

Three weeks before the attack, the artillery started working the area with their preliminary bombardment, the heavy guns working on the rear areas and trying to disrupt communications and reliefs while the lighter ones attempted to smash barbed wire. One artillery officer wrote that he had never seen anything like it:

> Even the Somme front has nothing that it can show to beat it. Every dug out has been completely blown in, and numbers of Germans must have been buried in them … What the difference in gun power is between this battle and the Somme I don't know, but the havoc each shell has done seems to be infinitely worse than anything further south.[2]

The ground was a morass:

> You cannot here walk between the shell-holes – you have to walk over and into them, and over vast parapets of clods of earth weighing over two hundred weights which the explosion causes. How any man could live in the hell it must have been I don't know.

Air activity was also intense in the run up to the battle. There were bombing raids against supply dumps, railways, counterpart aerodromes, billets and all of the scout activity associated with attempting to interrupt such missions.

At 5.30 a.m. on Easter Sunday, 9 April, the guns roared to life at Arras and two mines went up. Then the barrage began to creep forward. German batteries and ammunition dumps were targeted with high explosive and gas shells. Under a stringent artillery bombardment, two British armies went forward, keeping close to the torrent of shells. The infantry 'swept like a flood'[3] towards the enemy. In a little over half an hour almost the entire front line was overrun. Guns, thousands of enemy troops, pile upon pile of war material, fell into their hands as they went forward. Trying to rush the second set of objectives was harder as the element of surprise had diminished, but on they pressed. A dozen miles to the rear the 17th Middlesex had received orders to be ready to march at four hours' notice. At midnight they were finally pressed towards the battle. Trudging through a snowstorm, dragging their feet through the muck that covered the countryside, Bob Whiting and the Fulham men still with the Footballers' Battalion were ordered to make their way to help relieve a Scottish division. As their tortuous journey into the face of the storm continued on the following day, the Canadian troops charged with seizing Vimy Ridge fought on, as did the men who reached the outskirts of Monchy-le-Preux. By 9 a.m. on 11 April the British had seized Monchy but were experiencing difficulties elsewhere along the Hindenburg Line. The heavy snowfall was still affecting the 17th Middlesex's ability to move. Due to go into reserve at Roclincourt, exhausted, they were still attempting to take up their positions in the early hours of the 12th. That day to the north of them the success of the British offensive continued, as it did to the south, where on the other side of the River Scarpe some 2,000 yards of the revered Hindenburg Line had now fallen, causing a new salient to bulge in the German line. The Footballers' Battalion got to work, trying to make the saturated roads in their sector usable and constructing a track of duckboards up to the front lines. While Bob Whiting and his fellow soldiers and fans continued their back-breaking work, the battle raged in front of them.

The war was taking its toll on the Chelsea contingent involved in the battle, some more than others. Charles Dewar, in his mid-20s, was another Londoner with a proud Chelsea affiliation. Serving in the Royal Berkshire Regiment, he was one of the fifty or so lucky young men to receive a football from the club at the beginning of the war. Since then he had been put through the mill. Having arrived on the Western Front in 1915 he had seen the latter part of the disastrous Battle of Loos and survived the trauma of the opening throes on the Somme at Ovillers and Pozieres. At the beginning of 1917 Charles's division was marked for the Battle of Arras too and arrived in the sector at the beginning of the year. By the time they were relieved, having claimed some 2 miles of enemy ground in the middle of the month, over 2,000 men had become casualties, including Charles who had been slightly wounded in the arm. He was bundled off, presumably rather cheerfully, towards Havre for a sojourn back in Blighty.

Unfortunately the enemy had not quite finished with him. As the Battle of Arras raged, unrestricted U-boat warfare was reaching its terrifying zenith. In April 1917, almost 1 million tons of shipping would be destroyed, much of it by torpedoes launched from German submarines, an average of about thirteen ships a day.

At Havre, Charles Dewar was one of almost 700 slightly wounded British cases being ushered about the Scottish-built SS *Donegal*. Commandeered as an ambulance transport, it was now too dangerous for a hospital ship to be painted in the traditional white with red cross embellishment, so she was painted in an unsightly war camouflage. On 17 April the *Donegal* set off across the Channel escorted by two Royal Navy destroyers. At approximately 7.45 p.m., as Charles approached the South Coast, UC-21 launched a torpedo at his ship. The captain saw the track of the menace approaching and attempted to swing the ship out of harm's way, but she was unable to respond quickly enough and when impact occurred, the subsequent explosion almost took off the propeller.

The *Donegal* was doomed. One of her escorts threw itself alongside, smashing the port side lifeboats in between the two hulls in order to get close enough to take off several hundred wounded men and as many crew as possible, including two who had survived the *Titanic* disaster five years earlier. Forty-five minutes later the *Donegal* listed violently to starboard, ejecting those on her decks into the water, before she finally slipped underneath the waves and into the Channel. It had been a narrow escape at the last for Charles Dewar as he made his way home. Nearly fifty of his fellow passengers and ship's crew had perished.

By 14 April, 7 miles of the Hindenburg Line had succumbed to the offensive launched east of Arras, Vimy Ridge was in British hands and in front of the 17th

Middlesex's division the enemy had begun to withdraw again. At nightfall the battalion held the line opposite the battered village of Oppy, which was some 7 miles north-east of Arras and under heavy artillery fire. Patrols sent forward had already revealed that in front of them the German position was protected by an abundance of rifles and machine guns and lay behind a thick, imposing belt of barbed wire. The first phase of the Battle of Arras was coming to a close. Erich Ludendorff, in joint command of the German war effort, looked back on events as being a miserable start to 1917 for his army. 'April 10th and the succeeding days were critical days,' he wrote afterwards:

> A breach, 12,000 to 15,000 yards wide, and as much as 6,000 yards or more in depth is not a thing to be mended without more ado. It takes a good deal to repair the inordinate wastage of men and guns, as well as munitions, that result from such a breach.[4]

For all of the monumental effort put into its construction, a large portion of the Hindenburg Line was in tatters. After six days of fighting, Sir Douglas Haig proudly stated, the front had been advanced miles to the east and all of the key, dominating features of the landscape that he wanted were in the possession of his army. His troops had also seized well over 10,000 prisoners and 200 guns in driving a wide gap into the German lines. Additionally they had ensured that precious men who could have withstood the attack that the French were about to unleash on the Aisne had been transported north to hold back the British.

General Nivelle's grand attempt at winning the war commenced on 16 April. With the British fully embroiled in their own contribution at Arras much depended on him delivering his promise of a decisive action on the Western Front. Unfortunately for the Allies, in terms of its lofty objectives the offensive was a horrific failure. The Prime Minister was told by the French Minister of Munitions in the aftermath that France was categorically determined not to get involved in prolonged fighting such as that of 1916. Nivelle was determined to push on again, but his government were unimpressed with his efforts thus far. Unless a decisive break could be made, the French might break off their offensive and cut their losses. Fighting on against the Germans alone at Arras was obviously not in Britain's best interests. On 26 April Haig met with the French Minister of War, who was pessimistic, but as far as Haig was concerned, the French backing out of their contribution to the 1917 campaign was an unacceptable concept. As for his own army's part, though, in the meantime he would have no choice but to carry on until it became clear what the French intended to do.

While the political wrangling continued, the 17th Middlesex had settled down to yet another period of trench warfare. They began patrolling the Oppy area immediately 'under exceptionally trying circumstances'.[5] German shelling was prolific and the men were followed everywhere by the fire of machine guns and snipers. The weather had also deteriorated again, with heavy rainfall as soon as they took to the lines. It was

still tipping down the following morning, meaning that wading through mud was
necessary for the men to go about their business. The beginning of the Footballers'
Battalion's time in the lines was a tedious tenure of cleaning support lines, rebuilding
damaged trenches, strengthening their defensive positions and reconnaissance for
future operations. Then came digging assembly trenches, as well as edging the line
forward into a more favourable position on a railway embankment. All of the signs
pointed towards the fact that they would soon be expected to go into battle.

On 23 April the division on their right took to the offensive and seized the village
of Gavrelle. On their brigade's front, the situation remained quiet for the 17th
Middlesex until mid-morning when the enemy unleashed heavy artillery fire on them.
Reports arrived of a counter-attack massing on the other side of the village. Under
heavy fire the Footballers' Battalion lined the embankment, bracing themselves for
the enemy onslaught. Five counter-attacks came, all repulsed with crushing losses to
the German troops owing to accurate British artillery fire. By 7.30 p.m. the situation
had calmed and the battalion returned to their original positions before spending the
night digging a new defensive trench. The attacks continued the following day, again
with no success for the Germans when they came bursting out of Oppy Wood. That
night the 17th Middlesex was relieved and marched away from the front line, but Bob
Whiting was about to become involved in his first major offensive.

While Haig was away meeting with the French, his army commanders on the
Arras front were told that they were to go on with their campaign unless their allies
stopped their activity on the Aisne. In that eventuality, Haig would immediately
switch his attention to Flanders and the north, but until then preparations were
apace for continuing the existing offensive. On 28 April, on a front about 8 miles
north of Monchy, the British Army would attack again. During the afternoon of
the 26th orders were sent out to the 6th Infantry Brigade, to which the Footballers'
Battalion belonged. They were to assault and capture Oppy, the wood beside it and
the surrounding area. The objectives were threefold and indicated on a map again by
progressive coloured lines, blue, green and brown. The divisional commanding officer
made his way forward to observe their path, but visibility was minimal. 'There was
considerable shelling on both sides, and the general appearance of the country under
a leaden sky, mist and smoke of bursting shells was that of a manufacturing district.'[6]

The attacking strength of the 17th Middlesex's division was weak at this point and
their front was a lengthy mile and a quarter. As a whole it was down to roughly 3,500
fighting troops and the Footballers' Battalion was selected as one of its assaulting units
in the main because they were one of the strongest left. It was a serious undertaking.
Bob Whiting and the rest of the battalion marched from Roclincourt on the evening
of the 27th and formed up opposite Oppy, where the British line was being heavily
shelled. The 6th Infantry Brigade was on the right of the intended attack, with the
17th Middlesex forming the left side of the front and the 13th Essex the right. Men
of the South Staffords waited behind, ready to provide support and carry up supplies.

By 3.30 a.m. all were in position behind lines of tape and ready to attack, including five machine-gun teams on the flanks poised to follow the first wave, supporting the initial attack and then forming strongpoints to withstand enemy retaliation. Bob Whiting and his cohorts were weighed down with cardigans, capes, a groundsheet, box respirators in gas alert position and wearing uncomfortable tube helmets. Stuffed in their haversacks were spare oil tins, holdalls, iron rations. Mess tins and covers were strung to the outside along with water bottles. Each man also carried 120 rounds of ammunition, Mills grenades, two empty sandbags tied to his shoulders and field dressings. Different specialists had coloured bands tied to their arms, green for scouts, red for runners, blue for signallers, yellow for carrying parties and white for mopping up teams.

The 6th Brigade was to head for Oppy itself and the wood, as well as the area just to the south of both. Oppy and the village of Arleux nearby were already decimated. The 5th Brigade to the north were responsible for the ground almost up to Arleux, where they joined up with the Canadians who would attack the ruins of that village. As far as the 17th Middlesex were concerned, the first line (blue) on their maps took them to German trenches on the other side of the wood. The second, the green, followed the eastern outskirts of Oppy and the third, the brown, took them to the German support trench. The whole infantry attack would follow a creeping artillery barrage that would aim to regulate their pace. Conducting the bombardment was not easy, for the gunners either had to place their weapons on the wrong side of Vimy Ridge and fire at long range, or they had to place them on a forward slope where they were exposed and the task of getting ammunition up became extremely difficult. The barrage had nonetheless been planned in minute detail in terms of the progression and troops had been yet again primed with the importance of staying close on its heels and making sure that they attacked the Germans swiftly as it passed over them, before the enemy could man their weapons and fight back. 'They must assault any portion of the enemy trench or position opposite them immediately the barrage lifts off it.'[7]

The Battle of Arleux commenced at 4.25 a.m. It was a mild, bright day but with poor visibility. The barrage came down promptly and at 4.33 a.m. the leading wave of the 17th Middlesex hauled themselves up. By the time they got to the enemy wire, machine guns had opened fire and frantically showered them with bullets. The Germans had also retaliated with their own artillery and with mortars. Nonetheless the men of the Footballers' Battalion quickly entered the enemy front line and found the German trench almost empty. Pressing forward behind the creeping barrage, with Bob Whiting's company in the centre of the attack, the battalion's first objective was reached with few casualties. Shortly after the advance commenced, the officer commanding A Company on the left noticed that the 5th Brigade beside them was nowhere to be seen. As a temporary measure, he placed a Lewis gun section and some bombers in the enemy front line trench with instructions to block it and hold up any attempts by the Germans to move on their left flank.

At 5.50 a.m. the Footballers' Battalion appeared to have kept in touch with the 13th Essex on their right successfully, despite the latter having been hit by a German bombing attack. Fighting became much heavier from here on, though, with very heavy machine-gun and rifle fire cascading towards them from the shattered houses in Oppy itself. The enemy hid among the ruins. 'In places scarce one brick stood upon another and shelter for a dog could hardly be found.'[8] German troops lurked ready to pounce on their attackers, 'sheltering beneath the tumbled bricks and masonry in deep dug-outs'. Artillery had wrought havoc:

> For days the opposing guns had been engaged in mercilessly shelling one another and in subjecting the front line and communication trenches to such a storm of shell that it was a wonder that any living thing could emerge from that terrible holocaust … There were, indeed, instances of men becoming insane under that awful fire, and German prisoners when taken were not infrequently still shaking violently from the ordeal through which they had passed.[9]

The fighting was now 'fierce in the extreme',[10] with numerous counter-attacks being launched back at the 17th Middlesex. It was especially intense around Oppy, with heavy losses on both sides. The wood was a mass of tangled foliage – as had been proved at Longueval and Delville Wood the year before, attacking a village next to woodland was a complicated business. The artillery had been told to aim their shrapnel high in order to clear the remaining trees. The infantry had been warned that although the shells may be bursting over their heads or even a little behind them in order to destroy what was left of the foliage, that they must gauge the barrage by the strike of the shrapnel bullets on the ground in order to get as close to it as possible.

The first wave of troops began doggedly consolidating their new position while the rest of the 17th Middlesex pressed on. The second and third waves found themselves embroiled in a fierce scrap. Then, at battalion headquarters the steady flow of wounded men and runners bringing news of the fighting back slowed thanks to the enemy bombardment. On the left of the attack A Company were largely unaccounted for, possibly held up by a murderous volley of German fire and a senior officer had to be sent out to try and make sense of the situation and find headquarters a position more suited to the task of managing the battle. There was a reason for the way that the battle was playing out and the British hierarchy was expecting these fierce counter-attacks. The Germans had implemented a new system after the horrific casualties suffered on the Somme. No longer was the front line intended to be packed out with troops. Forward areas would now be loosely held, supplemented by concrete pill boxes and machine-gun nests. This explained not only why the initial attack swept over their front lines, but why they then retaliated with such well orchestrated counter-attacks. Higher numbers of defenders would be in the second and third lines; specific counter-attack formations intended to let the British come on a certain way before beating them back after they had tired themselves out. A battalion of the King's Royal Rifles had been sent up from reserve to help, but could not get out of the British front line. The German counter-attacks were becoming stronger and stronger, heavily hitting the Footballers' Battalion from both the left and in front. Large numbers of enemy troops were emerging from Oppy Wood, getting around the rear of the advancing British line and reoccupying the trenches already lost. An officer was sent to see to the situation, but disappeared without a trace.

The Germans may have learnt lessons about how to defend on the Western Front, but in turn the British method of attack was also evolving with the planning for each offensive. Crippling casualties from enemy machine guns had resulted in an emphasis on crushing any nests immediately. A massive amount of energy went into preparing designated mopping up parties. That day the Footballers' Battalion had six, each with specific, detailed tasks to ensure that threats were removed as soon as the assaulting waves passed over and that the enemy would not pop up from hiding and hit them in the rear. It was also ordained that advancing between Oppy and Arleux was to be delayed long enough for the villages to be secured. That way it was hoped that men advancing through the middle would not be caught in the flanks by machine gunners skulking in the ruins. With the enemy's evolution of counter-attack formations senior officers also recognised that although they might take front-line positions quickly, the need for consolidation of their objectives was paramount for when the enemy inevitably hit back. Consolidation had to be done quickly. Four strongpoints were planned to be put up immediately in detailed areas on 28 April. The men designated to construct them were ordered not to get involved in any of the fighting as they progressed across No Man's Land. Laden with shovels and picks, as well as poles, sandbags and barbed wire, as soon as they reached the last objective they were to attempt to go out 100 yards in front of the main lines and establish Lewis gun posts to hold up enemy counter-attacks.

Senior officers had also endeavoured to deal with the disastrous consequences of not being able to communicate properly on the field of battle. Special attention was to be paid to keeping in constant touch with one's flanks throughout the operations. 'Officers must pay particular attention to dispose their men so that the flanks were well defended with bombs, Lewis Guns and grenades most suited to the ground.'[11] There could also, if at all possible, be no repeat of previous battles, where headquarters sat in ignorance as to what was playing out in front of them. 'Exceptional diligence must be expended on reporting properly – at least every hour giving current position of units on both flanks, whether they were in touch as to what was going on on the battalion front.' The role of contact aeroplanes was evolving too. At 7 a.m. they were to begin flying over the battlefield, at which point flares would be lit and stuck in the bottom of trenches and mirrors would be flashed to furnish them with information about troop dispositions. They could also demand this by dropping Very lights or sounding a klaxon in passing. Outside divisional and brigade headquarters, bright groundsheets would be laid out on the floor to mark their positions for airmen. There would also be five relay posts, telephone stations, signal and visual stations and a power buzzer for maintaining communications. A minimum of four pigeons were also issued for the attack, each to a company commander to be sent up when required.

Oppy Wood, through which the Footballers' Battalion was first advancing, by this stage 'was but a scorched and shell-blasted mass of tree stumps'[12] which must have been all too reminiscent for survivors of Delville Wood the year before. Bob Whiting and the 17th Middlesex had got through, but the Germans were still putting up a fierce resistance from the village beyond, firing through specially cut holes in the walls of the battered buildings. It was now nearly 8 a.m. and a few minutes later a report came in from the left-hand company of the battalion to say that the enemy were working around both their flanks. Reserves to help put up a stronger fight were hard to come by. The only others that the Footballers' Battalion had were the men who had been designated to mop up the first objective and they had already been pushed forward to try and help further the other side of the attack. An officer sent up found enemy troops flooding down from the north, managing to drive two companies of the 17th Middlesex back through the wood to the original German front line. The men were doing their best to make a stand, but sustaining heavy losses. The wood was rapidly becoming a mass of uncoordinated troops, counter-attacking Germans, men consolidating the captured front line and the Middlesex men who had been pushed away from their assault on the second objective. The enemy was also counter-attacking from the south with bombs. A company of the Royal Berkshire Regiment was sent to try and stabilise the situation, but they could not get out of the original British line owing to German fire. All communication with the troops at the first objective was cut off and any runners who attempted to get through to the troops still holding the Oppy trench were either killed or wounded.

Despite efforts to improve communication, senior officers had little idea about as to what was going on in front of them. At 8.30 a.m. news finally filtered back redundantly to one of the brigade headquarters that the first objectives had fallen. At the same time, officers were finding out that troops on their flanks were proceeding well. The Canadians took Arleux and the 5th Infantry Brigade had made it to their second objective too. Others, however, were lagging behind. Although Oppy had been captured, on the right of the attack elements of the 17th Middlesex were among those being delayed at the old British front line having been unable to get through a patch of German wire. As a result, the rest of the 6th Infantry Brigade, who had pressed on to their second objective, suddenly found themselves being shot at from both sides and from the rear because they had lost touch with the men on either side. 'In the confused fighting that followed it was impossible to ask for fresh artillery barrages, for friend and foe were intermingled, and much of the fighting was of a hand-to-hand nature.'[13] The 13th Essex next to the Footballers' Battalion were ordered to fall back on the original enemy front line and hold it. Orders were one thing, reality was another. All of their officers were casualties and most of the NCOs too. Their ranks were a mass of fumbling, exhausted men. A few managed to carry out the order, but were eventually forced out of their position, dodging from shell hole to shell hole back to safety.

By mid-afternoon the remnants of the two Middlesex companies still holding the first German trench finally exhausted their supply of bombs. The ten remaining soldiers made a run for the original British line and abandoned their position. One officer and three men got through. The rest were missing all over the battlefield. Nothing more was known of the fate of those at the first objective until another officer staggered back after nightfall. 'His evidence made it clear that these troops had fought till they were practically exterminated by the superior pressure of the enemy, the few survivors probably surrendered.'[14] The Middlesex troops that had survived joined together with the remnants of the South Staffordshire carrying party and were eventually relieved by the Royal Fusiliers later that night. Except on the left flank, the entire division had now been driven back from the gains taken in the morning.

Orders came through for a renewed assault on Oppy by the 99th Brigade the following morning, due to begin at 4 a.m. The attackers had only reached the rear positions at 4.30 a.m. on the 28th and having been marching all day were tired. All of the supply dumps were filled up ready and on 29 April 'an Homeric struggle'[15] by exhausted troops was ultimately unable to fend off German bombing counter-attacks. All units were now seriously depleted. A battalion of the Royal Berkshires could only muster 265 rifles. By the end of the day, the Oppy line was in British hands to within 200 yards of Oppy Wood, but all beyond was still in the possession of the enemy.

In between the River Scarpe and Monchy the 12th Division had made progress. The 37th Division took a little more ground and the 2nd Division had picked up more gains around Oppy. As the Germans did not consider the retention of the area to be vital, as long as their line to the rear was held they declined to counter-attack further. It was only a local success for the British and Canadian troops, but at this stage of the battle it was better than nothing. For their efforts the 17th Middlesex was in bits. Four officers, three of them wounded, had found their way back with something like 150 men, over 100 of whom were also incapacitated in some way. Senior officers were of the opinion that had the flanks held, as they had tried to ensure, then the first objective may have weathered the initial attack on the 28th 'and possibly the 2nd Objective would have been gained in its entirety, although in view of the strength of the enemy in the village this may be doubtful'. Unfortunately for the Footballers' Battalion it was not to be:

As it was the sudden arrival of the enemy from both flanks which enabled them to re-occupy the wood combined with their vigorous counter attacks in front was disastrous; and in the confused nature of the fighting it was impossible to know where to ask for fresh artillery barrages to be placed.[16]

The Battle of Arleux, part of the middle phase of the Arras offensive, came to an end. The Canadian feat of capturing Arleux was the only glowing success in the operation. Eleven officers and 451 men were gone from the strength of the 17th Middlesex, a huge percentage of them missing. On the 29th they were moved to Roclincourt to reorganise and as the battalion departed, the last vestiges of the men who had answered the original call to join its ranks seemed to be gone. Thirty-three-year-old Alfred Andrew, one of the initially disruptive recruits at White City, was missing, as was young Fred Brown. Both were later found to be prisoners of war. The same could not be said of Bob Whiting, who died of wounds on 28 April 1917. His son, Joseph Frederick was less than 2 months old and Bob died without ever seeing him. Two weeks later his wife Nellie received a letter from the battalion adjutant informing her that her husband had been killed as the result of being hit by a shell during the attack on Oppy. According to the B Company commander, at the time Bob was trying to help wounded men who remained under fire. A condolence letter to the widowed mother of three with a newborn to take care of included the perhaps seemingly insensitive line: 'It is sad for those left behind but you must remember there is a world to come.' The British tried again to launch further attacks in the Arleux sector in the opening days of May, but having made little progress it was called off on the second day having accumulated yet more casualties. By the middle of May the Battle of Arras, like the one on the Somme before it, had ground to a halt.

Nellie Whiting's suffering was exacerbated by rumours that began circulating to the effect that Bob had been shot as a deserter. Distressed, by 1919 she was determined enough to put an end to it that she asked both local and national newspapers to publish evidence to the contrary. The secretary of Brighton and Hove Albion helped her and at the end of the year one newspaper stated that:

> for some time past a dastardly rumour has been in circulation ... to the effect that Whiting, who greatly distinguished himself as a goalkeeper in the service of Brighton & Hove Albion, and previously with Chelsea, was shot as a deserter in France.[17]

Of course, this was not the case, 'the real fact being that he fell gallantly in action'. It was all most stressful for Nellie:

> Unhappily the rumour has now reached the ears of his widow, and has come as a great shock to her. Fortunately Mrs Whiting, who is now living with her fatherless little ones ... has in her possession official documents and letters which disprove a foul calumny on the heroic dead.

Buried near Vimy Ridge, goalkeeper Bob Whiting's grave was subsequently lost and the former Chelsea keeper was commemorated on the Arras Memorial. His widow Nellie struggled to support her family, taking on laundry jobs again until the early 1930s when she was forced by ill health to give up work. She died in 1933 aged just 50.

16

'Hitting and Hitting with All of Our Strength'

The Third Battle of Ypres

Before the Arras offensive had even begun, plans were afoot to take the British focus northwards to Flanders. Backed by the government, representatives of it claimed that there was 'no measure to which the committee attached greater importance than the expulsion of the enemy from the Belgian coast'.[1] In the summer of 1917 the Germans held almost 30 miles of Belgium's sandy coastline, including key ports such as Ostend and Zeebrugge, making Britain distinctly nervous because of their proximity to her south coast. At the end of the First Battle for Ypres in November 1914 the original BEF, Cecil Dean among its number, had ultimately held their position in front of the town. As the battle wound down Churchill, at the time First Lord of the Admiralty, was already advocating going on the offensive in Flanders in a combined operation with the army but Joffre interceded, far more concerned with events threatening the French capital. A second Battle of Ypres took place in the spring of 1915. German attempts to press the issue again were not wholly unsuccessful, but still the salient remained. Again the Royal Navy reiterated the threat that Germany's ability to utilise their Belgian port possessions posed to Britain and to her own part in the war in supplying the army. Again they approached the issue of seizing back the coastline, but by this stage it had already been ordained that the bulk of Britain's contribution in 1916 would be committed to the Somme. Any plans for significant action in Flanders melted away as Verdun and the progress of the British campaign to the north of it consumed available resources.

After the early Chantilly outline for 1917 had been abandoned and Nivelle's offensive accepted, potential plans for a British effort in Belgium needed to be reworked. One of the officers given this responsibility was General Plumer, a distinctive figure with a bristling white moustache and a wealth of fighting experience gleaned from throughout the empire. It turned out that he was not wholly accepting of Haig's intention of destroying the German Army in the Ypres area and bringing about an end to the war. His plans to capture both the Pilckem Ridge and more high ground at Messines still retained an element of perceived caution that prompted Haig to write in the margin of the plans submitted 'our objective is to break through rapidly'.[2] Unimpressed with the sprit and dash of the seemingly cautious Plumer or General Rawlinson, who had been in charge of the Somme and had also contributed to the plan, Haig decided to make a change. Their work had reinforced the likelihood that the army could be in for another succession of turgid infantry offensives such as in 1916, instead of overrunning Belgium swiftly. In the end, unimpressed, the commander of the BEF settled on a third Old Etonian, General Sir Hubert Gough, to come up with an alternative. Still not 50 and a cavalry man like Haig himself, Gough was not familiar with the Flanders area of the British front, but was far more likely to exude the kind of offensive spirit that Haig was looking for. By mid-May he had been appointed the man in charge of the summer offensive.

After Nivelle's stunning failure there was no question of abandoning the idea of the Flanders offensive. 'Even if a full measure of success is not gained,'[3] Haig postulated, the Germans could not refuse to fight on the cramped Flanders front and the BEF could hope to wear down enemy resistance until the time was ripe to deliver the crushing blow he dreamt of. Conferences at the beginning of May resulted in the unanimous opinion that the Allies should somehow continue to bludgeon the German Army on the Western Front, giving them no time to recover from operations that had already taken place at Arras. David Lloyd George, who was wholly invested in the manner in which events had transpired as a result of his interference in the military strategy of 1917, stated that 'the enemy must not be left in peace for one moment ... we must go on hitting and hitting with all our strength'.[4] The Nivelle philosophy of crashing to a decisive victory was bypassed in favour of a more traditional approach of wearing down the enemy and pushing them to a state of exhaustion, a doctrine not necessarily suited to Gough, who had been placed in command of the oncoming battle.

Plans for the Allied Flanders advance made at the beginning of May were also constructed in ignorance of potentially catastrophic problems within the French army. It began when one division had refused to go up to their trenches after the misery of the Aisne. The disorder appeared to be contagious. Men went absent without leave and wilfully disobeyed orders. Insubordination gathered pace, revolutionary songs were sung, war material was destroyed, red flags were waved, railways sabotaged and there were increases in drunkenness. As much as the French military authorities tried to conceal their problems, word filtered out to the British hierarchy. The issue of whether or not the French could be relied on to co-operate with the summer operations was now gravely concerning. Aside from whether they were *able* to play their part, there was also the question of how *willing* the French authorities were to be involved. It was rapidly becoming apparent that their intention was to sit tight, build up material and not cede any ground until the endless resources of the United States, who had now entered the war, started flooding onto the battlefields in 1918.

The campaign in Belgium would commence with a fierce assault on the Messines Ridge at the beginning of June. Some weeks later, using this advantageous high ground it was intended that a large-scale offensive would begin further north in front of Ypres itself. The extent of how little France could help was not truly apparent until the first stage of the action at Messines was all but ready to begin. Further British offensives would now be as much about diverting German attention away from the dire state of the French army, before the enemy caught on and attacked it, as it was about Britain establishing dominance over the Channel coast. Russia was in no position to pick up the slack either; the Italians were relying on the Western Front to consume German resources so that they could not be used to support the Austrians against their own troops; and the Americans were nowhere near arriving as a large, battle-ready force to help forge a path towards victory. Huge responsibility now rested on the shoulders of the British Army at Ypres. It would be a formidable task, for as early as the middle of May the Germans began to catch on to the possibility of an attack around Ypres and started to shift men and guns up from the Aisne in readiness to face them.

The Messines Ridge lay between Armentières and Ypres, with Messines itself situated towards the southern end and the high ground running steadily upwards and north-west to Wytschaete. Possession of the ridge was essential to take away the Germans' view of the surrounding area, but getting ready for the battle was troubling as, from the higher position on the ridge that the British so coveted, the enemy could watch everything they were doing. 'Railways were built, huge dumps of ammunition and stores formed, roads made and pipelines laid to carry water.'[5] More importantly a large collection of mines was ready for action. Ever since initial plans to attack the German Army in Flanders were made, British specialists had been burrowing underneath the battlefield. Nearly two dozen of their efforts were lying underneath the enemy's line in a myriad of galleries primed, if all went according to plan, to cause a terrifying explosion on the Western Front.

Twenty-one-year-old Joseph Norman, who had suffered acutely from shellshock in the aftermath of Delville Wood and sustained damage to his right arm during the Footballers' Battalion's scrap at Guillemont, had rejoined the 17th Middlesex at the beginning of May 1917. Whether on account of his physical or mental wounds, the authorities must have deemed that he was no longer fit to serve in a front-line battalion and moved him into the 19th Middlesex two weeks later. A pioneer battalion, by 1917 each division had one allotted to them. Units such as Joseph's were there to take care of an immense amount of support work such as building, repairs and assisting the division's engineers. The 19th Middlesex had not been involved in supporting any significant operations since the tail end of the Somme campaign. Having played no part in the Battle of Arras, their division had been holding the line towards Ypres instead earlier in the year. Now on the Messines front, wiring parties had been busy putting out new entanglements and repairing existing ones that had been damaged by the enemy, or were in need of maintenance. Joseph and the rest of the battalion spent early June working on roads to help ready the fighting troops for battle, digging and maintaining communication trenches and carrying supplies. The day before the battle began, on 6 June, the 19th Middlesex moved into support lines. Once there, Joseph Norman and the other pioneers were ordered to garrison the entrance to one of the precious mineshafts in readiness for zero hour.

The 23rd Middlesex had been designated the 2nd Footballers' Battalion and was created when recruits continued to come forward on the premise of serving with such a unit. While Norman and the 19th Battalion waited to support the advance, the 23rd were due to attack. As the former settled in the support lines, the fighting men of their fellow Middlesex battalion drew rations, ammunition and flares. After a flurry of enemy artillery fire, the companies began moving up to their assembly positions. 3.10 a.m. was designated as zero and promptly the earth heaved. 'There was such a roar as no man had ever heard, and a sight which can only be likened to Etna and Vesuvius disgorging their volumes of flame and smoke and lava into luckless Herculaneum.'[6] The guns had opened fire, but in addition efforts had been made to detonate simultaneously nineteen mines beneath the battlefield. In the largest man-made explosion the world had yet seen:

first there was a rumbling and strange groanings from the very bowels of the earth; the ground shook, lurid tongues of flame and smoke, clouds of dust and debris shot up into the air, as if Satan and his legions had at last broken through the bonds which bound them, as if the inferno of Dante had indeed become a reality and Hell let loose.[7]

The 23rd Middlesex burst forward. The front line fell, then the enemy's support line in quick succession. They moved towards the Dammstrasse, a road to the east of St Eloi which had been pounded beyond all recognition by British artillery, trench mortars and gas shells in the weeks running up to the battle. The enemy hit back hard, but Joseph Norman and the 19th Middlesex had been sent up to help and together they had taken the Dammstrasse and rounded up a large number of prisoners. Then another brigade passed through to continue the attack, supported by tanks. The Battle of Messines, which lasted until 14 June, was a rare and stunning success. By the close of operations, commanded by General Plumer, the British line had swept forward and taken both Messines and Wytschaete, the ridge, more than 7,000 prisoners, nearly seventy guns, 100 trench mortars and nearly 300 machine guns from the Germans.

The 19th Middlesex had been put straight to work after the initial assault, joining the rear wave of the attack on 7 June as ordered and helping to dig communication trenches between the captured German positions and the British lines and to consolidate the positions gained. If there was a perception that a pioneer battalion was in a safe position during battle, Joseph Norman was proof that this was not the case. He was killed on 9 June, while still busily working to build new roads and tramways to help the forward momentum of the division. The 21-year-old was buried at Bus House Cemetery, 2½ miles south of Ypres. His fellow soldiers bundled up his letters, photographs, his broken cigarette case and in November 1917 they finally found their way to his father at the family home opposite Stamford Bridge.

Flanders had not even begun to gnaw through the ranks of the Chelsea men present on the Western Front in the summer of 1917. The preliminaries of the campaign taken care of, preparations now turned to the main offensive. The Fifth Army was to attack the enemy on a 7½-mile front from Klein Zillebeke, to the south of the Menin Road and then northwards to Boesinghe. On the right of them, the Second Army was to cover their flank and advance a comparatively small distance with the intention of drawing off the enemy artillery. The French First Army would advance to the north of Boesinghe and the Yser Canal, making sure that a counter-attack did not come from that direction. At the northernmost point of the battlefield, the Belgian Army and Rawlinson's Fourth Army filled the gap to the coast.

Roughly in the middle of the advance would be the three South Downs battalions. As well as the original volunteers with a Chelsea connection who still resided within their ranks, a former Blues striker was present with the 11th Royal Sussex Regiment. Arthur Wileman was born in Derbyshire in 1889 and began his football career at Gresley Rovers the year before Chelsea was formed, before moving on to Burton United for a short run until they were put out of the Football League. He and his brother then arrived at Stamford Bridge in 1909. Arthur scored on his Chelsea debut at Arsenal and his career with the Blues appeared to be going well until the club signed Bob Whittingham and he found himself displaced as a result. Since his tenure with the Pensioners, Wileman had played in brief stints for Millwall, Luton Town and Southend United before the war came and like other current and past Chelsea personnel volunteered for the Footballers' Battalion in December 1914. He didn't serve overseas with them, transferring instead into the Royal Sussex Regiment and departing in March 1916 with the South Downs battalions. Once there Arthur had taken part in the attack on the Boar's Head the day before the Battle of the Somme commenced.

The Third Battle of Ypres finally commenced on 31 July 1917 and the 116th Brigade, to which all of the South Downs battalions still belonged, was to form the right attacking brigade of the 39th Division. Once again the objectives for the day were marked out by coloured lines on the map. Simply put, Wileman and his fellow troops would assault the yellow line, followed by the red and then more troops would pass through to assault a blue marker. The final troops selected were to then pass through them and move on to a black objective. As they steeled themselves for battle on 30 July, Arthur and the rest of the Chelsea contingent listened to an exchange of heavy gunfire whipping itself up into a tempest around them. That night they moved off to their assembly positions. The enemy shelled their communication trenches with gas and explosives, but Wileman and his cohorts advanced across the open country and avoided the onslaught. Shortly before 2 a.m., the 11th and 12th battalions of the Royal Sussex Regiment assembled and the men sat down to a meal of hot coffee and sausages while they waited for zero hour.

At 3.50 a.m. the much anticipated British advance in Flanders got underway. The Sussex battalions went forward with the remaining South Downs men and the 14th Hampshires ready to come up behind. Immediately Arthur Wileman and his cohorts rushed up behind the creeping barrage, the rear waves closing up on those in front and battalion headquarters going up with their commanders too. They had eight minutes' grace before the German artillery began their response, by which time they were well into No Man's Land. The shellfire was 'weak and erratic' by the Germans' normal standards, but murderous nonetheless. It was a dark morning, making progress awkward. It was later said that waiting just half an hour more would have given the advancing troops a huge advantage, but preparations had been made to the contrary. Flares and bombs fired by trench mortars at zero hour lent the battlefield an eerie light, but helped the troops to keep direction in the dark. 'Lines of direction had been taped out, direction discs planted, and all officers knew the compass bearing they were to march on with the result that no loss of direction took place.' They met little opposition except from isolated parties and machine-gun units. 'The German machine gunner as a rule put up a fine fight and were only silenced by being rushed with the bayonet.'[8]

The men moved on towards the Steenbeek, a stream about 15 feet wide but shallow, 'whose valley, with marshes bordering the stream, and with its drainage upset by shelling, offered one of the bad patches of the battlefield'.[9] They went over the high point of the Pilckem Ridge trying to follow hard on the heels of the artillery bombardment, but the ground was saturated because of the heavy showers in the run up to the battle and slipping and sliding downwards they found it hard to keep up with the protective barrage. Eventually reaching their allotted objectives, with the sun up, Arthur and the rest of the two South Downs battalions got down to the work of consolidation shortly after 5 a.m., enemy shells crashing down around them with fierce intensity and ruining communications across the battlefield.

Key observation posts had been seized and the rest of the brigade passed through and carried on the advance, tanks trundling up to help them. They proved their worth when the 13th Royal Sussex and their Hampshire counterparts reached an enemy stronghold. Two tanks 'opportunely crushed the uncut wire and by their fire drove the garrison to cover until dealt with by the infantry'.[10] As was becoming the norm, the 116th Brigade were expecting heavy counter-attacks from German units designated to pounce on them after they had taken the enemy front line to attempt to push them back again. In this area these were sure to come from the ruins of farms which had been reinforced and manned with significant firepower. The British were working out ways to combat this new form of defence, approaching with parties that would try and outflank the strongpoint, engaging trench mortars, pouring grenades and Lewis gun fire into loop holes cut for the German machine guns to fire through to dampen their enthusiasm for a counter-attack. The tactics proved effective and by 8 a.m. the 116th Brigade had seized all of their objectives as planned. It was only later in the day, when the neighbouring 118th fell back and enemy counter-attacks intensified, the South Downs battalions had to retire back to the line of the Steenbeek. It was at St Julien that Arthur Wileman, who was destined to be awarded a Military Medal for his bravery, settled in with the rest of the surviving Chelsea men.

Rain set in on the evening of 31 July and continued for three days and nights almost without cessation. The shelled areas turned into a massive swamp blocking off relieving troops from reaching the new front line. Streams such as the Steenbeek overflowed and any route still passable was tormented by German artillery. Stepping off duckboard paths could result in men disappearing into the mud for good. Constant repair work did nothing as the downpour cascaded onto them and shell holes up to 3 or 4 feet deep were filled to the brim with disgusting water. As the rain continued on 1 August, St Julien remained under fire and the 11th Royal Sussex Regiment was subjected to both shell and bomb before being ordered up to relieve the Hampshire Battalion in the line. By 3 a.m. on the 2nd, Arthur Wileman and the rest of his battalion had occupied part of the line along the Steenbeek known as Canopus Trench, accumulating just two casualties. By mid-morning, though, the enemy had commenced shelling them heavily and at lunchtime it was reported by the division on their left that the Germans were massing for a counter-attack on the other side of the stream. The artillery were immediately advised and countered the enemy's fire. The rain-sodden torment went on and nearly 100 men were rendered casualties. That division appeared to have been saved from an assault by the artillery's efforts but at 7 p.m. the Germans appeared to be forming up again, this time in front of Wileman and the South Downs men. An SOS got through on the wire and once again any attempts by the enemy to fight back were put down by more British shells. The few German troops that did manage to get through were pushed back by rifle and Lewis gun fire.

Fresh troops arrived to end the Sussex battalions' part in the opening throes of the summer campaign that night. Shortly before 1 a.m. Arthur Wileman and the rest of the 11th Sussex, Chelsea fans still among them, had been relieved. The downpour finally stopped on 4 August, although the weather remained unsettled and damp, with no sun or drying wind and more rain was forecast. That morning Arthur's battalion boarded trains and moved to the rear. Safely out of harm's way they began the arduous tasks of cleaning their rifles, counting their losses and reorganising their companies.

When he reported back to the War Cabinet in the following days, Sir Douglas Haig claimed that the opening of the Flanders offensive had been 'highly satisfactory and the losses slight for so great a battle'.[11] Part of the high ground had been seized and generally speaking, a mile and a half of ground had been gained, more than on the opening day of the Somme. The enemy were rushing reinforcements up, having suffered severe casualties, but despite Haig's clinical assessment more than 30,000 British casualties had also been suffered in just four days. The 39th Division alone had lost nearly 4,000 of their number. The original waves of the BEF had been expected to take four objectives, then assault the high ground towards Passchendaele too before being relieved, but had actually barely reached the halfway point and some had lost as many as 60 per cent of their fighting strength. Their increasingly important tanks had already suffered greatly on the boggy ground, almost half of them being either knocked out or grinding to a halt, in the main with mechanical issues. The German counter-attack forces were proving strong, as was the enemy artillery. Just as at Messines, the majority of the British casualties were not suffered in the initial attack on the front lines, but rather afterwards as men tried to consolidate their new positions under heavy fire for prolonged periods of time.

After more rain and more failure, Haig saw fit to remove Gough from command of the battle, handing it instead to the orchestrator of the victory at Messines, General Plumer. His divisions would continue to assault the same ground, but this time in measured, meticulous jumps forward with more strenuous support and reserves and an increase in the proportion of heavy artillery insisted upon by the new man in charge. The first of these jumps began on 20 September. Four divisions battled on a front of more than 2 miles for the important Gheluvelt Plateau and a further attack was carried out by the Second Army to the south. Plumer's reasoned approach ended in success across almost the entire front in what was dubbed the Battle of the Menin Road, as his men managed to overcome the new counter-attacking principles of German defence.

Within twenty-four hours, Sir Douglas Haig had issued orders for a second jump forward that he had already discussed with Plumer. Always hoping that any of his efforts might cause the German Army to collapse, Haig was nonetheless committed to a step-by-step approach to round off 1917 in Flanders and advancing the line would absorb Polygon Wood and part of Zonnebeke. Haig was forecasting that this leap would be completed by 26 September and that a third would then take place to capture Broodseinde. A fourth and final step would then seize Passchendaele itself, establishing a solid base for any future north-easterly assault towards the Channel coast.

Orders for the second stage of Plumer's renewed advance were issued as the shots fired during the first were still ringing in the ears of those that had taken part. The main assailants were to be the Anzac Corps, but among the troops due to take over the southern part of the attack were, yet again, the South Downs battalions. Also coming up were the 33rd Division, which included the 1st Battalion of the Middlesex Regiment. Among their number was William Tillbrook. He had joined the battalion on 7 July 1917. Having suffered a gunshot wound to the ribs a few days before Guillemont he had never rejoined the Footballers' Battalion, ending up in the 1st Middlesex instead. The 23-year-old gardener had got married in March while home on leave at St John's in Fulham and his new wife was now pregnant with a son. Also marching forward with the battalion was Harry Ford, who had been so prolific during

Chelsea's 1915 FA Cup run. Like many Blues players, Henry Thomas Ford, as he was born, had joined the army when his profession was put on hiatus at the end of the 1914/15 season. Twenty-four years old, he had made his debut for Chelsea just two years before the war. Technically a winger, one of the fastest in the country and with fine precision, Harry brought a fighting spirit to his battalion. He would have played anywhere for Chelsea, and at just 5ft 7in even turned out in goal on one occasion.

In April, the 1st Middlesex had been by the River Scarpe during the Arras offensive. The battalion had come away with only eight officers and 230 men. From then until the end of September, they had had a quiet time. On the 22nd the men received orders to move up the line the following day and began preparing for their part in the next stage of the battle for Ypres. The Middlesex men were met by guides, but they too had little idea where they were going. Shellfire plagued the men as they made their way up and the troops became disorientated among the craters. The German artillery barrage grew worse and telephone lines were cut. One company reported that their relief was complete, but nerves were racked at headquarters as silence prevailed on the other three. It took until 4.30 a.m. for the entire battalion to report in. Once in position they began sending out patrols and cautiously covering their front with outposts.

On 24 September a collection of NCOs and officers from each company of the 1st Middlesex went up to see a battalion of the Yorks and Lancaster Regiment whose line they were going to take over in order to launch an attack on the 26th. Their new position ran in between Polygon Wood and a stream called the Reutelbeek to the south. The spot had been in British hands for a matter of forty-eight hours and was still actively being consolidated. It was so new that the men got lost frequently walking about while under heavy fire. Thus far the defences were mere shell holes filled with defenders, linked together by short lengths of new trenches, rather than a coherent line. Huge craters surrounded the trenches. The Germans opposite were in a much better state, with continuous lines and strongpoints sitting in yet more shell holes and the odd ruined building that had been converted into a machine-gun post. In No Man's Land was a wrecked farm, named Jerk House, that had also been claimed by the enemy. The Middlesex Battalion had hardly any time to prepare for the 26th, and the Germans were not to give them the chance to carry out their duties. Harry Ford, William Tillbrook and the 1st Middlesex were about to be attacked before they were even used to their surroundings.

Before dawn on 25 September, out of a thick mist the enemy suddenly began to drop a torrent of shells on the Middlesex front, support and reserve lines and the Australians to the left of them. Twenty-seven batteries of field artillery pumped their murderous fire towards the Middlesex Battalion, along with nearly forty more of heavy calibres, high explosive and worse, gas. One officer described it as 'one of the heaviest bombardments of the war'.[12] Referred to by the Germans as 'destructive fire', 'so vicious was this barrage, and in such great depth ... that it was impossible to move transports or troops upon the roads'. SOS signals began simultaneously shooting skyward, the British artillery immediately jumped into action and the gunners began firing a response. 'So great was the roar of the guns, that not only could they be heard in Boulogne, but it was possible in that place to hear the vibration of the ground.'[13]

Using the mist as cover, the enemy prepared to attack. Afraid that the British were about to take the Gheluvelt Plateau once and for all, the Germans were stalling for time in order to bring up reserves and organise their counter-attack defences, attempting to win back a collection of pillboxes and strongpoints in what they referred to as the Wilhelm Line. The day before the attack a senior German officer expressed concern about what would happen if the British attacked again too soon, 'as we have not sufficient reserves behind the front'.[14] Orders had been issued for four battalions to push forward and dump the troops opposite, including the 1st Middlesex out of their newly gained position. Heavy machine guns were going forward with the first waves, attached to each company. As soon as the German barrage lifted, the Kaiser's men were to hit and hit hard, giving the British no chance to gather themselves after the shock of the bombardment.

The morning was fine but hazy. The enemy were supposed to have come forward as soon as the barrage started, but their artillery bombardment fell short on their own assembled infantry and the men had to wait for it to lift. Then, protected by both their barrage and the limited visibility, the German infantry commenced their assault just before 6 a.m., popping up at distances of up to a quarter of a mile from the British lines. Strong waves came at the Middlesex Battalion, the enemy swarming across No Man's Land. The British defenders had arrived so recently that they had never seen their positions in daylight. Despite being attacked on both flanks and from behind, doggedly they hung on, but eventually the Germans worked their way around the strung out, new defensive posts and attacked the British troops from behind. In some areas they came brandishing flame throwers. 'The stream of burning oil thrown from these devilish weapons reached a length and height of 100 yards and set fire to the trees, which being as dry as tinder, immediately took fire.'[15]

At 6.30 a.m. the enemy came at the Middlesex men again from the direction of Jerk House with five solid waves of assaulting troops. The morning haze still masked them and it was being assumed by British commanders behind that the sound of the shelling was British and not German. By now the enemy had driven a wedge between A and B companies of the 1st Middlesex and within the gap were working from shell hole to shell hole, engaging in hand-to-hand fighting with the likes of Harry Ford and William Tillbrook. The Germans entered their trenches, bombing their way along. All of the officers in the front companies were killed and the remnants of A Company were forced back.

It was not until half an hour later that the 6th Brigade headquarters knew that the attack encompassed their own front. The brigadier immediately seized command of the situation, although he was still waiting for confirmation that all of the reliefs had even taken place and that the troops in the line were his own. 'The 1st Middlesex were driven in a little, accruing heavy casualties. The loss of ground was not great, but was sufficient to jeopardise the following day's operations.' Now the brigadier was in a quandary. Only three battalions were available to him for the attack planned for the following day, 'and knowing the importance of the operation … I was contemplating whether to counter attack at once with one of them or hold the enemy and combine the counter attack with the morrow's attack'.[16] Eventually divisional headquarters solved his dilemma when they despatched orders telling the brigadier to regain any lost ground and not worry about the consequences for the preparations for the forthcoming attack.

The remnants of A and B Company were now falling back on C and D behind them in the support line. Pinned down behind the thick mist these rear companies had not been able to advance past the heavy German barrage and the enemy's hostile machine-gun fire. It was also proving almost impossible to get small arms ammunition up to the troops at the front because of the rate of enemy fire and at times they were reliant on individual acts of madness/bravery to bring up supplies. Now suddenly aware when their fellow men came rushing towards them from in front, the rear companies steeled themselves to halt the enemy advance. Lewis guns were to cover the gap forced by the German attack, and men rushed forward and dropped into the surrounding shell holes to give themselves some cover. When the next waves of enemy troops arrived they were stopped in their tracks. As the mist began to lift though, the troops on the right of the 1st Middlesex were seen falling back, leaving their flanks bare and exposed. German infantrymen were pouring over the ridge in front. The 1st Middlesex pinned them back, but enemy aeroplanes, seemingly unchallenged by the Royal Flying Corps counterparts, began to shoot low over the battlefield, pouring machine-gun fire into their ranks.

By 8 a.m., the Middlesex Battalion's headquarters was aware that their front line had caved and the brigade sent up a company of Highlanders to help them. Just as this was being organised an NCO fell into battalion HQ to say that right up at the original front line, on the far left of their front a platoon was still hanging on, although being shot at from all sides. Senior officers responded by rushing to engage a heavy artillery barrage opposite them to relieve the pressure being exerted by the enemy. Information was sketchy, but news filtered back that heavy casualties were mounting. The rate of fire being aimed at the British batteries throughout was so heavy, that despite the fact that the artillery had guns 'locked almost wheel to wheel'[17] in the area, it seemed they grew weaker and weaker as the day progressed. It was taking runners three hours to get reports in, the only means of communication not destroyed by the enemy barrage. Directing a defence seemed impossible:

> It is improbable that any General knows what became of the troops he committed to battle five minutes after he had seen them disappear into the cloud of gun smoke and dust. Many of the platoons who were ordered forward in support of the shaken lines disappeared forever.[18]

However, something had to be done about the oncoming Germans, who had now gained back the British front line and summarily ejected its occupants. Scattered across the battlefield, the 1st Middlesex were still being fired at from all directions when orders came from brigade HQ to prepare for a counter-attack of their own. Along with two companies of Argyll and Sutherland Highlanders, the battalion was to strike back and re-establish their line. An artillery barrage was to come down at zero, 150 yards in front of where the likes of Harry Ford and William Tillbrook cowered. Three minutes later it would begin to jump back and the battalion would attempt to advance some 200 yards. The Middlesex men left their assembly trenches at 1.55 p.m. but in broad daylight every move was obvious to the enemy who responded with yet more artillery fire. Then came the machine guns, whipping up a storm of fire. Neither of the battalions could advance properly and a further artillery barrage was requested to support them. It never materialised.

German casualties were evidently high, because when artillery observers were going about their work they witnessed repeated attempts by the enemy to relieve their front battalions. Thoroughly determined, though, in the evening the Germans came on again, but this time were greeted by heavy fire from more organised troops. At dawn fresher units flowed through the battered Middlesex and Highlander companies on their way to the front line. In fact, they then went past it. The original victims of the counter-attack were relieved that afternoon with some difficulty. Finally, the platoon in the front line that had held out since the very first onslaught more than twenty-four hours before was relieved. On vacating the position they had held they went back along the main road where the Middlesex men sank into some empty reserve trenches to keep from harm. William Tillbrook was taken prisoner in the confusion and initially reported missing. Harry Ford was luckier, finding himself on the British side of the lines when the fighting died down. As far as the Polygon Wood attack planned for the 26th was concerned, the 1st Middlesex were out of position and as a result Plumer decided to reduce their division's intended contribution. Still this proved too much of an undertaking for units weakened the day before. By 28 September Harry Ford and the rest of their division had been relieved. The 1st Middlesex Battalion had lost a total of nine officers and almost 250 men since being thrust into their tentatively held position three days before.

Arthur Wileman had been back in action with the 11th Royal Sussex Regiment at the Battle of Polygon Wood. Away from the north side of the Menin Road, the South Downs battalions had attacked a spot known as the Tower Hamlets spur. A fierce strongpoint in their way known as the Quadrilateral caused problems. The area had been pummelled by artillery in the run up to the battle, though, and eventually the 116th Brigade managed to overrun the dogged machine-gun nests and shelter on the crest of the spur. The rest of the division, though, got left behind by the creeping British barrage owing to deep mud that often required men to yank each other out of a waist-deep morass. Although the division eventually reached the Quadrilateral, it was pushed out again by counter-attacks and the South Downs men; Arthur Wileman, and the collection of Chelsea fans among them, were forced to dig in at a nearby ravine and fend off a fierce German attack that evening. A final, heavy counter-attack was launched at 7 p.m. and managed to penetrate the British artillery barrage in places, 'only to be annihilated by machine-gun and rifle fire'.[19]

The 33rd Division, said Plumer, had done 'fine work'[20] and the 39th, to which the South Downs battalions belonged, had 'carried out their task most successfully'.[21] Despite sending up a mass of reinforcements, the German system of letting the British come on, only to counter-attack in force, had failed again during the second stage of Plumer's reformatted advance. 'Not a yard of ground lost by the enemy had been recaptured.'[22] Instead of throwing their formations back against the continuing British advance, the Germans had piled them into their new positions to the rear to try and halt the British from taking any more ground. Ludendorff ceded that the British Army had evolved a method to get around his counter-attack divisions. The failures experienced during the first two steps of Plumer's advance caused German high command to take a second look at their methods. The counter-attackers were arriving too late, struggling to co-ordinate their efforts with their artillery and the chaos of trying to organise an assault mid-battle was confusing the issue. Perhaps, it was stated, it would be better if instead of responding to the British assault straightaway, they waited until the following morning to organise and gather information before striking back to regain lost ground.

In the meantime, Haig began to think that his coveted breakthrough might be near, that Passchendaele itself might find its way into British hands by winter, perhaps along with even more gains depending on the weather. At a conference Haig told Plumer and Gough that he next wanted the area around Broodseinde to be taken early in October, but he provided less definitive objectives so that they might try and take any opportunity to exploit the situation. Both army commanders told him that talk of exploitation was jumping the gun. It was, after all, coming away from the tactics that had started to bring them success, and Haig responded that he merely wanted to make sure that the relevant reserves were prepared just in case an opportunity presented itself. He anxiously didn't want to wait and repeat the mistake made by German command back in 1914 at Ypres, when victory was so close and they failed to carry the attack through and seize it.

It was eventually decided that the third stage of the reformatted advance would go forth on 4 October. The enemy were, quite naturally, determined not to be undone again, making 'desperate final efforts'[23] not to lose any more of their precious high ground. 'The fine weather held over the turn of the month; warm sunny days were followed by bright moonlit nights.'[24] It was not all comfort, for the Germans took advantage of thick morning mists to prepare their defences and to harass the British with artillery. At 5 a.m. on 1 October a hurricane bombardment opened on lines in the same area in which the 1st Middlesex had operated at the end of September when William Tillbrook had been captured. The position was held, notably, against 'specially trained German shock-troops'[25] but the resistance did not manage to dampen the preparations for the British attack on Broodseinde.

Chopper Harris' family had been doing their utmost to contribute to the war effort, even if it was not entirely legal. His grandfather, Albert, was just 14 when he enlisted in the Rifle Brigade at Shoreditch in September 1915. Presumably he managed to carry off the falsehood that he was 19 to begin with (for added effect he claimed to be a tailor), but less than two weeks later he reported to Winchester to begin his training where it seems that he was being far too hopeful. Albert was sent home after twelve days in the army.

Taking part in preparations at Broodseinde though, would be Edwin Samain, a full eight years older than his over-enthusiastic brother, and at 25 more than old enough to fight. Edwin had originally served with the same battalion of the London Regiment as George Collison's unfortunate brother Jack, before transferring to the 1st Somerset Light Infantry.

At 6 a.m. on 4 October, the 4th Division, to which Edwin's battalion belonged, was to attack. A full moon was masked by thick clouds as the 1st Somerset Light Infantry formed the far right of their divisional front, with the 1st Hampshires of the same brigade on their left. They arranged themselves under cover of darkness, laden with equipment, the officers dressed exactly like the men and without their telltale walking sticks in order to blend in. Every man except machine and Lewis gun specialists was carrying two flares to answer the aeroplane klaxons and keep the authorities informed as to their progress.

Edwin and the rest of the battalion were waiting in three lines to advance when a creeping artillery barrage commenced 150 yards in front of them. For the first half an hour it was also accompanied by an arced shower of Lewis gun fire. The men had of course been primed with the idea of keeping as close as possible to their own bombardment. When Edwin, the great uncle of later Chelsea legend Ron 'Chopper' Harris went forward, however, his company joined by a machine-gun team, they found the barrage ragged, impossible to keep close to because so many shells were falling short. A senior officer later remarked that sadly, but undoubtedly, Somerset casualties were caused by the effects of their own shellfire. The brigadier acknowledged that this was always going to be the case in the rush of battle, but he thought that this time the sheer numbers falling prey to their own guns was not acceptable.

Elsewhere the Australians had burst forwards and reached the old British line of 1914/15. When they began digging in, they found scraps of khaki uniforms, all that was left of the men who had already fallen trying to hold this land, 'belonging to British soldiers who had given their lives to hold this gateway to Calais and London three years earlier. The gathered strength of the Empire had now arrived to make good the gallant defence by that small British force.'[26] Meanwhile, back on the Somerset Light Infantry's front, owing to the darkness it was hard for Edwin Samain and his fellow men to keep direction and the surrounding battalions became rather mixed soon after their advance commenced. A certain amount of veering off to the right was encountered, but thankfully a trail of tape was being left by the advancing troops to help those coming up behind them. It was a new innovation as far as they were concerned, but the brigadier was impressed, later commenting that 'rapid communication in the future would undoubtedly be facilitated by their wider use'.[27] The battalion had recently welcomed a draft of 200 men who were, in battle terms, babies, 'for the most part only 19 years of age'. They were acquitting themselves admirably thus far, 'having never been under fire before they showed the greatest [bravery] and determination and behaved ... excellently'.

The brigade continued on to their first objective, the Hampshire Battalion faring better than Edwin and their Somerset counterparts, who met with stiff resistance as they came up. An enemy machine gun was holding up the left-hand side of their advance, but they eventually seized the trench by the use of rifle grenades, despite the fact that they were being targeted by a German machine gun at the same time. The same vicious method of assault was required to overcome a number of enemy troops hiding in a large pile of stones. Added to the Somerset men's woes was the fact that British shells were still dropping short. Still, Edwin's battalion managed to overcome a reinforced concrete house under cover of a Lewis gun. Machine-gun fire was pouring onto them from weapons stationed on the roof and to the side of the building, but the battalion worked around an enemy flank and swept aside the threat from the rear, seizing sixteen prisoners and both of the German machine guns in the process. Although troublesome for them, the British bombardment appeared to have wreaked its havoc on the enemy lines.

On reaching their objective the Somersets attempted to reorganise themselves. It was a difficult task thanks to the total absence of landmarks on the pockmarked, muddy ground, which had also made it so problematic for them to maintain direction. Men who had become detached were not easily found in the confusion. Then at 2 p.m. troops belonging to the Seaforth Highlanders on their left were observed falling back in the face of as many as 300 German infantry who had emerged in the form of a counter-attack in front of them. The left-hand side of the Somerset battalion's brigade, formed of the Hampshire men, was pulled back in tandem.

As ever, battle tactics had evolved once again and on this occasion proved perfect to deal with the situation. A specific battalion of the East Lancashire Regiment had been designated as the 'counter-attacking battalion' of the brigade along with two platoons of the Somersets themselves who had also been given specific tasks should the enemy launch a counter-attack during the day. They were not required to wait for orders, which if communications were short would cause critical delays, but had been instructed to act on their own initiative the instant they saw the enemy emerge. Executing this concept perfectly, a captain in the designated East Lancashire Regiment immediately realised what was happening in front of him when the neighbouring brigade began to fall back, took his company forward, checked the retirement and restored their position with the support of the rest of his battalion. Rifles, Lewis guns and a captured machine gun were opened on the Germans as they came over the ridge in front, including from the heap of stones that had recently been seized from them. The counter-attacking enemy infantry suffered severe casualties and eventually the Seaforth Highlanders were able to push up again and re-establish their line. On this occasion the concept of the German counter-attacking units had been well and truly overcome. The brigadier was thrilled: 'The principle of detailing units by name on counter-attacking duties seems to have met with definite success during this action.'[28]

Confusion reigned that evening though as far as headquarters were concerned, trying to establish where all of their troops had finished the day. Those on the flanks could not assist with locating them as contact had been lost. When the battle recommenced the following day the 1st Somerset Light Infantry remained in reserve. Edwin Samain's battalion, with all of its new recruits, had done reasonably well, capturing eighty prisoners, six valuable machine guns and three trench mortars from the enemy. Their efforts were costly. In the assault on Broodseinde the 4th Division had suffered the loss of 157 officers and nearly 3,500 men.

The third stage of Plumer's advance had gained an average of about 1,000 yards of ground, and the general referred to it as 'the greatest victory' since the Marne in 1914. His response might have been a little over-enthusiastic. The success of the British advance declined after Broodseinde with failure at Poelcapelle in shocking conditions. Although the troops engaged in the Flanders campaign had suffered wet weather in August, when the autumn rain came down at Passchendaele it was hellish. The culmination of nearly three months of constant fighting and shelling in the area had destroyed the flat ground and any natural drainage had been obliterated. A senior artillery officer gave some idea of the nightmare:

> The mere movement of artillery and supply of ammunition under peace conditions would have been a Herculean task; it was scarcely possible to walk off the duckboards. All ammunition supply to the more advanced batteries was perforce carried out by packing, mules were constantly engulfed, and even guns in considerable numbers were swallowed up in the sea of mud.[29]

Nevertheless, thanks to confusion about progress on the battlefield, the slaughter continued. On the men advanced to Passchendaele, where after three days the ground initially seized was pulled back by way of enemy counter-attacks. The offensive stalled on account of the weather as the BEF attempted to restore its shattered lines of communication.

The final stage of the Third Battle of Ypres took place at the beginning of November. The capture and retention of Passchendaele Ridge by the Canadians was a significant achievement. Ludendorff wrote in his memoirs that 'the British charged like a wild bull against the iron wall which kept them from the submarine bases. They threw their weight against positions along the entire front.'[30] The total casualties suffered by the Canadians in the final stages of Third Ypres alone amounted to nearly 13,000 men. On 12 October a senior German officer wrote the words, 'Rain. Our best ally' in his diary.[31] It was becoming evident that the battle immortalised as 'Passchendaele' had almost run its course. Five British divisions were on their way to Italy. Four divisions of the Fourth Army were going to have to take over a length of the front on the Somme from the French and could not be used. The secretive Battle of Cambrai was also due to begin, using up more valuable resources and Haig decided to end the campaign in Flanders. Since 31 July the divisions engaged in the Third Battle of Ypres had suffered nearly a quarter of a million casualties. Nearly every British division on the Western Front had fought at some stage with minimal French support. 'The wonder is not that complete success was not achieved, but that so much was done by so few to break the spirit and reduce the numbers of the enemy.' There had, however, been no crushing victory over the Germans, despite how much enthusiasm and resources had been lavished on the area. Arthur Wileman had survived. Edwin Samain would soon be invalided out of the army as a result of being wounded in action. Harry Ford would fight on and William Tillbrook now sat in a prisoner of war camp. But what was to happen next? Ludendorff had to do something, for soon the Americans would arrive in France and Belgium with their massive resources and the Germans could not possibly hope to match them either in men or material. Decisive action would have to be taken, and quickly if Germany was to entertain any hopes of winning the war.

17

'With Our Backs to the Wall'

Spring 1918

As the war entered its final year, it was far from only the Western Front that had thrown up action for scores of Chelsea fans, players and those associated with the club. The conflict was truly a world war, raging on many fronts and the founder's son, Joseph Mears, had fought on two of them. Disembarking in Egypt with the London Yeomanry as an 18-year-old three days after the Gallipoli landings, he had fought dismounted in the latter part of that botched campaign. Horsemen found a type of warfare far more familiar to them on the wide expanses of Britain's eastern fronts. Later handed a commission, Mears joined a unit that eventually formed a new battalion of the Welsh Regiment. They would spend the latter part of the war on the offensive in Palestine, fighting at the Second and Third Battles of Gaza before being present at Allenby's capture of Jerusalem.

A handful of Chelsea players and fans would find their way to the campaign in Mesopotamia, the highlight of which was British and Indian troops' march into Baghdad. Harold Brittain was with the Leicester Regiment. Another former Chelsea player, the war was to wreak havoc on his football career and would eventually see him move to the United States to play. After the Great Retreat of 1914, Lawrence Catchpole continued to serve with motor-based ASC units in France. A small percentage of his time was spent tied to a fixed object, such as a gun wheel or fence post as punishment after he was caught urinating up against one of the park's lorries, but it was not much of a detriment to his army career which was curtailed as per his terms of service in October 1915.

However, Catchpole re-enlisted in September 1916 and was put back into the motor transport branch of the Army Service Corps. Shortly afterwards he was shipped out to the Middle East as part of the Mesopotamian Expeditionary Force, arriving in Basra in October 1916 when he was moved to 596 Motor Transport Company of the ASC. Like many young Britons, he fell foul of the climate in Mesopotamia at some stage

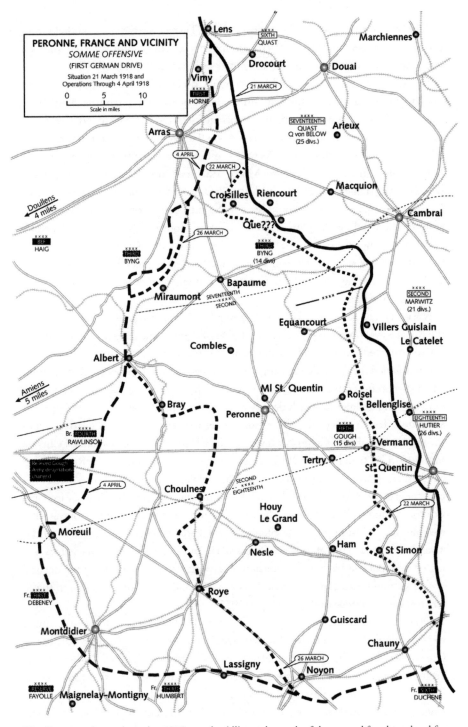

The German advance in spring 1918 saw the Allies cede much of the ground fought so hard for nearly two years earlier. (*Authors' collection*)

and his service was punctuated by a hospital stay. He recovered to join another motor transport company in February 1918, equipped with Ford motor vehicles, shipped from the United States, because of difficulties in meeting supply in the UK.

Having began his career with his local club, Brechin City, Colin Hampton had joined Chelsea just before the war and made his goalkeeping debut in April 1914. Enlisting when professional football was curtailed, like Lawrence Catchpole he served in Mesopotamia in a motor-based unit, but one that on the surface sounded far more adventurous than the reservist's. As well as mounted regiments, the open terrain of Mesopotamia made it ideal for the Motor Machine Gun Corps, which essentially saw men rampaging through the sand brandishing machine guns from their vehicles. A company such as Colin's would have included a collection of motorcycles with sidecars attached for the gunners, more bikes without this hindrance and a small number of armoured cars fitted with machine guns. Colin Hampton was in one of the latter when a shell struck their vehicle in 1918 and he was taken prisoner by the Turks. He was being marched into Ottoman captivity when peace was declared and was released to return home.

Not every man associated with Chelsea kept his feet on firm ground. Some served in the Royal Navy from the very outset, and a handful joined the fledgling flying services. Having survived the Boar's Head and having been awarded a Military Cross, Clifford Whitley joined the Royal Flying Corps and qualified as a pilot. He joined 21 Squadron, who flew bombers out of an aerodrome just north of Amiens at the time. The stress of flying, which sometimes included trying to fly these particular cumbersome aircraft as fighters, took a heavy toll on the young Blues fan and he saw out the latter part of the war being utilised as a ferry or test pilot. Jack Harrow, who had captained Chelsea in the 1915 FA Cup Final at Old Trafford, worked on the ground as the Royal Flying Corps merged with its naval counterpart and evolved into the Royal Air Force at the beginning of 1918. He was joined by Bill Richards, who recovered sufficiently from his wounds at Aubers Ridge to leave the Rifle Brigade and become a driver for the RFC well into the 1920s. Like Harrow, Blue's player Charlie Freeman also served as a fitter when his career was put on hiatus by the war. He had an association with Chelsea that lasted decades and having been employed as a player, a trainer during the Second World War and then a groundsman in later years, Charlie lived long enough to see Chelsea win the league championship in 1955.

Other Chelsea players were included in a group of British men who were assumed to be available for war service, but who would not fire a rifle in anger during the Great War. Angus Douglas was a firm favourite with the Stamford Bridge faithful after Chelsea won the battle for his signature against Rangers and Everton when he decided to leave his hometown club in Dumfries. Capped for Scotland, Angus had since, rather surprisingly, departed for Newcastle United in 1913 and spent the war working as a machinist at Armstrong-Whitworth's north-east factory providing shells for the artillery.

George Hilsdon was a prolific striker in Chelsea's early years and was the model for the lucky weather vane on top of the East Stand at Stamford Bridge. After returning to West Ham, he allegedly fled the authorities initially and hid in a chicken coop to avoid military service. Others took a more official approach. William Brawn was another former Blues player and he had taken his case, as was his right, to the Middlesex Appeals Tribunal in protest at the idea of military service. Originally from the Midlands, the giant outside right had spent four years at Stamford Bridge and played no small part in making Chelsea a top division side for the first time before moving on to Brentford. The tribunal upheld his claim that military service would bring him economic hardship on the condition that he worked thirty hours a week in the munitions industry. The great-grandfather of twenty-first-century Chelsea legend Frank Lampard had an eventful career in the same sort of work. Working a short walk from his home near West Ham, Arthur Lampard was fortunate enough not to be on duty at Silvertown when an incident involving purifying TNT in early 1917 left a string of casualties in east London when the factory exploded. He later joined the Royal Navy and had a troubled time serving at Scapa Flow.

Despite the abundance of Chelsea men scattered across the globe, as 1918 dawned, it became clear that it was to be the Western Front that would decide the outcome of the war. At the beginning of the year 'the stars in their courses',[1] according to General Gough, appeared to be aligning for the German army. On the Eastern Front the Russian contribution had survived the overthrow of the Tsar at the beginning of 1917, but not for long. An offensive launched in July was a magnificent failure. With their own interests in mind, the Germans let Lenin pass through their territory to return home and by the end of the year, following the Soviet Revolution, Britain's Eastern ally was out of the war. German divisions began rolling westward, giving them a window of opportunity in France and Belgium as far as numbers were concerned until the Americans began arriving in force. In early 1918 the Kaiser's army would outnumber their enemies on the Western Front by some fifty divisions and the fate of the Allies would rely more on the BEF than ever before.

Germany categorically needed to take this opportunity to end the war. Not only was she running out of men to throw forward into battle, but at home the economy was collapsing under the expense of the conflict. Ludendorff had anticipated that the Americans could be expected to begin flooding the battlefields sometime in spring. If the war was not over by summer, then everything indicated that he would not be able to win it. As such, planning for the essential offensive began in November 1917. One option was directing a hammer blow towards the British army. The alternative was another one against the French. Planning for all manner of possible spring attacks began. Suggestions for attacking the French varied from impressively titled operations such as Hector and Achilles around Reims, to the not so inspiring sounding Operation Roland in the Champagne region. As far as the British were concerned there were also myriad possibilities. Operation George looked at Flanders, Operation Michael would hit out from the south of Arras across the Somme and alternatively Operation Mars would attack Vimy and Arras itself.

Mars was never held in massively high regard because of the issue of having to reclaim the imposing Vimy Ridge. Given the early date that the attack was planned for, there was also a chance that German endeavours towards Ypres could be brought to a grinding, muddy halt in Flanders and so when Ludendorff decided to stick with his own preference and attack the British, attention naturally turned to Operation Michael. The German approach was not going to be subtle. There was no time for General Plumer-style bunny-hopping towards sensible limited objectives. Three armies were going to smash full force through the Somme sector and then pivot north-west. Then the catastrophically weakened BEF would be hit with Operation Mars a few days later, crushing resistance around Arras. Finally, when the ground had dried out, Operation George would be brought to fruition to kick the British Army out of Flanders and out of the war. In mid-February the Kaiser was informed that this was to be the greatest military feat an army had ever attempted. 'Upon the results of this offensive the very existence of the German Empire depended: failure would be the beginning of the end.'[2]

No matter how much the need for stealth might be urged, no campaign on this scale could be kept secret for long. Sir Douglas Haig was aware that he would not only have the full might of the enemy to contend with in 1918, but his own government too. Led by David Lloyd George, political interference in military affairs was to prove crippling for the British Army at this point in the war. The Prime Minister had orchestrated at the request of the Fench the occupation of yet more of the line, from St Quentin down to the River Oise. Additionally, Haig was refused the men he had requested to bring his army up to strength after the nightmare of the Third Battle of Ypres and further casualties suffered at the Battle of Cambrai had rounded off the year. Men with no concept of military reality withheld reinforcements and those already at the front would suffer heavily for it. The British Army now held a line longer than ever before, with less strength per mile. In order to man the length of the front that had now been ordained for him, Haig had no choice but to pull his army apart and reorganise it. Any semblance of familiarity among the divisions at the front was destroyed as they were broken down and reassembled. Each brigade was reduced from four battalions to three, which was not so much impossible to work with as the timeframe was ludicrous given the impending German attack. Therefore, just prior to the biggest blow that the BEF had yet dealt with, each division was significantly reduced by its existing standards. More than 130 battalions were disbanded and among the casualties was the Footballers' Battalion. What began as an attempt to bring together the football community to help contribute to the national crisis had lost all semblance of its identity by early 1918 when the bulk of its survivors were mainly fed into the 13th or the 21st Middlesex battalions.

The fact that in many cases the ordinary soldier's world might have recently been torn apart was just one small factor contributing to a mood of abject misery across the BEF at the beginning of 1918. By now, for the Fulham and Chelsea men who saw the 17th Middlesex disappear, the idea of rushing to Bert Palmer's office at the Bridge and then into a recruiting venue to sign up for the war was not nearly so attractive. Now that they had seen the reality of it, if they had survived long enough, they had forgotten the patriotism, the social pressure to enlist, the wave of enthusiasm that had driven them into the army. War was disgusting and there was no end in sight. The recently disbanded men of the 17th Middlesex were exhausted. Almost none of them had escaped unscathed from the battles that they had fought so far and nearly everyone had experienced some form of incapacitating wounds, physically or mentally, since their original arrival in France in 1915.

A prime example was Stamford Bridge local Charles Prentice, a coal porter who had enlisted in March 1915 with the first swathe of enthusiasts heading for the Footballers' Battalion. Charles was not a bad soldier. He displayed some issues with turning up for parade in the early days at White City and while the battalion was training at Holmbury St Mary he had to be apprehended by the local police when he wandered off for a week on two occasions. But he was far from an isolated case and since arriving at the front his behaviour had been exemplary. Charles was even awarded a Military Medal for his conduct on Christmas Eve 1917. At the turn of the year, however, he appeared to have reached the limit of his endurance. As the Footballers' Battalion was disbanded and Charles found himself routed to the 13th Middlesex instead, he went home for two weeks' leave at the end of February and failed to return for duty on 8 March. Charles would eventually be apprehended by the police in England six weeks later and shipped back to France where he was remanded for a subsequent court martial appearance.

Sir Douglas Haig had so much front to cover, with so few men, that inevitably there were going to be weak spots on the British line. Understandably he was categorically not prepared to let the Ypres sector be one of them. Losing even the smallest piece of ground could be catastrophic as the opposing armies were packed in so tightly in Flanders. The Second Army, who guarded it, and next to them the First Army, who protected key points to the south over the border in France such as the Vimy Ridge, could be safe in the knowledge that on no account would their strength be undermined if GHQ could help it. Next in line, with a relatively short front, was General Byng's Third Army, which guarded a salient at Flesquieres created at the Battle of Cambrai at the end of 1917. Early in 1918 the most southerly army of the BEF happened to be the Fifth, under the command of Sir Hubert Gough. With twelve divisions and some cavalry, weak in numbers by comparison to infantry divisions, he had responsibility for more than 40 miles of front, right where the Germans were planning to attack.

At this point, though, Sir Douglas Haig could not be completely sure where the enemy assault was going to take place and he had hard decisions to make. While Gough's concerns revolved around his own men, understandably Haig had to consider the whole picture. As unjust as it would have sounded to Gough, if Haig could afford for any army to be bludgeoned, coldly speaking it was Gough's. Behind the Fifth Army line was a stretch of 40 miles of terrain before the Germans, if they broke through, could reach a point of strategic significance: Amiens. And surely it was unthinkable that they could ever get that far if they did make a break for it?

Knowing that they were weaker in numbers and that an attack was brewing, the BEF, who were more experienced at launching big offensives than standing up to them, had to make a hurried attempt to build a system of defence akin to that which the Germans had developed over a period of years. It was based on the enemy's fluid system with a Forward Zone, loosely held by outposts. Behind that would be a Battle Zone. This was to be the main point of defence, roughly a mile and a half in depth and taking advantage of all of the most appropriate features that the countryside had to offer. Some distance behind that was to be the Rear Zone. It all seemed very impressive on paper, but in reality a lack of time and resources meant that too much effort had been placed on the Forward Zone, which was of course the first line of defence but one that was also expected to be overrun. In tandem, not enough time had been spent on the Battle Zone, which was supposed to be the point of the most fierce resistance, while the Rear Zone was, at best, generally still a line of shallow markers that showed where the trenches ought to be.

While the BEF struggled to dig in in depth, intelligence operatives, captured prisoners and the hardworking Royal Flying Corps were amassing more and more clues as to when and where the impending German offensive might take place. British aeroplanes had registered 'the greatest activity' opposite the Fifth and Third armies. Informants claimed that the enemy would be coming at them around 20 or 21 March. The British command was also privy to the same common sense about ground conditions that prompted the Germans to turn their attentions away from Flanders. When two generals who had overseen heroic victories in the name of the Kaiser further east at Riga and Caporetto arrived and headed straight to take command of troops opposite Byng and Gough, the coming offensive appeared to be coming into focus properly. The attack would come against the Third and Fifth armies. Haig was still mindful that this could all be a ruse and would not waver from his determination to keep his limited available reserves where they could help protect Ypres and the more northern aspects of the British front if necessary, Gough was understandably beside himself at the thought of his army, with its weakened divisions, facing off against the might of a determined German attempt to end the war. His cries for reserves to be positioned accordingly and his protests about his predicament were not unjustified, but there was little Haig could do about them. The junior man would just have to make do. If, as might realistically occur now, they were smashed head on by the German onslaught, his men now had a hypothetical 'Emergency Line' along the River Somme itself that they could retreat to. That was of course providing anybody was available to prepare it in depth, which they were not. It was not either man's fault, but it was the rank and file left manning the lines that were ultimately about to suffer the consequences for politicians meddling in matters that they quite obviously didn't comprehend.

The dubiously prepared zonal defences were going to have to stand up to immense scrutiny. By 19 March it was certain that it was Gough and Byng's armies that were going to be hit. One prisoner gave 9.30 a.m. on the 21st as a precise time. A multitude of Germans falling in to British hands up and down the lines were tellingly anxious to be sent back to the rear as they were seized, out of potential harm's way. By 20 March, with a thick mist beginning to settle over the battlefield, some units were hearing whispers of the attack that was to hit them on the following day; Thursday 21 March 1918 would indeed be the date that the Germans intended to strike out and win the Great War.

The Kaiser's army had prepared for their offensive by dragging up some 10,000 guns and heavy trench mortars. A monstrous bombardment opened at 4.40 a.m. across a huge swathe of the British front, even spreading to the First Army sector to the north. Fired in phases aimed at different types of target, it began with a stunning attack on British gun batteries, in particular, leaning heavily towards gas shells which sent out noxious fumes that curdled with the mist. Communications were brutally targeted too, severing the flow of information in the impermeable fog. This supreme effort was largely thanks to the work of Germany's airmen, who had photographed the positions of all such targets prior to the battle. Shell holes were punched in the ground in such close proximity by the enemy that the craters in places were almost touching. The British response was immediate but fraught with difficulty. The gunners opened fire on pre-preparation positions, but the awful visibility meant that adjusting their fire to aim for specific points relevant to events unfolding was impossible. The noise had sent General Gough running from his bed. He could not even see to the end of the garden outside his window. He had tried to do his best in dire circumstances to prepare for the onslaught; now surviving it was the responsibility of his subordinates and he could do nothing but wait.

The 24th Division was in the vicinity of Pontru, spread out over some 7,000 yards, 9 miles north-west of St Quentin and roughly in the middle of Gough's front. Its three brigades were all in the line, each with one battalion in the Forward Zone, one in the forward part of the Battle Zone and one to the rear of that zone with their relevant pioneer battalion. Back in reserve behind the centre of the front were the 13th Battalion of the Middlesex Regiment. Charles Prentice was at this point still unaccounted for somewhere in England, but still with the battalion was Edwin Siveyer, a Battersea labourer who enlisted in the Footballers' Battalion at Chelsea Town Hall as a teenager in 1915, was still 20 at Delville Wood and Guillemont and barely 21 when he went into action at Arras. Miraculously, the only physical injury worth noting that the now 22-year-old had suffered by 1918 was a superficial one to his right eyelid at the end of the previous year.

On 20 March Edwin and the rest of the 13th Middlesex were instructed that in the event of enemy attack, they were to form part of a garrison near Vermand. Men had already reconnoitred the position, which was useful because less than an hour after the deafening, brutal German bombardment began everybody was ordered to man their battle positions. By 7.30 a.m. Edwin had taken up his place and was listening to the shellfire raging on. Dawn failed to penetrate the mist. In the first five hours of the barrage over a million German shells would be fired at the BEF. Playing the role of sacrificial lambs in this scenario, those unfortunate enough to be manning posts in the Forward Zone awaiting their miserable fate would have been fully aware that a significant infantry attack was to follow. In front of Edwin's battalion, the majority of the division had been reporting that all was still clear of the enemy on their front, but that their plight was obscure on account of the fog. Shortly after 9 a.m. a telephone call revealed that the Germans were moving on nearby Épehy. The codeword 'Bustle' went out to make sure that a welcoming party would be waiting for them. In the fog Edwin Siveyer and the 13th Middlesex had to go up wearing their gas masks, holding on to each other 'like blind men as they stumbled forward in the darkness',[3] managing remarkably to stay largely on track with almost zero visibility.

The German infantry advance began at just before 10 a.m. The British wire had been obliterated across the front and masked by the mist, enemy troops had been out cutting more by hand. Advancing through the opaque fog, they came upon whole garrisons and outposts annihilated by their own artillery's bombardment. Those that had survived in the Forward Zone did not see the Germans until they were almost on top of them. Any SOS lights sent up were lost in the mist. In the Battle Zone men did not know whether to open fire or not; was the enemy coming at them or was it the Forward Zone troops falling back? Men were cut off and surrounded, 'in some cases before the garrisons behind them, except for hearing the sound of cheers, were aware that the enemy assault had begun'.[4] Offensive tactics had evolved once again by the beginning of 1918, building from experience at Cambrai at the end of the previous year. The idea of the storm trooper had been set in motion by the German Army and was a follow on from British offensive methods already developed in 1916 and 1917. Men had been pulled out of their existing units to form special teams. Armed with lighter weapons, they would sweep forward, accompanied by the odd flamethrower or mortar, and infiltrate the British lines, purposely leaving behind any points of resistance. Behind them would come the main infantry to occupy the ground, clear out dugouts and take care of any determined defences that had been bypassed. Despite some isolated pockets somehow evading the troops following up storm trooper units, the Forward Zone on Edwin Siveyer's sector was overrun. By lunchtime on 21 March the enemy had reached the all important Battle Zone along the entire, massively outnumbered Fifth Army front.

Having not occupied forward positions when the attack commenced, the 13th Middlesex had got off relatively lightly on the opening day of the overwhelming German offensive. The battalion struggled though to ascertain what was going on around them in the chaos. Information that did come in was sketchy and they spent the day frantically improving defences. Communications remained impossible across the board. Pigeons had been gassed, telephone wires smashed to bits by high explosive and the weight of the bombardment meant that runners could not get back and forth. All of the elements conspired to make the flow of communications across the battlefield utterly impossible. Added to that, even the men on the ground were running about with gas masks on until 11 a.m. and so, notwithstanding the bursting shells and the fog, troops engaged in the battle had next to no peripheral vision to enable them to see what was unfolding immediately around them, let alone at a distance. The all important airmen who could have assisted could not be of use either, unable to get up and see down on the battlefield. When they eventually could, any zone calls, asking for the British gunners to target a particular spot in aid of the infantry, went unanswered when they were most relevant to the artillery because telephone and wireless equipment was wrecked and instructions could not get through.

The Third Army was stationed to the north under General Byng, who had distinguished himself leading the charge on Vimy Ridge in April 1917. Here the German plan was to attack the salient at Flesquieres on either side in order to squeeze its British occupants into submission. To that end the area had been saturated with gas and the troops holding the line were in serious trouble. Deep in reserve were the 21st Middlesex, who had been training after being pulled out of the line over a fortnight before. Among the men that the battalion had inherited on the disbandment of the Footballers' Battalion was Cyril Dale, who had got away with enlisting at 16. The lottery that was life on the battlefield had turned out in the teenager's favour thus far, with the exception of the shellshock that saw a brief hiatus from the 17th Middlesex in the aftermath of Delville Wood. Alongside Cyril was Thomas Frost, a valet who originally hailed from Devon. He had married shortly before the war and at home off Fulham Road had twin daughters whom he had left at 6 months in order to enlist and a third little girl who had been born just a few weeks before he departed for the front with the Footballers' Battalion. Tom had done remarkably well too in keeping himself physically fit so far at the front and had not long returned from a period of leave at home with his family.

On the morning of 21 March when the enemy commenced his offensive, the battalion heard the bombardment hammering away in the distance and stood to for an hour and a half in case they were needed. Out of sight the enemy began raiding the trenches on their front but immediate counter-attacks pushed them out again. At lunchtime orders came for the 21st Middlesex to move off on the long march to join the battle. By 10.30 p.m. news had arrived that part of their neighbouring front had caved and that the enemy was thought to be preparing to attack again the following morning. This section of Byng's line had been pushed back to their third system of defences and it was these that the 21st Middlesex were sent to help hold. In the confusion they found friendly troops in front and so occupied their position without much opposition, taking up a front of about 1,400 yards and pushing out reconnoitring patrols to endeavour to trace the enemy. In front of them things did not look good. The Germans had already almost bludgeoned their way through the entire Battle Zone.

Things were even worse to the south. By the end of Thursday 21 March the Germans would be well into the Battle Zone the length of Gough's front. The enemy had blitzed through the Forward Zone along the whole Fifth Army line and as yet reserves had not managed to get anywhere near the fighting. More troops being summoned from the Ypres and Arras areas would take even longer to reach the battle. The lack of adequate preparation on Gough's front was telling. Although the loss of the Forward Zone was essentially the point of its existence, the success the Germans had had in advancing beyond that was deeply concerning. The BEF suffered almost 40,000 casualties in one day, more than half of them seized as prisoners as the troops holding the line were overrun. A quarter of those in the Forward Zone were lost along with valuable equipment such as Lewis and machine guns. Confusion was rife in the fog and the German artillery's efforts at disrupting communications were wholly effective:

> The battle was mainly carried on by battalions and small bodies, assisted by the divisional batteries … it was impossible for the artillery commanders to know what to shoot [at]. The heavy artillery batteries were mostly silent or firing slowly when the assault took place, and the first intimation which many of them received of the situation was the sight of the infantry retiring through or past them.

In terms of manpower, the opening day of the German offensive was almost as damaging as the day the Battle of the Somme began on 1 July 1916. Whole battalions had all but evaporated and hundreds of British guns were lost. An area roughly the size of modern-day Birmingham had been lost in a single day.

In charge of the German operations, Ludendorff's options for continuing the offensive were relatively flexible. As such he decided that rather than turn north-west towards Arras as planned, he would carry on smashing away at the Fifth Army, the southern portion of which was in absolute chaos. Already Gough did not think for one moment that he could fight back; he simply had to hope his men could cling on until enough reserves arrived to make a stand somewhere along the path of retreat. Orders sent out from his headquarters instructed the men to try and fight back in a coherent manner until they reached the front edge of their dubious Rear Zone. If necessary they could fall back to the Emergency Line, which as a coherent form of defence was actually non-existent. It was merely a hypothetical line that Gough's men should try and stick to in order to stop the Fifth Army from completely folding. Even if the positions had been properly constructed, the units being detailed to hold them were threatening to break apart. In such mayhem how was a battalion, a brigade, a division supposed to hold itself together? Men were variously dead, captured, still clinging to outposts somewhere forward or part of the main retirement backing away from the German onslaught. Figuring out who fell into which category or how troops were distributed so that orders might be given out was to become increasingly difficult.

On the 13th Middlesex front mist cloaked the battlefield again on 22 March when the enemy renewed his attack. Edwin Siveyer and his fellow troops managed to drive back several attacks, but against such overwhelming numbers they could not be expected to hold their position. When troops on the right withdrew, leaving them isolated, Edwin and the rest of the battalion were forced to pass through the end of the Rear Zone towards a set of crossroads in the evening under heavy artillery and machine-gun fire. There was no rest for the men once there, as they were forced to take up emergency battle positions throughout the night on account of enemy shellfire. Edwin's war was now over. Machine-gunned in both legs, he was captured by the enemy as the Germans swept forward. Once in captivity he would fight tooth and nail to prevent the authorities from performing a double amputation. Although he was successful, the 22-year-old would be left with a limp for the rest of his life.

The day had been no less of an ordeal for Tom Frost and Cyril Dale with the 21st Middlesex and General Byng's Third Army. As early as 3 a.m. the battalion had had to withdraw to support troops nearby. It was misty, foggy and inclined towards rain. During the morning the brigadier made his way around to all of the battalions to see the impact of the German offensive for himself. Just before lunchtime reports were received that the enemy was forming up, aligning themselves north-west with a view to attacking. Elements of the 21st Middlesex were sent up to man the lines. They reported that British troops in front of them were 'wavering'[5] and that St Leger nearby was under threat. By the day's end it appeared to have fallen. Ludendorff delivered himself to a meeting with the Kaiser and von Hindenburg on 23 March and the original plan for rolling north-west up the British line and dumping Haig's various armies out of the war one by one now went completely out of the window. Instead, Ludendorff wanted to pierce the spot where Gough and Byng's armies still met and force them apart, rupturing the British line. The question now was would this turn out to be a stroke of genius or a fatal choice that would cost Germany the war? As history would reveal, it turned out to be an appalling decision.

British troops falling on the rear positions were a ramshackle collection of various corps and regiments who happened to be going along together. Fighting men fled with cooks and troops usually charged with occupations to the rear such as sanitation. The make-up of various groups retiring back towards the River Somme was entirely random. German aircraft zipped low across the path of the British retreat, unleashing a hail of bullets on the fleeing troops. Any defences on the western banks of the Somme were negligible. At GHQ, Sir Douglas Haig was bull-headed in his instructions as far as the Fifth Army was concerned. The line of the river must be held 'at all costs' and no withdrawal should occur. Already, though, this position was beginning to disintegrate. For one thing the river didn't protect the whole front and so the Germans were flooding past it on either side. Some British troops retreated up to 6 miles. After three days of constant running and fighting, the fleeing men were utterly exhausted, but they had no choice but to continue to try and hold up the assaulting Germans.

Early in the morning of the 23rd the remaining Chelsea men of the Footballers' Battalion who had been transferred to the 13th Middlesex were ordered to occupy defensive positions. They moved off and had found their way there by 7 a.m. where they found no sign of the enemy. Less than two hours later, though, they were ordered to fall back across the Somme providing their own rearguard. This tenuous position was not a realistic place to mount a defence. The men that reached it could stay there in theory, but how were they to make a show of holding it with no reserves to help reinforce it when the enemy fell upon them? The battalion approached the Somme as preparations were made to destroy the bridges across it. If the Germans appeared at any of the crossings, there was to be no hesitation: blow them up. Masked by another thick mist the 13th Middlesex got across without any misfortune, but certain companies were required to spend a jittery night guarding the river with men of the Northamptonshire Regiment.

The Third Army were not in quite such a state on the 23rd, although the Germans continued to pound away at the salient at Flesquieres. The day began swathed in a crisp frost, which would later give way again to fine weather. At 4 a.m. news arrived with the 21st Middlesex that another battalion of the regiment was breaking under the strain of the enemy advance at Mory some 20 miles west of Cambrai towards the southern part of the Third Army front. The village had fallen and the Germans were now pushing towards Ervillers further west. Early on a brigade major visited the 21st's headquarters and gave verbal orders to concentrate at once and to launch an attack on Mory in conjunction with a battalion of the East Surreys, who were to operate on their right. The plan was for the Middlesex men, including Tom Frost and Cyril Dale, to help retake the village and a defensive line running north-east and east of the village. By 8 a.m. the battalion was concentrated in front of a quarry watching the East Surreys deploying south of Ervillers. Zero hour was timed for 8.45 a.m.

The Middlesex attack commenced. Reaching the high ground in front of them the men were met by a considerable amount of machine-gun fire but not much hostile shelling. By now the British artillery bombardment had commenced, but the gunners underestimated their range and a worrying number of shells began falling among British troops causing several casualties. Frantic messages from brigade headquarters managed to get the range lengthened and despite the continuous machine-gun fire, the advance jerked forward in short rushes, one section of Lewis gun team covering the next in line. On their right the East Surreys were being held up by machine-gun fire coming from an advanced post in front of Mory, but on their left the 21st Middlesex went swiftly over the high ground. When Cyril, Tom and the 21st Middlesex reached their objective the enemy were nowhere to be found, instead having taken up a position on the other side of a tangle of wire, from where they began to enfilade the advancing British troops.

By 10.30 a.m. the overstretched Middlesex line was faced with the rumour that German infantrymen were coming towards them and a reserve company was thrown in to strengthen their position as a request for more reserves went back down the line.

Some men had got close to Mory itself, but they went ominously quiet, suggesting that they had been cut off. A German airman zoomed overhead, spraying the attacking troops with bullets from his machine gun until he was eventually brought down by ground fire. As the advance continued, more men poured into the line until it was fully garrisoned. During the afternoon the Surreys went forward again from either side of the road running into the village from Ervillers. Their right flank got up well towards the outskirts of the village before they were again held up by machine guns showering them from higher ground. It was then realised that the amount of co-operation the East Surreys were apparently able to afford the 21st Middlesex would make it impracticable to press home the attack on Mory while keeping in touch with the Guards division on their left as they had been ordered. The attack on the village was broken off and orders issued to consolidate in depth. If at all possible the men were to send patrols out towards the village.

It was found that the line that the Middlesex men were supposed to be occupying was dug to less than 2 feet deep, ditch-like as opposed to a proper trench and far too wide. This gave them no cover and the enemy took advantage as such to rake their ranks with more machine-gun fire. Some 300 yards of this so-called line had not been dug at all. By dusk, though, a telephone line had been run out, the Surreys had taken Mory and the British position improved. Lewis gunners would have been able to take advantage of an unlimited number of targets, had they not been saving their ammunition. That night the men continued to dig in and when they were relieved the following day, almost all of the line had been properly turned out of the countryside as instructed.

The night passed quietly, but on the 24th Byng's army was retiring to keep up with the flank of the fleeing Fifth Army to the south. Heartbreakingly, British troops were now passing over the terrain that they had fought for, that their fellow men had died for, during the Somme battles of 1916. 'Units retired, took up defensive positions in the old trench lines, held on for as long as they could, until they were once again outflanked and they went back again.' Discipline was breaking down, panic was rife, men were starving and in need of rest. To the south the Germans accounted for both Teddy Foord's military and professional football careers by putting a bullet in his left knee. The 22-year-old would never now cement a place in the Chelsea first team. Having led by example in being one of the first to raise his hand at the original meeting in Fulham on the founding of the Footballers' Battalion, Teddy was subsequently assessed as having a 30 per cent disability. He had paid for his patriotism with his future. Invalided out of the army in October 1918, Teddy would arrive home to Fulham to a pension of 11s a week for the first few months only. The salary cap for a professional footballer before the war had been a comparatively huge £5.

On 25 March the battered Fifth Army were expecting the onslaught to continue and the enemy did not disappoint. The Germans continued to attack across the Somme and the last remnants of the defensive line continued to fragment. There was now a rabble-like effect to Gough's force, with little cohesion and structured command as little bands of men tramped along. It was every man for himself. While the Germans erroneously obsessed over separating the two British forces, Haig's preoccupation was keeping alongside the French to the south to ensure the ultimate survival of the BEF. Whether or not the French would adhere to this, or peel off in the direction of Paris and abandon their Allies to protect their capital, was unclear. The following day Haig orchestrated a conference at Doullens. He wanted French support and a reassurance that they were going to stay alongside his force. Amiens, which had seemed so far in the rear a week ago, was becoming threatened and it was agreed that protecting it was vital. A united Allied command on the Western Front seemed the way to make this happen. Haig didn't even have the support of his own prime minister, so he was not going to be able to get it for himself. To that end, he plumped for the least offensive suggestion and put forward General Foch for the role. If he had to be a subordinate, then Haig could at least live with the idea of deferring to him as opposed to other French alternatives.

The line along the Somme had been obliterated by 26 March. All that had been won in 1916 was being abandoned, but after five days of constant fighting the Germans were beginning to tire. They were moving too fast, outrunning their supplies, suffering from breakdowns in their own communications. On Byng's front the enemy were checked at Bucquoy. The playing field was levelling off, with the two sides facing similar problems as the offensive went on. By now Cyril Dale too had been wounded, although he was lucky enough not to follow Edwin Siveyer's fate and fall into enemy hands. With wounds suggestive of fleeing the oncoming German assault, gunshot wounds to the back of a foot and a leg, Cyril would reach a hospital in England within a week.

A mixture of French and British leftover troops now flooded into position to help stabilise the front. The Fifth Army was in tatters. 'Army' was stretching the truth considering the number of men that remained under Gough's control. It had taken catastrophic events, but at home the government had finally taken heed of what was happening on the Western Front strategically speaking. Having strangled the BEF of recruits, miraculously now the age for service came down, men were found and over the next few months they would be coming not only from home but from other fronts whose importance seemed to have receded into the background now that everybody suddenly acknowledged the primary importance of the fighting in France and Belgium. On 28 March Operation Mars struck out towards Arras. This time the British were far better prepared for what was coming at them. Although the German preliminary bombardment wreaked havoc and the enemy infantry rushed into the Forward Zone, the First Army had been able to pay far more stringent attention to the principle of the Battle Zone being all important during their preparations and the German attack ultimately failed.

The ragtag remains of the General Gough's army had now fallen back some 30 miles and Amiens had become a realistic target for the Germans. An 'Amiens Defence

Line' was cobbled together in front of the city. It had at least some military thinking behind it, in that it was based upon some old French lines from 1915, but Gough had no men to put in it. In the end it was manned by anybody that another general on the spot could throw into it. There was little recognisable military hierarchy or communications set up in 'Carey's Force'. Less than 4,000 men, many of them non-combatants such as labourers with no record of fighting in a cohesive unit, let alone together, manned the line. But somehow they held it. French divisions were arriving to reinforce the shattered British men on the Somme. The principle of the Allies operating under Foch's single command was beginning to take effect, but it would not benefit Gough, who was cast in the role of scapegoat. The fact that his army no longer existed as a fighting force was all but irrelevant. When General Rawlinson arrived on the Somme to replace him his fall from grace was complete.

On 29 March, more than a week after the BEF's southern armies commenced retiring, the Germans' initial offensive was well and truly dying down. Carey's force had successfully held its position until it could be relieved and the enemy were spent on the Somme front. A coherent defensive line was being formed and the attack had lost all sense of direction. There did not seem to be any strategic point to the German push anymore. A lull began in terms of large-scale fighting whilst they attempted to take stock and organise themselves.

Operation Michael had failed, but the Germans still had to attempt to win the war. They were running out of men, running out of money and running out of war material. The ground that Ludendorff had gained had largely turned out to be strategically quite useless and had done little but cause a bulging salient into the British front that rendered his men at risk from future attacks. It had all come too at the cost of hundreds of thousands of irreplaceable casualties. The Allies may have lost more than a quarter of a million men from the strength of their armies, but they had American troops flooding to their aid. Germany had lost nearly the same numbers and these could not be replaced. Ludendorff's response was to reduce Operation George, aimed at Flanders, in scale to 'Georgette' and strike for the Channel via the likes of Bailleul, Hazebrouck with its critical rail junctions, and Ypres, which guarded the way to Dunkirk, Calais and beyond it, Britain itself.

It was now crunch time for Haig, who had always recognised how important this area was, but who had had to siphon troops away from it to send to Gough and Byng's aid. The front could be shortened by a few miles if they abandoned the latter gains of the fighting around Passchendaele in 1917, but for now this painful possibility was shelved. Operation Georgette commenced. By 10 a.m. on 9 April the enemy had overrun the Forward Zone in front of Hazebrouck, sending the British and a poor contingent of Portuguese troops stuffed into the line running on the cramped front, where not an inch could be spared. The following day the Germans set out separately to claim back the Messines Ridge on the approach to Ypres itself. Haig issued a message to his troops. He knew that they were tired, but victory waited for whichever side could stick out this torment the longest. The French were on their way, they just had to hold on. 'With our backs to the wall and believing the justice of our cause each one of us must fight on to the end,' he told them. 'The safety of our homes and the freedom of mankind alike depend upon the conduct of each one of us at this critical moment.'[6] His rallying words contributed to the determination to hold the line, some of the efforts from men who had already endured the hell of Operation Michael on the Somme. Bailleul fell on 15 April, but this was the extent of the enemy advance. Once again the Allied defence was becoming organised, this time with the influx of more reserves arriving from other fronts. The ground that had been bitterly wrested from the enemy in the latter months of 1917 did have to be given up, although it was done so in the form of a measured retirement as opposed to turning and running. It was nevertheless heartbreaking for everyone from Plumer himself, who had orchestrated its seizure, down to the rank and file returning to the Pilckem Ridge behind. They had, after all, seen their friends and countrymen die to take it. Nonetheless, by the end of April the Germans had failed to blow away the British front. Ypres and Hazebrouck remained firmly in Allied hands. Ludendorff was all but out of both time and options if he was to ensure that Germany did not lose the war.

18

'No Wild Scenes of Rejoicing'

The Advance to Victory

After his ordeal during the Gallipoli landings at Anzac Cove in the spring of 1915, Harry Trusler was next ordered onto a ship bound for Cape Helles. The authorities in the Dardanelles had determined another attack was needed despite all that the men had already been through. In mid-July it was decided to attempt to follow up minimal gains made at the end of the previous month. The point of attacking was negligible. The government had approved the sending of more men to the peninsula, so using battered formations like the Royal Naval Division was harsh. One senior officer went as far as to claim that such attacks were 'cruel and wasteful' as well as 'wicked' and incompetently planned.

When Harry and the Portsmouth Battalion of the Royal Marine Light Infantry were unexpectedly summoned on the second day of the battle, communications were completely shot and thus far, despite taking heavy casualties, it had proved impossible to budge the Turks from their third line of defences. At 4.30 p.m., with Harry in the middle of their line, the Royal Naval Division would attempt to help the advance. One battalion of Royal Marines did not go forward, not receiving their orders until 9 p.m. Harry's went too far for their own good in the mayhem. 'Only those who actually witnessed the confusion of the battle, the sickness of the troops, intensified a hundred fold by the local conditions and the tenacity of the Turkish resistance' understood the misery of those involved.[1] In the indistinguishable chaos, a bullet grazed the side of Harry's head as the Portsmouth Battalion came out of the attack with only one unwounded officer. On the battlefield hundreds of troops both British and Ottoman lay dead or dying under a burning hot sun. Everywhere the stench of death followed the men.

Following his narrow escape, Harry had eventually returned to his battalion and remained on the peninsula until it was evacuated. In time for the Battle of the Somme the Royal Naval Division was transported to the Western Front and at the Ancre on

13 November 1916, Harry and his battalion, now titled the 2nd Royal Marine Light Infantry after the Portsmouth's merger with another locally named battalion, went into action just to the south of the Footballers' Battalion. It was disastrous from the start and the enemy artillery was so relentless that men fell in their droves before they could even reach the German front line. Harry would come through in one piece, but that was more than could be said for many of his battalion, which disintegrated as the battle wore on. When the 2nd Royal Marines marched off of the Somme, Harry Trusler was only accompanied by six officers and fewer than 150 other NCOs and men.

Harry had survived the Battle of Arras, too, again going into battle in close proximity to the 17th Middlesex near Arleux. Already in a salient thanks to previous operations, his battalion set out for the enemy trenches. They advanced well, but building German counter-attacks enforced miserable losses on Harry and his cohorts again and by dusk they had been forced to withdraw almost all of the way back to their original line. The enemy had been entirely underestimated and losses far outweighed any territorial gain. Total casualties in Harry Trusler's battalion topped another 600 men. The Royal Naval Division was still on this front during the opening throes of the Third Battle of Ypres, but were in the thick of it further north by the end of October as the BEF fought for Passchendaele before operations closed down from winter. Harry advanced in heavy rain at 5.45 a.m. on 26 October, and two hours later the 2nd Royal Marines were in pursuit of their advanced objectives. Unfortunately the rest of the naval attack had faltered and while elements of Harry's battalion clung to their gains under heavy fire, the main assault broke down.

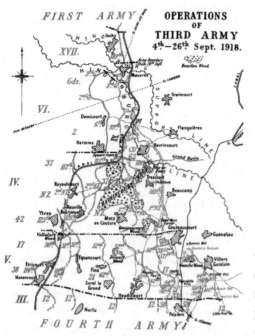

The forward momentum in which Chelsea fans and players participated in the final weeks of the war was previsouly unknown to most of them. (*Authors' collection*)

The 2nd Royal Marine Light Infantry were manning part of the line on Byng's Third Army front when the Germans launched Operation Michael on 21 March 1918. By now 22, Harry was pushed out of a salient that was more of a hindrance than an advantageous position. Without sufficient reserves his battalion was forced to fall back further towards the Rear Zone in the following days. As midnight approached on the 23rd it turned out that their flank was exposed, just as an ammunition dump went up in flames frighteningly nearby. Exhausted, it looked as if Harry and the men of the Royal Naval Division were about to be overrun, but despite suffering heavy casualties, the Royal Marine battalions held it together long enough to withdraw again. By the 24th they had reached the vicinity of High Wood on their way to the heights of Thiepval, all synonymous with the agony of 1916. The naval men settled in along the line of the Ancre. There they remained, cut by significant losses among officers as successive German attempts up and down the Western Front throughout the rest of spring failed to end the war.

May 1918 provided the BEF with time to breathe. At the end of the month the Germans advanced on the Chemin des Dames further south. Primarily attacking the French, they used tactics tried and tested in the initial assaults of March. Despite the fact that the Germans overran the Allied forward positions, causing a huge rupture in their defensive line and flooding towards the Marne, reinforcements arrived, including American divisions. Although exhausted men were bludgeoned, the combined Allied force began to dig their heels in and once again an enemy offensive ran out of steam. At the Second Battle of the Marne the Germans had once again failed to cause the decisive break they were looking for and the momentum swayed into Allied hands.

On the Somme, where the BEF and the French rushing to their aid had been well and truly ravaged, Sir Henry Rawlinson was investing time and effort in preparing defences lest the German Army come at them again. The same could not be said of the enemy opposite, for surprisingly they appeared to have lost interest in the business of war. Defences remained sketchy and ill-protected. Like the British before the March assault, they lacked the time or the manpower to invest in such a programme of work. At the front and at home in Germany a naval blockade was causing untold food shortages. The country was strewn with miserable, already wounded, ruined men and the young recruits needed to replace them were a scarcity. Divisions were hugely under strength after the failed offensive operations. Morale among the Kaiser's men and among the population at large was continuing to sink rapidly. But this did not mean that the war would end in the early summer of 1918. Sadly there was still much fighting to be done to forge a path to victory, even if Germany's long-term prospects seemed fated to end in failure.

Britain's fortunes were about to begin a swing from imminent defeat to certain victory. There was nobody left in Germany to send to fight, while thousands and thousands of American troops disembarked in Europe to continue to tip the balance in favour of the Allies, and their industry continued in overdrive to produce all of the equipment needed to win the war.

At the beginning of July the Germans gave way somewhat meekly when General Rawlinson launched his Fourth Army at them. Next he attempted to drive the enemy back from Amiens, which still sat under the shadow of the Kaiser's men after the spring offensives. With the Royal Naval Division, Harry Trusler had been continuously raided around Hamel throughout May and plagued by heavy shellfire. In return the Royal Marines had conducted their own forays into German territory, but for the most part it was a time for bedding in dozens of raw, young recruits that had arrived to replace those lost during the spring. It was all too reminiscent of Harry's experience when he was turned onto Anzac beach as a teenager three years before. The Royal Marines had suffered such losses that their two units were amalgamated into a single battalion. Throughout the summer they rested for nearly a month before taking over a section of the front again. On 20 July the Royal Naval Division were still in the lines when they heard that the French had thrown the enemy back across the Marne. The Allies were now ready to try and launch the decisive blow of the Great War. On 8 August the Royal Naval Division got unexpected orders to move towards Amiens and Albert. Something big appeared to be happening to the south.

In 1918 the combatants on the Western Front took everything they had learned, everything that had developed in four years of war and combined it to create the concept of the 'All Arms Battle'. Infantry now went forward not only with rifles, but with grenades and Lewis guns, closely supported by machine guns. Instead of assaulting in murderous long rows which exposed them to the enemy at battles such as that on the Somme in 1916, they crept forward with tanks to take out German strongpoints, before lines of men, 'worms' exposing as little of a target as possible, followed them. Poisonous gas, tanks and armoured vehicles had made their large-scale debut, as had trench mortars and smoke barrages. Aerial warfare had brought bombing raids, ground strafing and a level of observation of enemy positions that was unheard of prior to the Great War. And then there was the artillery. The part of the gunners was unrecognisable to that which they had known in 1914. There 'they had the wrong kind of guns, a preponderance of field artillery rather than medium or heavy guns, firing the wrong kind of ammunition, shrapnel rather than high explosive shells'.[2] The men of the artillery had swung from obscene shortages of equipment owing to the fact that nobody had anticipated that this would be *their* war, to a level of technical intricacy that was astounding, using complex tools such as sound-ranging to locate enemy batteries and meteorological data that would help focus the gunners' attack.

A powerful offensive was launched on 8 August, beginning the final phase of the Great War by first attempting to push the enemy back towards the River Somme. The German defensive situation was not much improved, especially in the face of every method of attack that Rawlinson planned to throw at them. Beginning shortly after 4 a.m., the enemy was subjected to a monstrous bombardment. It was a dark day for Germany. Rawlinson's Fourth Army advanced up to 8 miles, repelling them away from Amiens once and for all. Ludendorff was mortified, referring to 8 August 1918 as 'the black day' of the war.

As Rawlinson's Fourth Army advance continued, scenes among the German troops resembled that which they inflicted going eastwards in March. By 10 August the pattern of the spring fighting was mimicked further when the enemy front began to stabilise with an influx of reserves and the inevitable decline in quality of the British advance came as tanks fell by the wayside and the artillery struggled to keep up with the advance. Here a masterstroke was brought into action. What if, instead of mimicking the Germans and throwing everything the BEF had at the enemy until it too ran out of steam, the British hierarchy learned when it was appropriate to stop? Then, instead of pressing on until the enemy dug in its heels, Haig and his subordinates could switch the attacking focus to another army, in another sector and surprise the Kaiser's men with a new strike, switching their focus up and down the front and harrying the Germans, continuing to bludgeon the enemy at alternating locations until they could stand no more. Ludendorff was beside himself before this new strategy could even be put into action, offering to resign. The BEF had come up with an idea to always keep the advantage in their hands. Rawlinson and his Fourth Army would recuperate and prepare to go again at a later date, while the focus of the Allied advance was to shift north to Byng and his Third Army, including a whole swathe of men associated with Chelsea Football Club.

There was still no stroll to victory. Depleted, demoralised, with a bleak prognosis regarding the outcome of the war, the German Army was still no pushover and although open warfare was finally returning to the Western Front, there was no complacency within the ranks of the British Army at the beginning of summer 1918. Although the result was all but settled, thousands of lives would still be laid to waste in the exhausting, non-stop act of driving the Great War home to a conclusion. The bigger picture emerging was alien to the likes of Harry. Although the enemy was low in spirits, such things as the Allied superiority in terms of war material were a mystery to him at Beaumont Hamel. It didn't feel to the rank and file that the end might be coming.

Byng's Third Army launched an attack just to the south of Arras on 21 August. Harry Trusler and the Royal Marines had marched through the night. Forty-eight hours later, they were to wait for another division to seize the first objective, before passing through and making south-east for the railway line running between Achiet-le-Grand and Arras. Their personal objective would be a brown line that had been drawn across their maps some way towards the tracks, where the artillery would halt and tanks would take forward another contingent towards the railway line. The first waves of assaulting troops moved off and Harry followed into strange terrain through thick mist. Somehow the Royal Marines managed to carry on in the right direction and reached the brown line with hardly any opposition at all. A half-written message discovered by some naval men revealed that the enemy had departed the spot very suddenly indeed, and that they would find no resistance here.

The following day Rawlinson's men went forward again in the Albert area to the south and on the 23rd the Third and Fourth armies advanced side by side. The constant aggressive movement was harrowing for the Germans, who were also harassed by preparatory raids and small operations when the British and French offensive slowed. The enemy were still proving to be formidable opponents, though, and the BEF were finding that there was no let up in their own work rate. The nature of the British advance was a culture shock to Harry Trusler. Regular reliefs by whole divisions which had signified the end of an assault were history. Now the men revolved around and around as the Germans were pushed back with all haste. The tired British troops were sent into action over and over again so as not to lose the advantage of forward momentum.

On 26 August the First Army began to advance in the Arras sector. With increasing numbers of French and British troops pressing on his beleaguered armies, Ludendorff had the Germans withdraw over the Somme. There was no rest for the Royal Naval Division, who were now shifted north to take part in yet more offensive action. If the British could force their way towards a powerful German system at the northern end of the Hindenburg Line that the enemy had purposely retired to in early 1917, then they would split the German forces. In theory this would make the enemy fall back towards the Canal du Nord and Cambrai. This attack, on a position known as the Drocourt-Quéant Switch, was critical if the Allies' forward momentum was to continue.

The Germans were now roughly back in the position they had occupied before the Battle of Arras in 1917. The Drocourt-Quéant Line was a powerful addition that ran from the top of the Hindenburg Line, across the ground east of Arras and north, linking up with defences that protected Lens. By 31 August the BEF had reached this position thanks to the efforts of the First Army. They were to continue their attack, but with the support of the left flank of Byng's men, which included the Royal Naval Division. On 2 September the Canadians, along with two Third Army divisions, attacked. The Canadian objective was Magnicourt, which lay a mile and a half beyond the Drocourt-Quéant Line, and once they had reached it and reinforced their position on the flanks, Harry Trusler, the Royal Marines and with them the rest of the Naval Division would come into play. The highly original codeword 'Move' would signal them on past the Canadians and the railway line that ran east to Cambrai and onto the high ground east of Quéant. If the RND managed to get that far, then they were to press further eastward to Inchy which would bring them up towards the west banks of the Canal du Nord. This was ultimately an advance of several miles, reliant on the Canadians rupturing a strong line, something that would have been absolutely unthinkable until 1918. Yet rupture it they did and the naval men performed their tasks following in record time. Despite a tough counter-attack by the Germans when they ventured back across the canal to retake Inchy, Harry and the rest of the Royal Marines managed to throw the enemy eastwards again as the light faded on 4 September before finally being relieved. Total losses for the whole division for this period were under 1,000 men killed, wounded and missing. On the scale of the Great War, during which human life was painfully cheap, this was remarkable. The BEF had well and truly grasped the concept of when it was sensible to *stop* attacking, as well as to start. As soon as the Germans had begun to dig their heels in, the British attack on the Royal Naval Division's front was halted.

Lens fell to the Allies along with the gains taken by the Kaiser's men around Lys in the spring, but although open war was proving an acceptable concept, it was not without its complications. There were few officers and men who had received proper training in such warfare still in the field in 1918. They had been replaced by frighteningly young ones who had been prepared for the war in a hurry. More than three years of trench warfare had developed a slant towards lengthy, intricate orders and advances that could be rehearsed over and over again on practice courses before the men set off to their objectives. This new experience had produced an army which could survive incessant static pressure, 'but was practically devoid of real tactical sense'.[3] As such there was almost a reluctance to really take hold of tactical advantages and advance unless both flanks were meticulously covered, a concept that was no longer quite so essential faced with a fleeing enemy. One officer remarked that it was all 'too much blue, red and green line'[4] and initiative appeared to have suffered. Officers hesitated without having minutiae outlined to them through no fault of their own, but because they lacked training or experience, or both. Simple things like map reading had been neglected simply because they were so used to not going anywhere. Units lost direction, turned up in the wrong places and got in each other's way.

Momentum now slowed as the BEF took stock and acknowledged that in order to pierce the Hindenburg Line, a much more systematic preparation would be required. Communications were breaking down with the rapidity of the advance. The 'over-organisation bred of trench warfare' continued to be an issue.[5] Now the Allies were at a crucial juncture. If they could smash through the Hindenburg Line, perhaps the war could be over. If not, the Germans might drag the conflict into 1919. The formidable system stretched from Arras all the way down to the Aisne and was one defensive position that had not been neglected by the German army. At least 3½ miles deep and strongly fortified, as well as occupying this position, the enemy had seized upon the old British ones in front of it. Now the Allies faced three disused British lines, a line of outposts, the Hindenburg Line, a support system behind it and a reserve one behind that. On 10 September on a quick trip to London, Haig reinforced the notion that they must attack it now. To give the enemy the whole winter to reinforce their position further was surely inviting disaster. Foch orchestrated a flurry of offensives to be launched at the enemy at the end of the month, giving the German armies on the Western Front no chance to mount a coherent resistance to the now superior strength of the Allies. The French and the Americans would strike out into the Forest of Argonne on 26 September. A day later both the First and Third armies would advance on the Hindenburg Line. On the 28th the French, Belgian and British troops stretched across the Ypres sector and up to the Channel coast would go forward before finally on the 29th Rawlinson's men too would strike for the Hindenburg defences. Preparations began in earnest for what was to be a massive venture and included preliminary operations aimed at paving the way for the main offensive.

Byng's army would be attacking towards the Germans last defences in front of Cambrai. On 17 September a conference was held to begin arrangements. In front of Cambrai, where Harry Trusler and the Royal Marines would be sent into the battle, there were canals masking the town from the assaulting British troops. The first of these, the Canal du Nord, was a formidable obstruction. On Harry's front, the west banks of the canal had never been completely cleared of the enemy. Once those men had been overcome came the canal itself. Construction had been abandoned on the outbreak of war, so water was not their problem, as it was empty, but nonetheless it was up to 120 feet wide in some places and upwards of 50 feet deep. Additionally, men would have to scale sheer man-made sides from the empty canal bed to find their way to the other side. Parallel to the waterway on the eastern banks was the Hindenburg Support Line and then 3 miles beyond that was the Canal d'Escaut and a narrower river of the same name. The Royal Naval Division's first objective was to be cross the Canal du Nord opposite Moeuvres and then assault the high ground beyond it. They were then to angle southwards and secure the Hindenburg support system. The Third Phase, which was where Harry's battalion entered the fray, was then to push further on to the south-east before another division would pass through and bring them up on the Canal d'Escaut. On 26 September a long French/American offensive began on a front nearly 50 miles in length in the area around Reims. That day the RND were informed that zero hour for them would be at 5.30 a.m. the following day. Prisoners being brought into British lines revealed that opposite, the enemy were nervously anticipating an attack, waiting to be relieved.

Harry marched towards battle in difficult conditions. Rain soaked the men and caused them to slip and slide in the dark. Trench mortars took pot shots in their direction but failed to affect the Royal Marines as they moved along and in the early hours of 27 September all units reported their arrival in their allotted positions. Just after 5 a.m. the barrage opened and the Germans began responding. 'The hardest problem to be faced,' wrote one senior officer, 'is the maintenance of communication during the first hour of the battle.' Despite having ten alternative routes for telephone wires not one of them lasted more than ten minutes. 'Spark wireless suffered in the same way,' he reported. 'The aerials are too vulnerable under concentrated shelling.'[6] Use of a power buzzer was attempted, but with canals and railways bisecting the battlefield it was an inconsistent method. Pigeons became invaluable as smoke on the battlefield obscured any attempts to maintain communications. Despite these difficulties the first waves began to successfully cross the Canal du Nord and at 5.30 a.m., Harry Trusler moved off from his assembly point to prepare to advance. Intermittently held up by machine guns, they were required to mop up nests as they went, but soon enough reached the dry canal bed. Although some men had got across the Canal du Nord, others were being held up on either side of the Royal Marines when they arrived at the unfinished waterway, but Harry edged his way across the canal as battle raged and the men formed up behind a reverse slope ready to attack. Promptly the artillery barrage lifted at 7.58 a.m. allowing them to go forward.

Harry Trusler's battalion formed the left-hand side of the advance and with Anson Battalion they rushed over the crest of Bourlon Ridge. 'An original and daring manoeuvre,'[7] it seemed that the men of the Royal Naval Division might have taken too big a risk. The Royal Marines followed the line of the road to Cambrai and came up to meet the Canadians south-west of Bourlon Wood, but the Anson Battalion were being raked with machine-gun fire and held up and Harry and his cohorts could not go any further without their support on their right.

At 2.15 p.m. the attack was resumed successfully. Enemy strongpoints were overrun and by 4 p.m. the Royal Marine Light Infantry had entered the village of Anneux and begun reorganising themselves and digging in while they waited for the final division to pass through on their way to the Canal d'Escaut. Just as Harry and his battalion were finishing their consolidation, reports came through that the enemy was reportedly massing in front of Anneux for a counter-attack. SOS rockets were fired up along an extended front held by both British and Canadian troops but a protective barrage, aided by rifles and machine-gun fire dispersed these attempts and by 7.30 p.m. all was quiet. Harry settled in for the night as food and ammunition was brought up. It had been a successful day. The Hindenburg support line had been pierced and the way lay open for the Third Army to advance on Cambrai.

Considering what had been asked of them the First and Third armies had fared well. There was no time for self-congratulation, though, the Third Army must push on and attempt to prevent the enemy from reorganising themselves on the Rhine, else Ludendorff's hope that being on German soil might generate a renewed fighting spirit among his men when asked to defend their homeland might play out. For now, the enemy showed no sign of folding in front of the Royal Naval Division. Further north on 28 September an offensive went forward east of Ypres with astounding success. On Harry Trusler's front other troops had been ordered the night before to focus on the crossing of the Canal d'Escaut. At about 9 a.m. information was received by the Royal Naval Division that the men in front were busily trying to secure the crossings of the canal. When this was done the naval men, including Harry and the Royal Marines, were to pass through and begin circling round to advance on Cambrai itself, seizing the eastern approaches and the high ground en route. It was a glittering prize, a hub of rail connections, billets and headquarters.

The first of the Royal Naval Division troops moved off just as it became apparent that the division in front were struggling to consolidate the canal crossings. It was a frustrating day, difficult to ascertain exactly what was happening. The first naval waves went forward at 4 p.m. A wooden footbridge had survived across the canal, but it was fully exposed to German machine-gun fire. It was a chaotic, frantic scene until a heroic seaman set out across a broken bridge with a machine gun, swung down, set it up and began firing on his German counterparts before they could turn around. His feat enabled a handful of men and an officer to get across while dusk fell and more little pockets of men joined them under cover of darkness. Meanwhile the engineers, under heavy fire, worked through the night to get pontoon bridges up for the men such as Harry Trusler that still had to cross.

Shortly before dawn on 29 September two companies of the Drake Battalion succeeded in establishing a number of outposts across the canal. Lewis guns were now posted about the relevant lock to try and suppress enemy machine-gun fire. The plan of attack that day was for the RND to continue trying to force the passage not only of the canal, but of the River de l'Escaut, much more narrow and winding and just beyond it. By 8 a.m. little progress had been made but then gradually the belligerence of the Naval Division men began to wear the enemy down. At 11 a.m. Harry was ordered to stand to and an hour later they were told to cross the canal. Two and a half hours later the Royal Marines had mounted the high ground on the eastern side. If the Germans were going to make a run for Cambrai, then they would certainly not be allowed to go unmolested. By early evening Harry and his battalion had been informed that they would continue their assault on the town the following day. The Marines had reached the outer limits of the Cambrai; although the Germans were making a concerted effort to leave as many booby traps behind them as possible, once brave sappers had dismantled them, the enemy's options for defending the town did not look encouraging.

That night heavy rain fell, turning the ground to a muddy slime. At 8.30 a.m. on the 30th the Royal Naval Division advance began again, punctuated by heavy machine-gun fire coming from both the north and south ends of their front. After a morning of failure the attack was renewed again at lunchtime. Again Harry Trusler and the Royal Marine Light Infantry were held back by German machine guns and it took until almost dusk for their brigade to take their objectives. In four days, the RND had advanced, scrapping all the way, more than 7 miles. They had captured sixty-three officers, 2,138 men and hundreds of artillery pieces and machine guns. The end of the war was surely now in sight.

A letter written by his elder brother Alf was chasing 'Dear old Harry'[8] towards Cambrai. Posting home a belt he had borrowed, Harry had assured all at home that he was well and in return Alf had filled his reply with news of home. 'We thought of you a lot lately,' the former Royal Marine told his still-serving brother. 'Especially as I actually saw the Royal Marines mentioned in the daily papers.' Their brother Tom, who alone of the family served with the Hampshire and Wiltshire regiments instead, had been strangely silent, causing Harry to worry at the front. 'Well what do you think?' Alf informed him. 'He actually condescended to write to us last week. I think he is in a perfect state of health. Says if all well, he will be home before long. I expect he means about 1920.' Alf also sent news of Harry's nephews. He wouldn't recognise little Eric when he saw him in his grown-up trousers and miniature blue jersey. As for baby Jack, he was (Alf stated proudly) fat: 'He looks like a football with legs on.' Their father looked well, mum too; even the family horse seemed to have gained weight. As for their sister Nell, she was about as elusive as Tom, but it was known that she was busy courting with a Scotch sergeant. 'So when Nell brings her family home they will be dressed in kilts "Hoot Mon."' Alf signed off in more serious fashion, 'with fondest love and kisses from the boys'. His letter would never reach his brother, for Harry fell on 30 September as the Royal Marine Light Infantry continued their assault on Cambrai. The 23-year-old was evacuated back to a casualty clearing station but all efforts to save his life were in vain. He was awarded the Military Medal twice in 1918 for his brave service in stemming the German tide and then beginning the advance towards victory. Harry Trusler had served with the Royal Naval Division since the start of the war. On two fronts he had seen this unique formation go from a laughing stock in 1914 to an effective fighting force when he lost his life just five weeks before the end of the war.

To the south the Fourth Army attack had obliterated the Hindenburg Line and the support behind it. This formidable defence system was fragmenting up and down its length, leaving the path to Germany open behind it. At the beginning of October the Kaiser's army was falling apart, with no significant defences to the rear waiting to help them stand their ground. Having lost a quarter of a million men as prisoners alone in a matter of months, the chances of them being able to construct such a thing were nil. The German hierarchy had already met to discuss their options, which as far as they were concerned at the moment still included making a stand closer to home or an armistice.

The Allies were almost free to run rampant over open ground towards the enemy. As such a forceful line of troops protecting each other's flanks became less important and commanders were able to exercise a flexible approach to continuing the advance, exploiting local advantages. By mid-October the Third Army had reached the line of the River Selle beyond Cambrai, but Byng's men were then checked. Germany's soldiers were by no means incompetent, but they were prolonging the inevitable. Holding up the Allies on one part of the Western Front was futile when they would inevitably break through on another. The British were attempting to move again, including on the strategically important town of Douai.

A Chelsea player was still in action with Byng's Third Army. George Lake had been on Manchester City's books before signing for the Blues just prior to the outbreak of war. The promising position had managed just one appearance against West Brom at the Hawthorns before returning north to enlist on the outbreak of war. Having originally been part of an East Lancashire cyclist unit, George had since gone to the front with the 2/4th Battalion of the Hampshire Regiment. They had been east before being summoned late from Palestine, not arriving on the Western Front until the middle of summer 1918. With no time for much-yearned for leave to

England, the men were quickly trained in how to operate their gas masks and shown the trenches held by the 62nd Division, which they were to join. It was not an easy introduction for a battalion that had become used to a different kind of warfare in the east, with an abundance of enemy fire coming onto their static position at Bucquoy from rifles, artillery, trench mortars and machine guns.

After a brief spell in action with the French further south, culminating in the Allied victory in the Second Battle of the Marne, the Hampshire ranks were decimated. George Lake survived and fought on when the battalion returned to the British front and the Third Army. After just a fortnight's rest the 2/4th Hampshires went into action, seizing back Ervillers and Mory at the end of August. On 12 September they set off in the early hours through the remains of Havrincourt Wood amidst shellfire to help clear out the village and along with Harry Trusler's Royal Naval Division, were instrumental in pushing the advance of General Byng's army towards Germany. Like Harry, George Lake also made an approach towards Cambrai before the Hampshires were halted at Rumilly just outside the town.

The beginning of October was quiet as far as the battalion was concerned, as the focus of the fighting fell upon different parts of the Western Front. By 17 October, however, the Fourth Army was advancing again in the Battle of the Selle. In turn, Byng's men prepared for their next move. On 20 October George Lake made off across the River Selle to secure the high ground on the east bank. It was not an easy journey. The river was up to 20 feet wide and 6 feet deep and George's brigade was detailed to take the town of Solesmes, which was strongly defended. It was also still full of French civilians. The artillery sent a full barrage past either side, but as far as the town was concerned limited their fire to shrapnel and machine-gun bullets, which would not harm locals if they were to take refuge underground in cellars. The Hampshires followed up in support and by 7.15 a.m. had entered Solesmes from a north-westerly direction and mopped it up. This process was so intricate now, thanks to accurate aerial photography, that objectives had been dealt out right down to platoon level once the Hampshires got inside the town, and the men recognised each other by a series of passwords and armbands to keep organised.

The second phase of the Battle of the Selle began on 23 October 1918 and once again George Lake's division went forward successfully despite the fact that the advance was taking on an awkward north-eastern slant in the direction of Charleroi. The Germans were making a determined attempt to halt them, even though it would not influence the outcome of the war. A depressing sense of inevitability had taken over the Kaiser's men. The German perspective of George's advance did his battalion much credit. One German historian supposed that fifteen full strength, or completely fresh, divisions had made the assault in the area, and that 'it was the heaviest day of fighting since the great defeat of the 8th August with its direful results'.

The Third Army was now east of Le Cateau and still pushing forward, towards the Roman road running down the side of the Forest of Mormal that Chelsea fans had retreated south on in 1914. On 26 October Ludendorff walked away from his post, coinciding with a brief lull in major operations that gave the exhausted, dirty men of the BEF a rare chance to rest. The point of the scrapping had gone, and yet men were still dying. British airmen were dropping leaflets on German troops, encouraging them to throw in the towel and bring an end to the futile slaughter. Sporadic fighting continued until the end of the month, but once again the Allies were preparing for another large-scale assault on the retiring German army.

On 24 October a successful push began in Italy that would end the war on that front. Bulgaria had ceased hostilities the month before and further east in Mesopotamia and Palestine advances continued. Troops entered Aleppo on 26 October and four days later the Turks on the Tigris surrendered. Revolution was now rife in Austria, which had agreed terms, and in Budapest. The Central Powers were crumbling. The Germans themselves were not averse to calling it a day, but mindful of when they would be able to extract the best terms for an Armistice out of the Allies. They were playing for time. An Allied conference on 28 October led by Foch discussed potential terms. American and French suggestions were too severe for Haig, who drove home his point that if Germany failed to agree on account of this, then her army was more than capable of retiring to a shorter defensive line and causing a problem with a continued defence. In the meantime his men were exhausted, as were their French counterparts. The Americans may have been huge in potential number but they were inexperienced. He didn't believe yet that the enemy was desperate enough to accept peace at any cost.

George Lake was destined to be involved into the last days of the war, but for now the rest the 2/4th Hampshires were able to take was much appreciated. The pause was essential, for supplies of ammunition needed to be brought up and communications needed to be attended to. George and his battalion had now been on the move almost since their initial arrival on the Western Front. Many extremely young, inexperienced boys among their number, the troops had been sleeping rough for weeks. After a few days rest the battalion moved up towards Maubeuge over gently undulating countryside, dotted with villages, orchards and muddy sunken roads. It was an area that had been all but forgotten by the British since it was retreated through in 1914. Wargnies, Bavay, names which were familiar to the likes of Arthur Timoney and Thomas Bason when they stopped by on their lengthy retreat to the Aisne in 1914, were now coming back into play.

In the meantime Haig continued to be adamant that the enemy must be pushed relentlessly in order to end the war as soon as possible. Three large-scale offensives were to take place at the beginning of November. In the north an attack on Flanders began. The following day the French and the Americans would attack in the south, before in the centre of the Allied line on the Western Front, one French army and three British, including Byng's, would advance on 4 November on a front from Avesnes to Mons. George Lake would be advancing over hallowed roads, 'patrolled by the ghosts of [1914]'.[9] This final movement would assault the River Sambre and the Forest of Mormal. George's division was on the offensive just to the north-west of Le Quesnoy and the Hampshires would be leading the line. The battalion formed up roughly along the Le Quesnoy–Valenciennes railway in the direction of Maubeuge. Zero hour was set for 4.30 a.m. Once George and his battalion had advanced to their objectives more men would pass through, while the Hampshires prepared to go again the next morning.

Low embankments, no more than 3 feet on either side of the railway line, gave the men little cover. Half an hour before zero, the enemy sent up 'a brilliant firework display'[10] of multicoloured flares along the front line. The Hampshires were expecting very stiff resistance on the way to their first objective, as there were enemy machine gunners ensconced in a copse 80 yards in front; but although they picked up heavy casualties, the leading companies went off in such blistering fashion that they swept down a steep slope on their way to the enemy line. On the other side of the advance the battalion found themselves held up by machine guns. Together the two forward companies struggled up the slope of a ravine into heavy fire, but within an hour and a half George Lake and the rest of the Hampshires had conquered their objective. Any further forward movement after the initial three stages was postponed until the morning of the 5th. Civilians waved the division by as the battalion moved up in support, singing The Marseillaise for the passing soldiers.

Advancing alongside George in the neighbouring division throughout the final month of the war was another Chelsea player. Harry Wilding had joined the Grenadier Guards in 1912 but had signed for Chelsea in 1914. He had, though, managed only a single appearance before the war had interfered with his fledgling football career. Harry had thus far survived everything that the Great War had thrown at him, having landed in France way back in August 1914.

The 2nd Grenadiers slowly felt their way forward in the dark to their assembly area on the night of 3 November, heavily shelled as they went after having been gassed throughout the day. They would advance behind a battalion of the Coldstream Guards and then pass through them on their way to their objective. Rain had tailed off but a heavy mist still prevailed when Harry and the rest of the Grenadiers moved off and they could not see more than 200 yards. Unfortunately, their path obscured by the fog, more Coldstream troops on the right began to arc away from the advance. Seeing men in front of them, confusion descended as they followed them, thinking they were men of their own battalion only to discover that they were in fact retiring Germans. As soon as one company emerged from a wood near Wargnies-le-Petit the Grenadiers were showered with rifle and machine-gun fire. Harry's officers were struck down one by one. It took fierce scrapping to overcome the resistance but eventually the 2nd Grenadiers pushed on.

The enemy folded on the Third Army front at the beginning of November 1918. Byng's men burst forwards up to 5 miles. The advance on George Lake's divisional front had gone with 'almost clockwork regularity'. Yet again scores of invaluable

German troops and heaps of war material had fallen into British hands to compound the loss of ground. That night incessant drizzle began. 'The surface of the roads and tracks became churned into slush and mud by the continuous traffic.'[11] There were not enough pioneers and sappers to make good the damage or bring up materials to construct bridges and the advance now slowed considerably.

On 6 November the 2/4th Hampshires were ordered forward again towards the road running between Bavay and Avesnes. At noon the men were called up to advance through the troops that had conducted the initial assaults. Although they did not meet significant numbers of the enemy, the Hampshires were heavily shelled and pinned down by machine guns. The battalion wrestled their way through the village of Cognaux and its surrounding orchards. In the course of the day's fighting, Chelsea player George Lake fell, an agonising five days before the end of the war.

Rain cascaded down as the war entered its final days. Germany was in freefall, both at home and at the front. Troops were refusing to go into the trenches, others had mutinied. 'In the back areas wandered thousands of deserters and marauders.' Disaffection had spread to the navy too. As the Allies passed through occupied France and Belgium the locals welcomed them as heroes, but a lack of food, lack of sleep and German efforts to sabotage the advance in the way of their booby traps suppressed any mood of exaltation. By 10 November the fighting had reached Mons. At the final hour the Great War had turned full circle. The following day representatives of the combatant nations emerged from a railway carriage in the Forest of Compiègne with the news that at 11 a.m. on 11 November 1918 the fighting would stop.

By this time Harry Wilding and the Grenadier Guards had entered Maubeuge to a rapturous reception from the locals. On the 11th a short message arrived. 'Hostilities will cease at 11am today.'[12] The officers announced it to Harry and the rest of the men at the allotted hour. It was a surprisingly quiet reaction:

There was no exuberant outburst of enthusiasm, no wild scenes of rejoicing. Officers and men went quietly about their ordinary duties, scarcely realising at first that the end had really come, that the long strain was over, and yet dimly conscious that they had lived through an epoch and that a great and wonderful success had crowned their efforts.[13]

News spread slowly across the front. Four years of rumour and intrigue; could anybody really be sure that this one was true, that it was over? The sudden realisation that they had survived did not necessarily result in immediate jubilation, more stunned disbelief. Then came flooding back the memory of all of those who hadn't lived to see this day. Now that the pursuit of the enemy was over how would they ever settle the score?

Demobilising the largest British military force in history was a slow and laborious process, along with seeing them back into the lives they had left behind. Players like Teddy Foord and Vivian Woodward and fans like Edwin Siveyer would bear the scars of the Great War for a lifetime. Others were finding that it would be quite some time before they were able to return home for good. Harry Wilding marched with the Guards into Germany, where peacetime duties were interspersed with a considerable amount of football in Cologne. Soon after Christmas the authorities began breaking down the division. By the end of March, Harry and the rest of the Grenadiers had finally returned home. The survivors of the Grenadier battalions paraded with the rest of the men who had made up the Guards Division, past the King at Buckingham Palace and on through London towards Mansion House. Thousands lined the streets and hung out of windows, waving and cheering. Demobilised officers and men marched behind those still in the ranks in their civilian clothes and bringing up the rear were those who would never walk again. Wounded men filled lorries and were conveyed along the path of the procession so that they too could take their part in celebrating victory. Harry's division was no more, but in his speech King George V had some profound words for those returning to their pre-war lives as changed men. 'As your Colonel in Chief I wish to thank you all for your faithful and devoted services, and to wish you God speed. May you ever retain the same mutual feelings of true comradeship which animated and ennobled the life of the Guards Division.'[14]

At Stamford Bridge four years of economic struggle were coming to an end. The makeshift London Combination League had been a profitable venture. The Blues had won it comfortably over Millwall in 1915/16 and again by a single point in 1917/18 at the expense of West Ham United. The club searched for other ways to fill Stamford Bridge while the war raged on. One was by providing a home ground for the US Army in the new Anglo-American Baseball League. Designed to entertain vast numbers of American and Canadian troops in training near London, it was planned for eight teams to battle it out every Saturday afternoon and on public holidays in the summer of 1918. The London Victory Cup was played in the opening months of 1919, shortly before the Football League was reinstated. Chelsea entered in the second round, knocking out QPR, and in the semi-final Crystal Palace were crushed 4–0. On 28 April 1919, almost four years to the day after the Pensioners inaugural FA Cup Final, Chelsea beat Fulham 3–0 at Highbury. Harry Ford turned out as did Harry Wilding, who scored a rare goal at the advent of what was to be a nine-year stint with the Blues.

Cuthbert Headlam, the historian charged with writing the history of the Guards Division, suggested that in part, victories were owed to a mutual feeling of confidence between the officers and their men. 'And this confidence can only exist when all ranks are imbued with the same pride in their regiment, and are inspired by an ideal of a great tradition and of a common patriotism.' That same reference to pride and patriotism could be applied to a football club. Across the country, despite having been pilloried by the press, after four years of fighting, clubs from grassroots up to the higher echelons of the First Division had a right to feel proud of their footballing communities' reactions to the national crisis. 'The individual may perish, but the regiment lives forever,' wrote Headlam.[15] It was the same at Chelsea, as those left behind counted the cost of the war. Familiar faces at Stamford Bridge, of fans, players and staff associated with the club would not return, but the Blues had survived being shaken to the core by events on a worldwide scale. One hundred years later Chelsea Football Club lives on. And sharing the same traditions as long ago, in the remembrance of all of those associated with the club at the centenary of the Great War, so too does a sense of gratitude for the individuals that left the pitch and the terraces to fight and never came home to west London.

Epilogue

Thomas Bason

Thomas Bason remained with the Army Service Corps. In September 1914, shortly after the retreat from Mons, he was transferred to the Motor Transport 1st Heavy Repair Shop in Paris. He remained there until March 1915 when he was transferred to the 5th Auxiliary Petrol Company, still controlled by the Army Service Corps. Between April 1915 and December 1915 Bason was transferred between other units within the Army Service Corps. In December he moved to the 3rd Heavy Repair Shop at St Omer. He remained there until February 1916 when he was sent back to England. Upon arrival back in England Bason spent just over ten days in the Motor Transport Reception and Discharge Depot before being discharged from the army on 7 March 1916, when his engagement with the army was terminated on account of his age under his terms of service.

James Broadbridge

James Broadbridge survived the First World War. He remained with the Royal Field Artillery for its duration and at some point he was promoted to sergeant.

Lawrence Catchpole

Between July and October 1918 Catchpole was on leave in India. Upon his return to Mesopotamia, he was admitted to hospital in Basra. He was still there when the Armistice of Mudros was signed with the Ottoman Empire on 30 October 1918 signifying the end of the hostilities on that front. He was discharged from hospital shortly afterwards, remaining in Mesopotamia until March 1919 before sailing back to the United Kingdom. He arrived back at the beginning of June and was demobilised on 1 July that year.

George Collison

George Collison's body was never found. He was presumed dead for official purposes by the War Office on 4 December 1917, a full year after his disappearance on the Ancre. He is commemorated on the Thiepval Memorial. Standing on the ridge overlooking the River Ancre, it lists the names of 72,195 soldiers who were killed on the Somme before 20 March 1918 and have no known grave. It was designed by Sir Edwin Luytens and officially opened on 1 August 1932.

William Daley

William Daley was killed in the Footballers' Battalion attack on Guillemont on 8 August 1916. On 24 February 1920 the Infantry Record Office wrote to his wife, Harriett, who by this time was living on Woolwich High Street, to inform her that her husband's body had been exhumed from its original place of burial just south of Longueval and had been re-buried in Delville Wood Cemetery on the outskirts of Longueval. Exhumations and reburials happened on occasion where soldiers had been buried in scattered individual graves or in small cemeteries which were situated in places not suitable for permanent cemeteries.

Cecil Dean

After his death in 1915, Cecil Dean's body was never found, or if it was recovered it was not capable of being identified. Cecil Dean is commemorated on the Le Touret Memorial, which is located not far from where he fell at Richebourg, in north-east France. The Le Touret Memorial lists the names of over 13,400 British soldiers killed in this area of the Western Front between October 1914 and late September 1915 and that have no known grave. Almost all of those soldiers commemorated on it were either regular or territorial soldiers. The memorial itself was designed by John Reginald Truelove who served as an officer with the 24th Battalion of the London Regiment during the war.

William Dean

William Dean was transferred several times in 1917, first to the 7th Battalion of the Royal Welsh Fusiliers in January, and then on to a Labour Company of another battalion in February before ending up in the Labour Corps in May. The Labour Corps were formed in early 1917 and was an amalgamation of previous military labour arrangements. Nominally the ranks consisted of unskilled men who were not fit enough to fight, either as a result of age or injuries or sometimes both. The men who served in the Labour Corps played an important role in enabling the army to function effectively, building and repairing roads and maintaining railways in addition to other tasks, sometimes under dangerous conditions. William Dean remained with the Labour Corps as a quartermaster sergeant until he was demobilised in 1920. In all, he had given the army nearly thirty-five years' service as man and boy.

Charles Grant Dewar

By April 1917 Dewar was in Reading and spent some time in hospital before being sent to Ireland on 26 May 1917 where he was treated at the Military Hospital at Ballyvonare. He returned from Ireland in June 1917. At the time of his discharge from the army in January 1919, Dewar was claiming that he was still suffering from heart disease and shock caused by the wounds he suffered in France and the torpedoing of the SS *Donegal* mid-Channel. Despite the injuries he suffered and the fact that the hospital ship he was being transported in was torpedoed by a German U-boat, his family remember that he bore no ill will against the Germans until the chip shop at the end of his road was bombed in the Second World War. This was not to be the last influence Germany was to have on his life. On 24 September 1940, Charles Dewar was killed, aged 50, when the Luftwaffe bombed Shoreditch during a particularly heavy raid during the Blitz.

Alf Dorsett

After his death in March 1915 Alf's body was never found. He is commemorated on the Le Touret Memorial along with Cecil Dean.

Angus Douglas

Having lost a finger owing to blood poisoning, Angus Douglas continued his munitions work throughout the war. In 1918 he fell ill. His doctors were convinced that his strong constitution would ensure his survival, but sadly the 30-year-old player became a victim of the influenza epidemic which accounted for millions of lives across the world as the Great War came to a close.

Harry Ford

After Passchendaele, Ford was transferred to the Royal Sussex Regiment. He survived the war and afterwards returned to play for Chelsea. Between 1919 and 1925 he went on to make a further 136 appearances and scored 22 goals in all competitions.

William Goddard

William Goddard's body was never found and he is commemorated on the Thiepval Memorial.

Colin Hampton

The Chelsea goalkeeper returned to Stamford Bridge after the war where he remained until 1925. He later returned to Scotland where he ran a small sweetshop until the outbreak of the Second World War when, nearly 60, he took a position at a tool company and acted as a special constable. He died near his hometown of Brechin in 1968.

Henry Jarvis

Henry Jarvis survived the Great War. He remained a gunner in the Royal Field Artillery for its duration.

Sidney Jerram

Sidney Jerram was repatriated back to England in December 1918. He was demobilised on 28 May 1919. At the time of his demobilisation the Ministry of Pension acknowledged that he was suffering from a disability and the degree of his disablement was adjudged 30 per cent. As a result of this he was awarded a pension of 8s 3d per week with effect from 29 May 1919, and this was to be reviewed in a year's time. He later returned to his apprenticeship as a cabinet-maker, married and had a family. He never spoke of the Great War.

William Krug

In the first few months of 1917, William Krug was suffering with sciatica. It appeared bad enough to require him to return to England. Between May and November 1917 he was treated for it at the Eastern Command Depot at Shoreham-by-Sea. (Command Depots were established by the army in 1916 and used to rehabilitate wounded soldiers who had not recovered sufficiently to return to active service, but were too fit to be kept in hospital.) In November 1917, Krug was posted to the 5th Battalion of the Middlesex Regiment at Chatham. The 5th Middlesex was a Reserve Battalion used for home service and from 1917 until the end of the war it was part of the Thames and Medway Garrison. In 1918 Krug was promoted twice, to lance-corporal in January 1918 and to corporal in February 1918. He was demobilised in February 1919 and despite his fitness being described as 'A1' at the time of his demobilisation, there is no record of William Krug ever playing professional football again.

Albert Edward Ponman

Albert Ponman transferred from the Army Service Corps to the Royal Field Artillery in January 1917. In September 1918 he was back in the United Kingdom being treated for syphilis at the Military Hospital in Hemel Hempstead. He appears to have died from anaphylactic shock following an injection he received as part of his treatment on 17 September 1918. He was buried in Streatham Cemetery, near Tooting, in an unmarked grave, although he is commemorated on a screen wall memorial in the cemetery.

Charles Prentice

Having been apprehended by the police, Charles was returned to his unit in April 1918. His time with the battalion was short-lived. During the third week of May his hand was maimed when his rifle went off in some support trenches. Even with a witness, it could not be ascertained whether or not it was an accident, as Prentice claimed, or an act of self-mutilation in order to avoid service. He suffered extensive injuries to his palm and a compound fracture of a finger. Initially classed as fit to return, it appears that it was later acknowledged that his state of mind did not allow for service in the front line and by the end of the war he was serving at an officer's school in France.

Patrick Ronan

After the war, and after receiving a request from Patrick Ronan's wife Annie, the Imperial War Graves Commission wrote to her enclosing a photograph of his grave in Mailly Wood Cemetery. It is thought unlikely that she was ever able to visit it.

Arthur Timoney

Arthur Timoney remained in the Army Service Corps throughout the war. He received a Mention In Despatches for his conduct sometime in 1915. (The Commander-in-Chief of the British army, at this stage, Field Marshal Sir John French, was required to send a report of his army in the field to the War Office on a regular basis. These reports were referred to as Despatches. A Mention In Despatches is the lowest form of gallantry award in the British army.) The last paragraph of Sir John French's Despatch, dated 15 October 1915, reads, 'I have many names to bring to your Lordship's notice for valuable, gallant and distinguished service during the period under review, and these will form the subject of a separate report at an early date.' The first page of the *London Gazette* dated 1 January 1916 goes on to say, 'In accordance with the last paragraph of my Despatch of the 15th October 1915, I have the honour to bring to notice the names of those whom I recommend for gallant and distinguished conduct in the field.' Acting Company Sergeant Major Timoney is mentioned on page 62. Timoney was also awarded the Meritorious Service Medal on 18 October 1916. The Meritorious Service Medal could be awarded for Gallantry, Devotion to Duty or for Valuable Service. Timoney received his for Valuable Service. Arthur Timoney died in Watford in September 1953.

Henry Trusler

Henry Trusler was buried in Sunken Road Cemetery at Boisleux-St Marc, almost 5 miles south of Arras. His immediate family were never able to visit his grave.

Ernest Wenden

The *London Gazette* of 20 August 1915 included a notice confirming that 'Temporary Second Lieutenant Ernest Wenden is removed from the Army for absence without leave.' In late 1931, Wenden's wife wrote to the War Office, informing them that she wanted to marry a Swiss national and the Swiss government were requesting an official statement from the War Office confirming Wenden's disappearance and the circumstances surrounding it. The War Office responded in December 1931 stating that it was 'contrary to the general practice of the Department to furnish information relative to a member or ex-member of His Majesty's Forces except to such a member or ex-member himself'. Nevertheless, the letter went on to confirm that Wenden had been removed from the army having been absent without leave from 2 July 1915. The author has uncovered a promising lead, but as yet the fate of this missing young officer after the summer of 1915 is completely unknown.

Arthur Wileman

In April 1918, the 11th Battalion of the Royal Sussex Regiment were involved in the defence of Ypres against the German attack known as Operation Georgette, part of the German Spring Offensives. On 22 April 1918, Wileman and the battalion took up front-line positions near Elzenwalle Chateau, 2½ miles south-west of Ypres, where they remained until the 27th. During their time in the front line the battalion were subject to very heavy German artillery fire and frequent attacks. On 27 April, the battalion withdrew to support lines. Arthur Wileman was killed on 28 April 1918, aged 36, leaving behind a widow, Blanche Wileman, in Bristol. Arthur Wileman is commemorated on the Tyne Cot Memorial. This memorial is a long curved wall at the rear of Tyne Cot Cemetery listing the names of almost 35,000 officers and men who died in the Ypres Salient between 17 August 1917 and the end of the war and have no known grave.

Norman Wood

The Stockport County player, who spent fifteen months on Chelsea's books without actually making a first team appearance, has no known grave and is commemorated on the Thiepval Memorial.

Vivian Woodward

Woodward's wounds were so severe he was moved back to the United Kingdom for treatment. He arrived back on 6 February 1916 on the hospital ship *Cambria* and was immediately granted one month's leave. Between March and August 1916, Woodward was subject to regular examinations by the Army Medical Board. His wounds and general condition were slowly improving, although, in June 1916, the board reported that Woodward was suffering from complications, 'dermatitis with the occasional elevation of temperature', attributed by his medical attendant to the effects of his wound. On his return to France the army were determined to make the most of Woodward's physical prowess and leadership skills. In April 1917 he arrived at the Third Army training school in Auxi-Le-Château for a trial with a view to becoming a physical and bayonet training instructor. By October, Woodward was with the 1st Army Training School in St Pol, France. He remained there until February 1918 when he was ordered to return to England and report to the Headquarters of Physical and Bayonet Training in Aldershot with a view to him qualifying as a supervising officer. Woodward's time at Aldershot was a success; by May 1918 he was back to the 1st Army Training School which by now had been moved to Hardelot Plage following the German Spring Offensives and, in November 1918, Woodward was moved to the headquarters of the Physical and Recreational School. Before his demobilisation in May 1919, Woodward was transferred back to the First Army School.

Woodward did take to the pitch at Stamford Bridge again. On Saturday 23 February 1918 he played for Chelsea against Tottenham in the London Combination League, with Chelsea winning 3–0. In March 1918 he played again at Stamford Bridge for the British Army against a Belgian Army team, who went on to beat the British side 2–1. In 1919 he made two further appearances in the London Combination League against Fulham and QPR. These were to be his last appearances for Chelsea.

After the war, Woodward retired from playing and moved to Weeley Heath in Essex to concentrate on dairy farming. His connection with Chelsea continued; he served as a director of the club from 1922 to 1930. In 1949 ill health forced him to move to a care home in Ealing. He died on 1 February 1954 and at the time of his death he remained England's leading goalscorer despite having played his last international game forty years before.

Notes

1 'Entry by Storm'

1 'Entry by storm', Sewell, p.13.
2 'The audacity ...', Ibid.
3 'Now for the struggle', Ibid.
4 'Is that almost everything ...', Sewell, p. 15.
5 'To the very last game ...', Ibid., p. 17.
6 'What a struggle', Ibid., p. 17.
7 'Steering a middle ...', Ibid., p. 18.

2 'A New Stick for an Old Dog'

1 'Under the shadow ...', *Chelsea FC Chronicle* (*CFCC*), 27 August 1914.
2 'Who publicly voted ...', Ibid.
3 'Even if the crowd ...', Court hearing.
4 'Rolled up on to football ...', FA Minutes.
5 'To have to play under ...', Veitch, p. 368.
6 'Another travesty of the game ...', FA Minutes.
7 'Football proved to be the medium ...', Ibid.
8 'Time for paying off ...', Bailey, p. 5.
9 'That some of the noisiest ...', *CFCC*, 12 September 1914.
10 'A word from him ...', Lloyd George (Vol. I), p. 499.
11 'Having regard to the great ...', FA Minutes.
12 'That you only admit ...', Ibid.
13 'Agreements between clubs ...', Ibid.
14 'That the Football Association is prepared ...', Ibid.
15 'I am commended by the Army ...', Ibid.
16 'Take all steps in their power ...', Ibid.
17 'Football Association are of the opinion ...', Ibid.
18 'On the other hand ...', Simkin, p. 69.
19 'Provided the army medical ...', *CFCC*, 12 September 1914.

20 'First let us be told …', Ibid.
21 'Far be it from us …', Ibid.
22 'Which is essentially the pastime …', FA Minutes.
23 'Throughout the country …', CFCC, 12 September 1914.
24 'Luckily for Drake …', CFCC, Ibid.
25 'Because my patriotic …', CFCC, 26 September 1914.
26 'They are all of the well …', The Times, 11 September 1914.
27 'I am determined …', CFCC, 26 September 1914.
28 'The increase of distress …', CFCC, 12 September 1914.
29 'This side of the question …', CFCC, 26 September 1914.

3 'Cook's Tourists'

1 'For nations do not build …', CFCC, 27 August 1914.
2 'Twenty five acres of airless …', Forbes, p. 10.
3 'The Duke of something …', Ibid., p. 10.
4 'The position might be compared …', Ibid., p. 12.
5 'The articles were in …', Ibid., p. 12–13.
6 'In spite of protest …', Ibid., p. 13.
7 'The farthest limit of the railway …', War Diaries WO 95.
8 'Willing, honest, sober …', WO 363.
9 'Timoney the fiddler …', ASC Magazine, 1910.
10 'I should have thought …', Clifton-Shelton, p. viii.
11 'I stopped every despatch …', Ibid., p. 42.
12 'He said that he would be …', Ibid., p. 80.
13 'A compact and well cared …', War Diaries WO 95.
14 'For the sun beat down fiercely …', Ibid.
15 'Huge and unwieldy thing', Ibid.
16 'Bundled on out of the way …', Ibid.
17 'The only two survivors …', Ibid.
18 'The terrific nature of …', Clifton-Shelton, p. 67.
19 'Outside, the town …', Ibid., p. 61.
20 'Transport and mounted …', War Diaries.
21 'All of this had to be done …', Corbett-Smith, p. 187.
22 'Contemptible little army …', War Diaries.
23 'The weather was terribly …', Clifton-Shelton, p. 41.
24 'Paste of dust …', Ibid., p. 54.
25 'Hours passed as a week …', Ibid., p. 71.
26 'They looked more as if …', Ibid., p. 52.
27 'As the sugar was chucked in …', Ibid., p. 73.
28 'Who are you?', Ibid., p. 35.
29 'From the moment we started …', War Diaries.
30 'Shall we go?', Clifton-Shelton, p. 39.
31 'We did our best to cheer …', Ibid., p. 63.
32 'We used to get awfully bored …', Ibid., p. 86.
33 'With the spare men …', Ibid., p. 59.
34 'After a wild gallop …', Ibid.
35 'That the section with my horse …', Ibid., p. 74.
36 'But the poor jaded …', Ibid., p. 41.
37 'The dust on the roads …', War Diaries.
38 'We held nothing beyond …', WO 95.

39 'No other source existed …', Ibid.
40 'Nothing was taken …', Ibid.
41 'There were cases of …', Ibid.
42 'Some we put up …', Clifton-Shelton, p. 76.
43 'An old worldy …', Ibid., p. 87.
44 'It was pitch dark …', Ibid., p. 92.
45 'It sounds like a little thing …', War Diaries.

4 'England Expects Every Man to Do His Shooting'

1   'Pay up and look pleasant', *CFCC*, 7 November 1914.
2   'It'll dae fine …', *CFCC*, 3 October 1914.
3   'So satiated with luxury', PARL HC Deb, 19 November 1914.
4   'The worst nonsense', *The Sportsman*, 16 December 1914.
5   'Ninth Commandment …', *CFCC*, 25 December 1914.
6   'Civvies', *CFCC*, 31 October 1914.
7   'Almost without exception …', *CFCC*, 21 November 1914.
8   'Actually these soldiers …', Ibid.
9   'Fuller comment when …', *CFCC*, 14 November 1914.
10 'England expects …', *CFCC*, 5 December 1914.
11 'You don't know how …', *CFCC*, 24 October 1914.
12 'Let football continue …', Ibid.
13 'He almost hoped …', *CFCC*, 21 November 1914.
14 'Gentlemen of his type …', Ibid.

5 'Thus Far Shalt Thou Go and No Farther'

1   'There are Scotch …', *The Times*, 1 March 1900.
2   'Having deemed it desirable …', Verney, p. 4.
3   'As no greater Irishman …', Ibid., p. 5.
4   'With a benevolent …', Ibid.
5   'Ardent devotee', *Household Magazine*, 1904.
6   'During the first six days …', Greer Papers.
7   'We fully believed …', French, p. 142.
8   'The Germans had established …', Ibid., p. 145.
9   'The heavily wooded …', Kipling, p. 17.
10 'Suddenly a hail of bullets …', Greer Papers.
11 'He was shamming dead …', Ibid.
12 'The horrors', Ibid.
13 'We feel it shows …', *CFCC*, 10 October 1914.
14 'If it is true …', IWM Trefusis.
15 'That the stakes …', French, p. 215.
16 'In my inmost heart …', Ibid., p. 218.
17 'The enemy was daily …', Ibid., p. 225.
18 'We alone remain …', IWM Trefusis.
19 'All my worst forebodings …', French, p. 227.
20 'This, taken with the speed …', Ibid., p. 228.
21 'To the scandal of discipline …', IWM Trefusis.
22 'If we could keep our positions …', Ibid.
23 'For the ground was …', Ibid.
24 'The Germans had come between …', Ibid.

25 'Isolated in darkness …', Kipling, p. 34.
26 'We had been digging all day …', IWM Trefusis.
27 'Which, if it could be held …', French, p. 236.
28 'Expense in blood …', IWM Trefusis.
29 'They must have lost …', Ibid.
30 'In a perfect hail …', Ibid.
31 'October 31st and November 1st', French, p. 237.
32 'The incessant roar …', IWM Trefusis.
33 'Personally I felt …', French, p. 252.
34 'I think this is one of the worst …', IWM Trefusis.
35 'Triumphal entry …', French, p. 257.
36 'Twas like a football scrum …', Verney, p. 34.
37 'I want you to convey', IWM Trefusis.
38 'This was a popular obsession', Ibid.
39 'Whatever may have been …', French, p. 271.
40 'Most of them suffering …', IWM Trefusis.
41 'And told me that without relief …', Ibid.
42 'It is frightfully lonely …', Ibid.
43 'It was one of those mild …', French, p. 330.

6 'Any More Chelseaites for Berlin in the Spring?'

1 'The idea is that the players …', *CFCC*, 12 December 1914.
2 'He did not care …', *The Sportsman*, 16 December 1914.
3 'Hypocrisy and sham …', *CFCC*, 12 December 1914.
4 'What about a Press Battalion?', *CFCC*, 16 January 1915.
5 'Mind your own business …', Ibid.
6 'They can enlist today …', *CFCC*, 19 December 1914.
7 'Keep smiling …', *CFCC*, 25 December 1914.
8 'Here We Go Again', *CFCC*, 6 February 1915.
9 'The poor fellows …', *CFCC*, 20 March 1915.
10 'It is all football with them …', Ibid.
11 'I have the opportunity …', *CFCC*, 23 January 1915.
12 'Chelsea has already obtained …', *CFCC*, 13 February 1915.
13 'Only 122 professionals …', *CFCC*, 9 January 1915.
14 'When Lord Durham's …', *CFCC*, 5 April 1915.
15 'Probably the large majority …', *CFCC*, 16 January 1915.
16 'It seems to me …', PARL HC Deb, 1 March 1915.
17 'There he is credited …', *CFCC*, 2 April 1915.
18 'If racing continued …', PARL HC Deb, 19 May 1915.
19 'So let it go on …', *CFCC*, 2 April 1915.

7 'Carry Them Right Off Their Legs'

1 'The advance to be made …', Prior and Wilson, p. 31.
2 'The great point …', Ibid., p. 56.
3 'The divisional commanders …', War Diaries.
4 'Indeed everything was planned …', Ibid.
5 'No special preparations …', War Diaries.
6 'Smashed on their own parapet', Ibid.
7 'You can scarcely …', Rifle Brigade, p. 105.

8 'A Sterner Battle to Be Fought'

1 'England, Ireland and Wales ...', *CFCC*, 2 January 1915.
2 'Never-to-be-forgotten', *CFCC*, 9 January 1915.
3 'Our lads will have to play ...', Ibid.
4 'Plenty of time to beat ...', *CFCC*, 16 January 1915.
5 'Gave rise to a scene ...', Ibid.
6 'Old fashioned Yorkshire ...', Ibid.
7 'Buns vs. Guns', *CFCC*, 30 January 1915.
8 'Playing a game ...', Ibid.
9 'Erstwhile left winger ...', *CFCC*, 6 February 1915.
10 'Surely there are still a few ...', Ibid.
11 'It came as a surprise ...', *CFCC*, 6 March 1915.
12 'If I can run as fast ...', *CFCC*, 20 March 1915.
13 'An impromptu tango ...', Ibid.
14 'Went dotty', *CFCC*, 2 April 1915.
15 'A brilliantly dashing ...', *CFCC*, 27 March 1915.
16 'I was awfully pleased ...', Ibid.
17 'Rough on the Blues supporters ...', Ibid.
18 'Nearly killed at Fulham', *CFCC*, 17 April 1915.
19 'There must be ...', *CFCC*, February 1914.
20 'He made the ball ...', Buchan, p. 56.
21 'It was splendid to see ...', *CFCC*, 17 April 1915.
22 'Firm in his expressed ...', Ibid.
23 'All over 'em', *CFCC*, 28 April 1915.
24 'Wait until we reach the final ...', Ibid.
25 'That Germany will ...', *CFCC*, 17 April 1915.
26 'And, sinking the natural feelings ...', Ibid.
27 'It seems fairly certain ...', *CFCC*, 2 April 1915.
28 'Farewell until ...', *CFCC*, 28 April 1915.

9 'Clinging by Our Eyelids'

1 'Bearded, ragged ...', Australian (Vol. I), p. 535.
2 'The sides of the gully ...', Jerrold, pp. 116–7.
3 'As if it came through ...', Herbert, p. 89.
4 'Nothing but a series ...', Ibid.
5 'Giving off an odour ...', Bruckshaw, p. 41.
6 'Sniping squads ...', Australian, p. 539.
7 'The din was terrific ...', War Diaries.
8 'Thickly covered with scrub ...', Ibid.
9 'Men from the firing line ...', Jerrold, p. 120.
10 'In the half light of dawn ...', War Diaries.
11 'The end of the great assault ...', Ibid.
12 'Scallywag officers ...', Herbert, p. 91.
13 'The beach produced ...', Ibid., p. 90.
14 'Spy mania ...', Ibid., p. 86.
15 'There were enough spies ...', Ibid., p. 88.
16 'The first convincing proof ...', War Diaries.

10 'I Really Wonder We Had Any Left At All'

1 'I am very proud of my guards ...', IWM Trefusis.
2 'Some of the communication trenches ...', Ibid.
3 'Dead-blown to pieces ...', Ibid.
4 'Which is their height of bliss ...', Ibid.
5 'One cannot describe it ...', Ibid.
6 'The enemy contenting himself ...', Ibid.
7 'I sat out on my rustic chair ...', Ibid.
8 'So sodden and sticky ...', Ibid.
9 'I think it was heavier ...', Ibid.
10 'Wreaths of driving rain ...', Kipling, p. 87.
11 'A bad piece of map reading ...', IWM Trefusis.
12 'Where are you hit ...', Dean Papers.
13 'I am only sad to know ...', Ibid.
14 'To be kind I must say ...', Ibid.

11 'For King, Country and Chelsea!'

1 'Commandeering the ...', *CFCC*, 24 October 1914.
2 'After the weary monotony ...', Ibid.
3 'There really ought to be no ...', *CFCC*, 14 November 1914.
4 'They are fed up ...', Ibid.
5 'Whilst some units ...', War Diaries.
6 'Platoon training ...', Ibid.
7 'Gradually mutual esteem ...', Ibid.
8 'Cleanliness and smartness ...', Ibid.
9 'It has been noticed ...', Ibid.
10 'Trench refilling point ...', Ibid.
11 'If singing is permitted ...', Ibid.
12 'The best methods ...', Ibid.
13 'The large church ...', Blunden, p. 53.
14 'Accidental discharge', War Diaries.
15 'Those ideas sank instantly ...', Blunden, p. 57.
16 'Heavier and more effective ...', War Diaries.
17 'Moreover, the least failure ...', Ibid.
18 'At all costs', Ibid.
19 'Come on Sussex', Ibid.
20 'No straggling or 'souvenir' ...', Ibid.
21 'Ginger', Ibid.
22 'We were in the third line ...', Blunden, p. 58.
23 'Wise discretion', War Diaries.
24 'I consider that though ...', Ibid.
25 Boar's Head Massacre ...', Blunden, p. 59.

12 'Merely Murder If You Show Your Head'

1 'At all costs', Ewing, p. 108.
2 'Like ducks to water', *CFCC* Chroncle 11 November 1914.
3 'Admonished', WO 363.
4 'Unlawfully disobeying an order', Ibid.

5 'Chiefly oak and birch …', Official History, WO 95.
6 'The Devil's Wood …', Mddx, WO 95.
7 'The immediate digging …', War Diaries.
8 'The fighting in which …', Ibid.
9 'It must be impressed …', Ibid.
10 'In addition to covering artillery fire …', Ibid.
11 'The British soldier thoroughly …', Ibid.
12 'Two Tommies …', Official History.
13 'Every endeavour …', War Diaries.
14 'Soon portions of the trenches …', Ibid.
15 'Heavy artillery has …', Ibid.
16 'We are in a place …', Collison Papers.
17 'There is only a few …', Ibid.

13 'All Ranks Behaved Magnificently'

1 'Belched death and destruction', Mddx, p. 216.
2 'The resources …', Hart (Somme), p. 330.
3 'Many a hard won …', War Diaries.
4 'It is, I hope …', Ibid.
5 'I would like to point out …', Ibid.
6 'All ranks behaved magnificently …', Ibid.

14 'A Fair Chance of Success'

1 'The least rewarding …', Hart, p. 344.
2 'Our trenches were knocked …', War Diaries.
3 'We immediately sent working …', Ibid.
4 'A fair chance of success', Official History.
5 'Reliefs took hours …', War Diaries.
6 'Which was no easy matter …', Ibid.
7 'All the rear communications …', Ibid.
8 'Marching by compass …', Ibid.
9 'Gaping shell holes …', Ibid.
10 'I do not for a moment …', Ibid.
11 'No wonder you joined …', Ronan Papers.
12 'I can't help thinking …', War Diaries.
13 'Reports of individuals …', Ibid.
14 'I went over with …', Collison Papers.
15 'The sanguinary struggle …', Middx, p.232.

15 'Fatherless Little Ones'

1 'I daresay …', Whiting Papers.
2 'Even the Somme front …', Official History.
3 'Swept like a flood', Ibid.
4 'A breach, 12,000 …', Ibid.
5 'Under exceptionally …', War Diaries.
6 'There was the considerable …', Mddx, p.252.
7 'They must assault …', War Diaries.
8 'In places scarce one …', Ibid.

9 'For days the opposing ...', Official History.
10 'Fierce in the extreme ...', War Diaries.
11 'Officers must pay particular ...', Ibid.
12 'Was but a scorched ...', Official History.
13 'In the confused fighting ...', War Diaries.
14 'His evidence made it clear ...', Ibid.
15 'An Homeric struggle', Ibid.
16 'As it was the sudden ...', Ibid.
17 'For some time past ...', Whiting Papers.

16 'Hitting and Hitting with All of Our Strength'

1 'No measure to which ...', Official History.
2 'Our objective ...', Ibid.
3 'Even if a full measure ...', Ibid.
4 'The enemy must not be left ...', Ibid.
5 'Railways were built ...', Ibid.
6 'There was such a roar as ...', Wyrall v. 2, p. 86.
7 'First there was a rumbling ...', Ibid.
8 'The German machine gunner ...', War Diaries.
9 'Whose valley ...', Ibid.
10 'Opportunely crushes ...', Ibid.
11 'Highly satisfactory ...', Ibid.
12 'One of the heaviest ...', Official History.
13 'So great was the roar ...', Ibid.
14 'As we have not sufficient ...', Ibid.
15 'The stream of burning oil ...', War Diaries.
16 'Knowing the importance ...', Ibid.
17 'Locked almost wheel ...', Ibid.
18 'It is improbable ...', Ibid.
19 'A final, heavy ...', Ibid.
20 'Fine work', Seton Hutchinson, p. 73.
21 'Carried out their task ...', War Diaries.
22 'Not a yard of ground ...', Ibid.
23 'Desperate final efforts ...', Ibid.
24 'The fine weather held ...', Ibid.
25 'Specially trained ...', Ibid.
26 'Belonging to British soldiers ...', Ibid.
27 'Rapid communication ...', Ibid.
28 'The principle of detailing ...', Ibid.
29 'The mere movement ...', Ibid.
30 'The British charged ...', Official History.
31 'Rain. Our best ally', Ibid.

17 'With Our Backs to the Wall'

1 'The stars in their courses', Gough, p. 302.
2 'Upon the results of this …', Official History.
3 'Like blind men …', Ibid.
4 'In some cases …', War Diaries.
5 'Wavering', Ibid.
6 'The safety of our homes …', Hart (1918), p. 237.

18 'No Wild Scenes of Rejoicing'

1 'Only those who actually …', Jerrold, p. 275.
2 'They had the wrong …', Hart, p. 4.
3 'But was practically devoid …', Official History.
4 'Too much blue, red …', Ibid.
5 'Over-organisation bred …', War Diaries.
6 'Spark wireless …', Ibid.
7 'An original and daring …', Ibid.
8 'Dear old Harry …', Trusler Papers.
9 'Patrolled by the ghosts …', Wyrall (62nd), p. 147.
10 'A brilliant firework …', Ibid., p. 148.
11 'The surface of the roads …', War Diaries.
12 'Hostilities will cease …', Ibid.
13 'There was no exuberant …', Headlam, v. 2, p. 247.
14 'As your Colonel in Chief …', Ibid.
15 'The individual may perish …', Ibid., p. 248.

Bibliography

Original Documents

Private Papers relating to:
George Collison
William & Cecil Dean
Herbert & Sidney Jerram
Patrick Ronan
Henry Trusler
Robert Whiting

National Archives:
WO95 Series
WO363 Series
WO324 Series
AIR 79 Series
WO393/374 Series

Imperial War Museum:	Diary of Trefusis
Royal Logistics Corps Museum:	Papers relating to the ASC and the AOC
Brighton & Hove Albion [...] Whiting	Papers and photographs relating to Robert
Luton Town Football Club:	Photograph relating to Arthur Wileman

Newspapers & Periodicals

Chelsea FC Chronicles
Birmingham Daily Post
Evening Despatch
Manchester Courier
Birmingham Daily Post

Books

Atkinson, Christopher Thomas: *The History of the South Wales Borderers, 1914–1918* (London: Medici Society, 1931)

Bean, Charles Edwin Woodrow (ed.): *The Official History of Australia in the War of 1914–1918* (Sydney: Angus & Robertson, 1921–1943)

Bell, Matthew: *Red, White & Khaki: The Story of the Only Wartime FA Cup Final* (Peakpublish, 2011)

Boraston, John Herbert: *The Eight Division in the War, 1914–1918* (London: Medici Society, 1926)

Bruckshaw, Horace (Martin Middlebrook ed.): *The Diaries of Private Horace Bruckshaw, 1915–1916* (London: Scolar Press, 1979)

Cheshire, Scott: *Chelsea FC Players Who's Who* (Private, 1987)

Corbett Smith, Arthur: *The Retreat from Mons* (London: Cassell & Co., 1916)

Edmonds, James: *Military Operations France & Belgium* (multiple volumes 1914–1918) (London: Imperial War Museum, 1992)

Forbes, A.: *A History of the Army Ordinance Services* (London: Medici Society, 1929)

French, Field Marshal John Denton Pinkstone: *1914* (London: Constable & Co., 1919)

Gough, General Sir Hubert de la Poer: *The Fifth Army* (London: Hodder & New Stoughton, 1931)

Gray, J.G.: *Prophet in Plimsolls* (Edinburgh: Edina Press, 1978)

Hart, Peter: *1918: A Very British Victory* (London: Weidenfeld & Nicolson, 2008)
– *Gallipoli* (London: Profile, 2011)
– *The Somme* (London: Cassell, 2006)

Headlam, Cuthbert: *History of the Guards Division in the Great War, 1915–1918* (London: John Murray, 1924)

Herbert, Aubrey: *Mons, Anzac & Kut* (London: Hutchinson & Co., 1930)

Jerrold, Douglas: *The Royal Naval Division* (London: Hutchinson & Co., London, 1927)

Kipling, Rudyard: *The Irish Guards in the Great War* (London: MacMillan, 1923)

McColl, Brian: *A Record of British Wartime Football* (Lulu.com, 2014)

McGreal, Stephen: *The War on Hospital Ships, 1914–1918* (Barnsley: Pen & Sword, 2008)

Mace, Martin & Grehan, John: *Western Front 1914–1916 – Mons, Le Cateau, Loos, the Battle of the Somme* (Barnsley: Pen & Sword, 2013)

Ponsonby, *The Grenadier Guards in the Great War of 1914–1918* (London: MacMillan, 1920)

Seton Hutchinson, Lt Col Graham: *The Thirty-Third Division in France & Flanders, 1915–1919* (London: Waterlow & Sons Ltd, 1921)

Sewell, Albert: *Chelsea, Champions! The Story of the 1954–5 Football League Champions from 1905 to Their Jubilee Year* (London: Phoenix Sports Books, 1955)

Simkins, Peter: *Kitchener's Army : The Raising of the New Armies, 1914–1916* (Barnsley: Pen & Sword, 2007)

Starling, John: *No Labour, No Battle: Military Labour during the First World War* (Stroud: Spellmount, 2009)

Verney, Peter: *The Micks: The Story of the Irish Guards* (London: Peter Davies, 1970)

Williamson, Howard: *The Great War Medal Collectors Companion* (Harwich: Anne Williamson, 2011)

Wyrall, Everard: *The Die-Hards in the Great War: A History of the Middlesex Regiment 1914–1919* (London: Harrison & Sons, 1926)

– *The History of the 62nd West Riding Division, 1914–1919* (London: John Lane, 1924–25

– *The History of the Second Division, 1914–1918* (London: Nelson & Sons, 1921)

Young, Mike: *Army Service Corps 1902–1918* (London: Leo Cooper, 2000)

Index

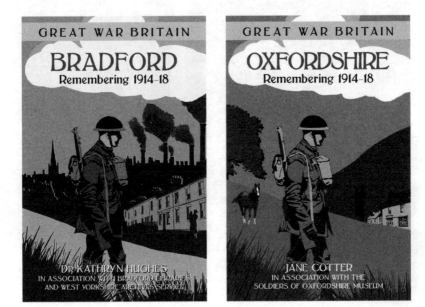

Also from The History Press

BACK OF THE NET!

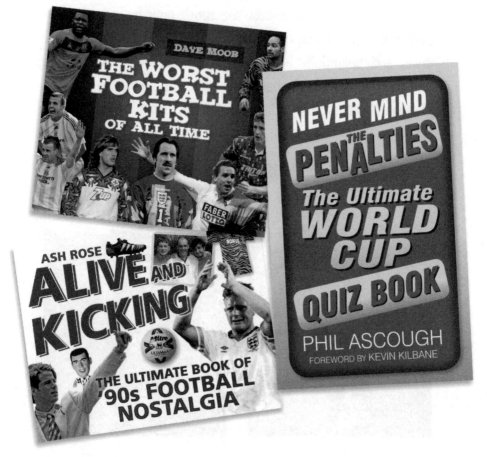